MASTERING 1 2 3

MASTERING

Carolyn Jorgensen

SYBEX® Berkeley • Paris • Düsseldorf • London

Cover art by Thomas Ingalls + Associates
Book Design by Joseph Roter
Project Editor Barbara Graves

Dedication

To my cousin, Judy Gabriel, who helped me to survive the ups and downs of writing.

And to David Weldon Norris, a writer who taught me the sounds of writing patiently without reward.

The author wishes to recognize Aisling Guy as co-writer of this book in every sense. Without her work, this book would not exist.

ACKNOWLEDGMENTS

This book would not have been possible in the three month period it was written in without the guidance and help of many other people.

First of all, thanks to P. Schwartz, who started it all.

To my colleagues who helped the day of the Disk Disaster: Mary Lee Smith Bingham (Gerbode Foundation), Sam Sternberg (my neighbor), Dan Alford, Bob Higby (both of 800-Software) and Dan (formerly of 800-Software). Without them, I would have lost my mind.

To the helpful staff of SYBEX who acquired, prepared, and directed this book: Ray Keefer, technical editor; Aidan Wylde, proofreader; Brenda Walker, typesetter; David Clark, word processor; and especially Mr. Karl Ray, managing editor, for his patience.

I want to thank contributors Joe Fusco and Karen Parker for their work on Chapter 11, "Macros," and Chapter 4's engineering @ functions respectively. They worked while most people were celebrating the holidays.

Thanks also to Tim Cooper who made testing the early chapters' exercises fun.

To the students at the Golden Gate University Computer Center who gave me support, especially Filemon Tanchoco, who helped a great deal at the last minute.

And thanks to Kay Nelson, the editor who polished the book.

Mildred Jorgensen, my mother, deserves special thanks for her help in proofing the galleys and making sure I didn't become a starving writer during this project.

David Weldon Norris read more of this book and rewrote more sentences than he probably cares to remember, especially the introduction. Thanks, darling.

And finally, Rick Nielson, Laurie Williams, David Jenkins, Alice Henretig, and Bill Grout were there for moral support, advice, and understanding when the times were rough. Thanks for your confidence.

To all these people I am forever indebted for their efforts on my behalf. I have learned a great deal from them.

CONTENTS

Chapter 4:   Using @ Functions   68

Chapter 5: Data Analysis Techniques 164

Chapter 6:   Graphing Results   204

Chapter 7: Formatting, Printing, and File Handling   234

Chapter 12: Using @ String Functions   400

Appendix **B**: Add-ons to 1-2-3   438

Part I

Introduction

Chapter *1*

Using Mastering 1-2-3

Mastering Lotus 1-2-3—getting really good at it—can save you time. There are hundreds of shortcuts and features of Lotus 1-2-3 that are not obvious and are not explained in the manual. You could, of course, learn these by trial and error—or this book can help you.

Experienced business people often have not taken advantage of 1-2-3's full power because they have not allowed themselves the time and freedom to learn, experiment, and practice the program. Furthermore, there has been a lack of structured models to work from. This book provides models that solve real financial and statistical problems that, with a little imagination, can be adapted to many other applications. It also provides a well-indexed structure for users who know exactly what they want to do. To make explanations more immediate and visible, illustrations and exact screen displays are used whenever possible.

Who Should Read This Book

Mastering 1-2-3 is for everyone who uses Lotus 1-2-3 or wants to use it. For those of you who are new to 1-2-3, simple tutorials precede each major topic. You can build on your skills by completing each tutorial as it is presented. If you're already familiar with 1-2-3, you can go directly to the chapters that discuss the more advanced information you need—we'll tell you which these are. (If you are totally unacquainted with 1-2-3, or perhaps unfamiliar with computers altogether, you will be better able to benefit from this book after working through the tutorial in the Lotus *Tutorial* manual.)

If You're a Lotus Wizard. . .

If you've been working with 1-2-3 for several years now, you've become a member of a special club. You may know people who know more about Lotus 1-2-3 than you do, but you're no novice yourself. To the uninitiated, your proficiency with the computer looks something like wizardry. Your incantations are macro commands and database functions; your potions are spreadsheet files and graphic displays.

Wherever you may have started, you've come to a place where

elementary 1-2-3 books aren't doing the job anymore. You need a bag of new tricks, including the proverbial philosopher's stone for turning lead into gold.

While perhaps not quite that philospher's stone, this book is written for the Lotus wizard in you.

What This Book Can Teach You

For example, you can learn how to quickly link different pages of various Lotus 1-2-3 reports from different files. Or you can include a Lotus report in a standard word processor text report, instead of having to retype the material into the document line by line. People often do these things in roundabout ways because they don't know there are other, faster ways. It may take you a while to learn such techniques, but once you have learned them, they can save you many valuable work hours.

Many users shy away from 1-2-3's database functions. If you take the time to learn, you will be surprised at how easy it is to use database management as an organizer. Coupled with various spreadsheet functions and formulas, this feature lets you take advantage of Lotus 1-2-3's true integration capabilities. You can even create relational databases—those that allow you to query and sort across multiple files—or share information from mainframe computers or other database programs.

Even more people stay away from macros. With this book you can learn how to use macros to make customized templates for less experienced users. You'll also find that in some situations macros can save an enormous amount of time. You can build an entire library of macros, or custom design a menu that will take the repetition out of using Lotus 1-2-3 spreadsheets and databases. If you work extensively with macros already, you will be especially interested in the possibilities the new string @ functions provide.

How It's Organized

Most reference manuals are structured to offer information about commands one at a time rather than grouping commands around the tasks they perform. Manuals tell how to use commands, but not when or why to use them.

This book groups commands and functions into the logical contexts in which you use them, beginning with simple applications and moving to more complex ones. Within each section, the feature or function and its parameters are demonstrated with a quick, straightforward example. This is sufficient for many experienced users solving problems with 1-2-3. Additional information provides more detailed suggestions, cautions, limitations, and, where necessary, more complex examples.

Mastering 1-2-3 is divided into four parts: The Introduction (Chapters 1-2), The Spreadsheet, The Database, and Macros and Advanced Functions. The Spreadsheet chapters (3-7) introduce the basics: creating, printing, and saving a spreadsheet; using @ functions in a variety of applications; creating, printing, and saving graphs; data analysis techniques, and security measures. The Database chapters (8-10) show how to build and use a database, discuss database functions, and illustrate how to transfer information to and from databases. The Macros and Advanced Functions chapters (11-12) emphasize simple macros, the new Command Language, and @ string functions.

If you need help in getting started, Appendix A contains concise information for installing the program, changing the default drive, and starting 1-2-3. Appendix B, "Add-Ons to 1-2-3," reviews several new products designed to work with 1-2-3 and expand its capabilities.

Here's a brief look at the contents of each chapter so that you can see which topics are of most interest to you. If you're a beginner, you'll see where you should begin; if you're more experienced, you'll see where to go directly.

CHAPTER 2: 1-2-3—OLD AND NEW

Summarizes the new features of Release 2, including updated hardware options as well as additional program functions.

CHAPTER 3: BUILDING A SPREADSHEET

Introduces the beginner to 1-2-3's spreadsheet with step-by-step instructions for building a budget: entering data, correcting mistakes, using formats, computing values, using what-if analysis, creating text notes with spreadsheet values, using windows, and saving and printing spreadsheets. The budget created here is used to exemplify features and functions presented throughout the rest of the book, but experienced users can follow the examples without building the spreadsheet.

CHAPTER 4: USING @ FUNCTIONS

Presents the program's functions and practical examples of their use. It defines and gives examples of 1-2-3's built-in functions: statistical, mathematical, engineering, logical, financial, date, and special functions (including VLOOKUP and HLOOKUP), and the new depreciation methods DDB, SYD, and SLN.

To maximize their usefulness for the people most likely to use a particular kind of function, the examples are drawn from actual applications. These examples assume that you are familiar with specific professional concerns and terminology. Consequently, financial analysts might find the engineering problems difficult and vice versa, but all the examples contain methods that can be adapted to other specialized uses.

CHAPTER 5: DATA ANALYSIS TECHNIQUES

Shows the intermediate and advanced user how to set up data for regression or what-if analysis using the Data Fill, Range Value, and Transpose commands. It demonstrates the new Data Regression and Data Matrix functions and discusses the Data Table command, which uses data to predict and perform automated what-if analysis. The functions introduced in this section are seldom used outside a fairly complicated data analysis structure. Representative examples are used.

CHAPTER 6: GRAPHING RESULTS

Covers creating, displaying, saving, and printing graphs. Two sample spreadsheets are used to create line and bar graphs, and a pie chart. Each of 1-2-3's graph types—line, bar, stacked bar, X-Y and pie—is illustrated. The chapter also explains naming graphs and discusses all the options for displaying graphs. Printing graphs with the PrintGraph utility and the options for size, fonts, and color are also described.

Because graphing in 1-2-3 is such a simple matter, most experienced users will seldom need instruction, and for the most part will want to skip this chapter.

CHAPTER 7: FORMATTING, PRINTING, AND FILE HANDLING

Illustrates housekeeping and cosmetics: spreadsheet-specific and global format options and defaults, hiding and protecting cells and columns, password protection, file handling (including translating files to and from Symphony, dBaseII and III, Jazz, and DIF), disk space management, and printing (changing font and type styles in a report and altering print option defaults).

CHAPTER 8: BUILDING A DATABASE

Steps you through the creation and design of a personnel database. Experienced users note: Release 2 allows 256 fields in a database. Topics covered are: database design; assigning range names; entering, formatting, and printing records.

Further chapters use this database to demonstrate data management. Experienced users may want to take a few minutes to create the file.

CHAPTER 9: USING A DATABASE

Discusses intermediate aspects of data management and introduces sorting and querying a database, including the options for outputting, finding, editing, and deleting selected database records. Chapter 9 also discusses bin classification for frequency distributions and database statistical functions, including setting up data tables for statistical analysis.

CHAPTER 10: DATA SHARING TECHNIQUES

Covers the most advanced features of 1-2-3, including linking different databases, translating files produced with other database or word processing programs into 1-2-3 databases with the Data Parse command, and transferring data back and forth between 1-2-3 and dBASE.

CHAPTER 11: MACROS

Defines and discusses 1-2-3's macro capabilities, new Command Language, automatic macros, and custom menu creation. Sample problems show you step by step how to use the advanced Command Language features.

CHAPTER 12: USING @ STRING FUNCTIONS

Introduces 1-2-3's string functions for editing text. An exercise using the @CHAR function to display international characters is combined with the Compose function to produce special characters like the British pound sign.

APPENDIX A:
INSTALLING AND STARTING 1-2-3

Supplements the 1-2-3 manual's instructions for installing the program. It lists the hardware components—printers and monitors—that can be used with 1-2-3 and summarizes the procedure for their installation. Intermediate and advanced users may find these brief instructions sufficient and preferable to the longer detailed instructions beginners get in the Lotus manual.

An important section for all 1-2-3 users is "Setting Up the Default Directory." Hard disk owners should read the instructions and warnings about COPYON, the new utility that eliminates the key disk requirement for installing 1-2-3 on a hard disk.

APPENDIX B: ADD-ONS TO 1-2-3

Reviews Lotus Development's new products: Report Writer, designed to work with the 1-2-3 database to print formatted reports; and Spotlight, a desktop manager that complements 1-2-3 with tools such as a note pad, phone book, and calendar. Another useful product that works with 1-2-3 is the Cambridge Spreadsheet

Analyst, a spreadsheet auditor used to check the accuracy of formulas in large spreadsheets.

Summary

This chapter has provided a quick overview of what you can expect to find in *Mastering 1-2-3* and has suggested a few ways you can use this book to suit your needs. The next chapter summarizes the new features provided in Lotus 1-2-3's Release 2, including expanded memory, advanced database features and @ functions, additional menu commands, printing and graphics enhancements, and increased macro capabilities.

Chapter 2

1-2-3—Old and New

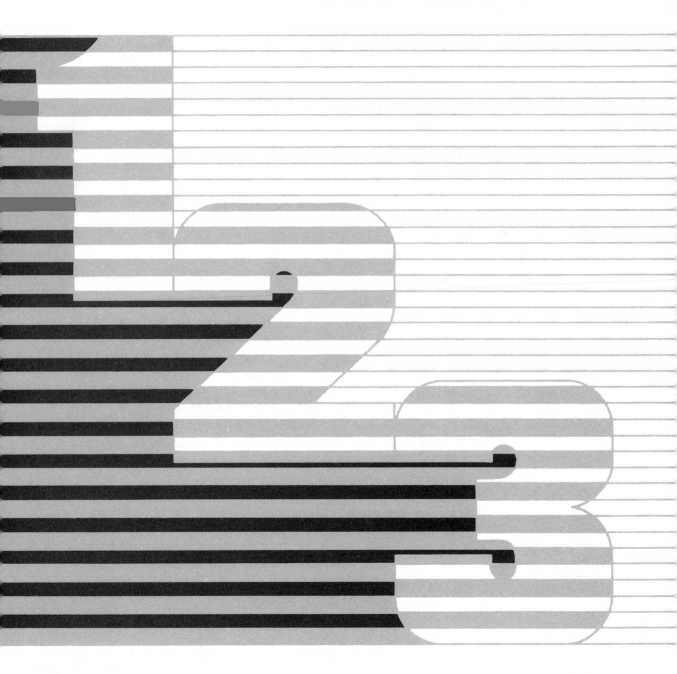

Lotus 1-2-3, as the name implies, is three different programs combined into one integrated package: spreadsheet, database, and graphics. The integrated program accomplishes an almost magical blend of the three features. On top of that, it is organized in a common-sense way, with commands tied together logically in menus. Add to that the ability to automate repetitive tasks with macros, and 1-2-3 is almost the perfect package for most business uses.

For specialized applications beyond its capabilities, 1-2-3 provides ways to turn to other programs specifically designed to handle those problems. For example, you can convert 1-2-3 files to ASCII files and edit them in most word processing programs. You can import files generated in word processing programs into 1-2-3 and convert them into spreadsheets or databases. If the database features in 1-2-3 prove inadequate, you can convert your 1-2-3 files for use in packages such as dBaseII and III, and most dBase II and III files can be converted for use in 1-2-3.

1-2-3's New Look

If you have been using Lotus 1-2-3 purchased before October 1985, you have been using Release 1A. As software companies make improvements to their programs, they create new editions and offer them to current users in exchange for their old version of the program. Each edition of the program is assigned a number. This exchange of the old edition for the new is called an *upgrade*. Lotus Development calls the issue of a new edition of 1-2-3 a *release*. As of the publication of this book, the most current edition of Lotus 1-2-3 is Release 2, which contains several new and useful features.

The sections that follow take a look at each of Release 2's new features and enhancements.

THE SKY'S THE LIMIT: GREATLY EXPANDED MEMORY

The single most important new feature is an improvement in the way 1-2-3 uses RAM (random access memory) so that you can create bigger spreadsheets without spending money on memory upgrades. For example, if you have reached the full memory limit of your 640K IBM PC using 1-2-3 Release 1A but need to add several more formulas and figures to an important spreadsheet, you should upgrade to Release 2, which gives you 40% more memory.

In some cases, even with 640K and using Release 2, you will still not have enough RAM. To allow for your really big spreadsheets, you can now add up to 4 million bytes of RAM (4 Mb) to your IBM PC and Release 2 will be able to use that memory.

FULL SPEED AHEAD

With Release 2, you can now increase calculation speed by using the 8087 math coprocessor (the "math chip"). If you're using very large spreadsheets, you've probably had to wait, sometimes up to several minutes, for them to recalculate. If you install the 8087 on the 640K IBM PC with Release 2, your waiting time will decrease significantly.

HARDWARE IMPROVEMENTS

Many new hardware options are now supported in Release 2, including printers such as the Hewlett-Packard LaserJet and new monitors such as the IBM Enhanced Graphics model. In addition, the new 1-2-3 installation procedure allows you to use 1-2-3 with more than one set of hardware.

Good news for hard disk owners: Release 2 allows you to run 1-2-3 without loading the floppy 1-2-3 System disk.

SECURITY MEASURES

New security measures are available for keeping unauthorized users out of spreadsheets. You can assign passwords that require users to enter a code to retrieve a spreadsheet file. You can hide columns and individual cells with the Hidden Format option and easily exclude information from printed reports.

PRINT ENHANCEMENTS

Printing enhancements include the ability to specify more than one text printer directly from 1-2-3 before printing. Zeros may also be blanked out from printouts to improve legibility. You can insert page breaks to force the printer to go to a new page before printing spreadsheet sections. Printer codes can now be entered in cells for changing the size, style, or degree of darkness or lightness of printed characters.

NEW @ FUNCTIONS

New @ functions have been increased to include all of Lotus Symphony's string, logical, and special functions. Several new financial functions have been added to calculate depreciation, terms, and rates of investments. You can now reference text labels in formulas and @IF functions, and locate circular references with the Worksheet Global Status command.

IMPROVING THE PICTURE: NEW GRAPHICS FEATURES

Now you can shade and explode pie charts, using several different patterns and colors. You can also use the PrintGraph program with several new plotters and printers to print both black-and-white and color graphs. Indicators for units can now be hidden from the graph's axis.

AT YOUR COMMAND: NEW MENU COMMANDS

Other commands have been added to the 1-2-3 menu. One such is the System command, which allows you to exit to DOS to use DOS commands and then reenter 1-2-3 without reloading the program. Another is the Data Regression command, which performs multiple or single regression analysis. The new Data Matrix command multiplies and inverts matrices.

These new commands are always located at the end of the menu, so that users who are already familiar with the command menu will not have to deal with a new menu structure. In the back of this book, you will find a guide to each menu as a quick reference. Throughout the book, new commands will be defined in detail and demonstrated in examples as the need arises. Under

"New Commands" in the index you will find each new command listed with the page number where it is introduced.

DATABASE IMPROVEMENTS

The Release 2 database can now contain 256 fields (the old limit was 32 fields). The Query Find command (to select specific database records) will now allow you to make changes to the records, rather than just to view or copy them. Hiding columns allows you to print selected fields from the database easily.

ADVANCED DATABASE FEATURES

You can now import mixed text and numeric data and break it into database fields using the Data Parse command. Databases can be linked using common text fields as keys and @VLOOKUP tables. Report Writer, the new add-on product from Lotus Development Corporation, can take 1-2-3 database information and print it as custom forms, computing totals and subtotals.

TAKE YOUR PICK:
MACRO COMMAND LANGUAGE CHOICES

Even the most complicated of financial analyses boil down to the repetition of a small number of steps, over and over. The more information being analyzed, the more tedious and time-consuming these repetitions become. For example, you might have a cash report that must be updated and printed every Friday. You can outline the exact steps you will take every week: bring the spreadsheet to the screen, insert a column for the new week, format it appropriately, enter the week's revenues and expenditures (moving down through the columns and rows automatically as you do so), copy the formulas for the totals from the previous week's column, recalculate, save the spreadsheet, and print it. Even this description, which might sound thorough, is only a summary of the exact steps you take each week to update your report.

Macros are a simple method offered by 1-2-3 for automating steps such as these. Basically, you indicate to 1-2-3 that the steps you are about to name are to be recorded. Then you type in the exact steps you take (including every cursor movement and every Enter command) and give the whole procedure a name. When you use the macro described in the example above, all you will have to do is enter the actual information for the week as prompted by 1-2-3. You can use the macro only for one spreadsheet, or save it in a "library" with other macros that can be used for other purposes.

Macro commands now include Symphony command language macros that allow you to structure more powerful routines using logic similar to that found in programming languages. Of course, you can still write macros using the 1-2-3 Release 1A method. All macros written using Lotus 1A will still work with Release 2 and need no conversion.

The new @ string functions, combined with the logical functions, are ideal for designing macros that execute different commands, depending on the value of the data.

NEW DIMENSIONS: 256 × 8,192

The new release contains 256 columns and 8,192 rows or 2,097,715 cells—4 times as much space as the old 1-2-3 (which had 256 columns and 2,048 rows and 524,288 cells). The world of spreadsheets has come a long way since the days of VisiCalc's 64 columns and 256 rows. In Lotus 1-2-3 Release 1A, you couldn't type anything in cell A2048. Now with improved memory management, you can use any of the 2,097,715 cells. This lets you store formulas in cells that are far away from areas of the spreadsheet seen by casual users. You can also create larger databases, as you can store more records in the 8,192 rows. Although typical applications don't use all of this space, when you need it, you will have it.

Boosting the Power:
Add-On Packages That Do What 1-2-3 Can't

Lotus 1-2-3 has been designed so that functions not offered in the package itself can be added on by hooking up with other programs. Why not just add these functions to 1-2-3, as was done with graphing and data management? Many of these functions are specialized, not needed or wanted by most 1-2-3 users, who should not have to pay for them and make room for them on their computers. One of these add-ons is Report Writer, which allows you to extract various pieces of information from your databases, combine it, and print it in reports. Others are the Cambridge Spreadsheet Analyst, which helps you debug your spreadsheets, and Spotlight, which gives you access to features such as a calendar and notepad while you are working in 1-2-3.

Notes on DOS

You must use DOS 2.0 or higher with the new release. A valuable new feature is a new menu option called System that allows you to exit 1-2-3 directly to DOS.

A disadvantage to the new release is that the amount of physical disk space the System disk programs take up is more than one floppy can hold, which means that if you are using a floppy system, you have to insert more than one disk to load the program into memory.

TEMPORARY EXIT TO DOS

While you are using the System option, 1-2-3 stays in the background, keeping the 1-2-3 program and any work you have on the screen in RAM, regardless of whether it is saved to disk. The System option allows you to use DOS to copy, rename, and erase files and format disks. To return to 1-2-3 from DOS, type **exit** at the A>, B>, or C> prompt. To use the System command in a floppy drive system, you must have the file command.com on the System disk or have a disk with command.com in drive A. If not, you receive an ERROR message when you select the command.

DISK SPACE LIMITATIONS

Because of the increased file size of the 1-2-3 System disk programs, you cannot use the SYS B: DOS command to make your 1-2-3 System disk bootable. To start your computer, you must first load a DOS disk and then insert the 1-2-3 System disk to load the program. (Release 1A users could use the 1-2-3 System disk to boot their computers after using the SYS B: DOS command.)

Hard disk users need not worry about this limitation, because a subdirectory is used to store 1-2-3 programs and the main, or root, DOS directory starts up the system.

To Upgrade or Not

Most 1-2-3 users are opting to upgrade to Release 2. The cost to those who already own the program is negligible and the benefits are considerable:

- You can use your 1-2-3 program on several computer systems with different hardware characteristics.
- You can build larger spreadsheets with less RAM.
- You can do financial analysis more easily with many new @ functions.
- You can do statistical analysis without purchasing another program.
- You can better organize the information in your databases (fields are increased from 32 to 256).
- You can put more information in your spreadsheets and databases by adding up to 4 Mb of RAM.
- You can password-protect your files.
- You can write more efficient macros.
- You can manipulate text and values using @ string functions.
- You can save time with increased recalculation speed.
- You can use many new print features.

And, of course, hard disk owners can finally throw away the key.

CONVERTING RELEASE 1A FILES

Converting data files from Release 1A to Release 2 is a simple matter: use the File Retrieve command and select the file name from the list of files that appears on the screen. It may take a little longer than usual for the program to retrieve the file, but this should only happen the first time you retrieve it.

THE DARK SIDE: RELEASE 2 BUGS

There are two bugs (that is, errors) that are known to date in Release 2. One involves using the IBM AT and the new COPY-HARD utility. This bug is discussed in Appendix A in the section "Installing 1-2-3." The other bug appears after transferring 1A spreadsheets to Release 2. It is discussed below.

If a formula in the converted spreadsheet references a cell that contains text, you will receive an error message. In Release 1A, a text string had no value; in Release 2 it does. Because a label must be converted to a number in Release 2 in order to calculate, 1-2-3 displays an ERR message in any cell that references a label in a formula.

To correct any such formula in the converted spreadsheet, edit the formula by deleting the label cell reference or convert the label to a number by using the @N function. This function is discussed in Chapter 12, "Using @ String Functions."

New Hardware Options

Release 2 allows for some different hardware choices than did Release 1A, with implications for memory management, the speed of processing, and the relationship with the DOS operating system. For lists of hardware that can be used with Release 2, see Appendix A.

THE EXPANDED MEMORY BOARD

Memory management is the optimal combination of your PC's RAM and your software. Many users mistake hard disk storage (permanent memory) for RAM (working temporary memory). Even though you might be able to permanently store 10Mb of information, you may not have sufficient RAM to look at that same information on the screen.

Lotus 1-2-3 increases your PC's capacity to work with information by allowing you to expand RAM to 4Mb by installing a Lotus/ Intel (or compatible model) memory board in your computer.

THE MATH CHIP

The math chip, or the 8087 or 80287 math coprocessor, is used to speed up real-number processing. *Real numbers* are numbers with decimal points such as prices, percentages, or fractions. Lotus 1-2-3 works with the 8087 in the IBM PC or XT and the 80287 in the IBM AT. With the math coprocessor installed, spreadsheet recalculation speed can be from two to thirty times as fast, depending on the complexity of your formulas.

Summary

This chapter has given you an overview of Release 2's new and expanded features, each of which will be looked at in detail in later chapters.

The next chapter will introduce the Lotus 1-2-3 spreadsheet and give you practice in using its basic techniques. If you're already experienced with 1-2-3, you may want to turn to Chapter 4, "Using @ Functions," for examples and practical uses of the program's functions. If you need to install 1-2-3 on your computer, turn to Appendix A, which contains instructions for installation and important information about using the program with a hard disk.

Part II

The Spreadsheet

Chapter *3*

Building a Spreadsheet

In this chapter, you will learn to:

- Use basic 1-2-3 techniques
- Create a budget spreadsheet
- Modify the appearance of a spreadsheet
- Save the spreadsheet on a disk
- Date your work
- Compose a report with a paragraph of text and key budget spreadsheet values
- Use simple what-if analysis
- Fix column and row labels and split the screen into windows
- Print a spreadsheet and a report

The first few sections in this chapter are intended for beginning users of 1-2-3. If you're more experienced, you may wish to go directly to the tutorial entitled "Creating a Spreadsheet" in this chapter. You will use this spreadsheet later for more advanced problems; you can create it quickly by following the numbered steps, or simply follow the examples if you're an experienced user.

A note to beginners: One of the best ways to familiarize yourself with 1-2-3 is to use the on-line tutorial, "A View of 1-2-3," which you received on a disk when you purchased the program. The on-line tutorial consists of lessons that lead you through basic features and commands. After you have completed the tutorial lessons, you can use this chapter to refresh your memory and expand your techniques.

If you need to install the Lotus 1-2-3 program on your computer, or if you need help in starting the program, see Appendix A, "Installing and Starting 1-2-3."

Spreadsheet Basics

The 1-2-3 spreadsheet, shown in Figure 3.1, is divided into columns (that you read across) and rows (that you read up and down). A *cell* is formed where each column and row intersects. All entries in 1-2-3 are made one cell at a time. Each cell can hold one piece of information—a number, a label, a formula, a date— whatever you want to put in it. Columns are referenced by letters

(A for the first column, B for the second, and so on) and rows are referenced by numbers. The column letter and row number form each cell's *address,* such as A1 for the cell in the first column of the first row. While 1-2-3 automatically makes each column 9 spaces wide on a new spreadsheet, you can make each column wider or narrower as you work. Figure 3.1 shows the basic structure of the 1-2-3 spreadsheet.

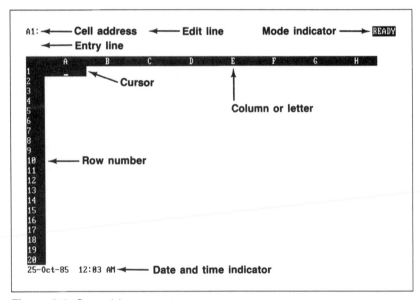

Figure 3.1: Spreadsheet structure

MOVING AROUND THE SPREADSHEET

The *cursor* is the rectangular box (or blinking underline) on your screen. In a new spreadsheet, it is always located at cell A1. The cursor indicates where the next character you type will appear on the screen. To enter data into the spreadsheet, your cursor must be located in the cell where you want the data to appear. You can move the cursor in several ways:

- By pressing any of the four arrow keys located on the right side of your keyboard.

- By pressing the Home key, which takes you to cell A1.

- By pressing the F5 (Goto) key and specifying a cell address.
- By pressing the PgUp or PgDn key, which moves the cursor 20 lines up or down, respectively.
- By pressing the Tab key, which moves the cursor right one screen, or Shift-Tab, which moves the cursor left one screen.
- By pressing the End key, which takes you to the last cell in the spreadsheet.

USING FUNCTION KEYS

Lotus 1-2-3 uses the function keys on the IBM PC and IBM-compatible keyboards. Each of the ten keys has been assigned a unique task. These tasks are commands that you may frequently need, such as editing a cell's contents, asking for help (explanations of commands), or moving directly to a particular cell address. Table 3.1 explains each key's function and lists the chapter in this book where you practice the use of the key.

Key	Name	Use	Discussed in
F1	Help	On-line explanations of commands	Chapter 3
ALT-F1	Compose	Make special characters	Chapter 12
F2	Edit	Correct mistakes in cell contents	Chapter 3
ALT-F2	Step	Help debug macros	Chapter 11
F3	Name	View a list of range names	Chapter 9
F4	Absolute	Make a cell constant in a formula	Chapter 3
F5	Goto	Move the cursor to a cell	Chapter 3
F6	Window	Move the cursor to or from a window	Chapter 3
F7	Query	Extract, find, or delete records from a database	Chapter 9
F8	Table	Recalculate a data table	Chapter 5
F9	Calc	Recalculate a spreadsheet	Chapter 3
F10	Graph	Redraw a graph	Chapter 6

Table 3.1: Function Keys

The Lotus documentation provides a plastic template—a guide that fits around the function keys. This template labels each key and key combination. Don't worry about memorizing these keys. You will naturally begin to remember their functions as you use them. Two important function keys, the Help key and the Goto key, are explored in the sections that follow.

Accessing On-Line Help Screens

One of 1-2-3's most innovative features is its index of on-line Help screens. By pressing the F1 (Help) key, you can see lists of various commands and features of the 1-2-3 spreadsheet (Figure 3.2). Move the cursor to the heading you want to learn about and press ←┘ to see an explanation of that topic on the screen. In addition, the screen displays the page number in the reference manual where you can read further about that command or feature. A sample Help screen is shown in Figure 3.3.

You must have the 1-2-3 System disk in drive A (or have installed the program on a hard disk) to access Help. If it is not in the drive, you will receive an ERROR message in the upper-right

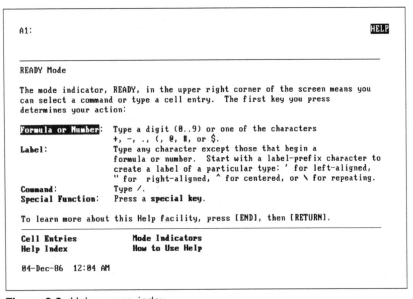

Figure 3.2: Help screen index

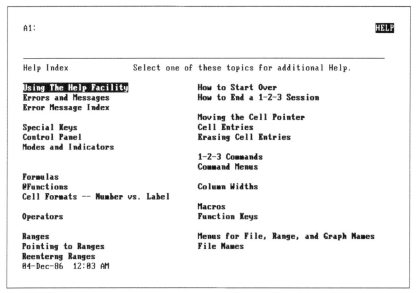

Figure 3.3: Help screen for formula or number

corner of your screen. To return to the spreadsheet from the Help screen, just press the Esc key.

Using the F5 (Goto) Key

You can use the F5 (Goto) key, located on the left side of the keyboard, to move the cursor quickly to a specific cell. After you press the F5 key, type the address of the cell you wish to go to; then press ◄┘.

You can also use the F5 (Goto) key to move to a range of named cells. This technique is discussed further in Chapter 9.

1-2-3 COMMAND MENUS

When you press the / key, Command Menu options appear on the screen, beginning with Worksheet (Figure 3.4). Each command option is discussed as the need arises for it during the exercises throughout this book. Each option on the Command Menu presents a submenu of further options related to the general option you select.

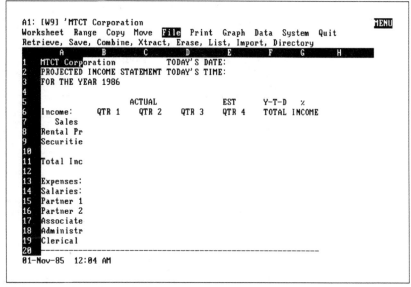

Figure 3.4: The Command Menu

A quick way to move around in any of the 1-2-3 menus is simply to type the first letter of the option you want, and 1-2-3 takes you directly to that option.

A Spreadsheet Tutorial

Now that you've reviewed the basic techniques, let's go on to create a budget in 1-2-3. In the tutorial that follows, you will learn how to enter labels, values, and the formulas that have 1-2-3 total values for you, how to insert rows and columns, and how to repeat underlines across cells, along with all the basic skills you need to create any spreadsheet from the first entry to the printed product. Intermediate and advanced users are welcome to sit in on this tutorial and review the basics of planning a good budget spreadsheet—one that works not only today, but next week and next year as well.

The budget you will create is displayed in Figure 3.5. It tracks the actual income, expenses, and net income for the first three quarters and the estimated income, expenses, and net income for the fourth quarter for a company called MCTC Corporation. The budget displays the year-to-date totals for each line item as a percent of total income. You will be given step-by-step instructions for creating, modifying, saving, and printing this spreadsheet.

```
MTCT Corporation                    TODAY'S DATE:     10/23/86
PROJECTED INCOME STATEMENT          TODAY'S TIME:     06:17 PM
FOR THE YEAR 1986

                ~~~~~~~~~ ACTUAL ~~~~~~~~~  EST      Y-T-D    %
Income:          QTR 1    QTR 2    QTR 3   QTR 4    TOTAL  INCOME
        Sales  110,000  125,000  135,000 140,000  510,000  81.3%
Rental Property 15,000   15,000   15,000  15,000   60,000   9.6%
     Securities 25,000        0   32,000       0   57,000   9.1%
               =================================================
   Total Income 150,000 140,000  182,000 155,000  627,000 100.0%

Expenses:
    Salaries:
Partner 1        13,750   13,750   13,750  13,750   55,000   8.8%
Partner 2        12,000   12,000   12,000  12,000   48,000   7.7%
Associates       10,500   10,500   10,500  10,500   42,000   6.7%
Administrative    9,000    9,000    9,000   9,000   36,000   5.7%
Clerical          7,000    7,000    7,000   7,000   28,000   4.5%
               -------------------------------------------------
Total Salaries   52,250   52,250   52,250  52,250  209,000  33.3%
Mngmt Expenses    4,000    5,000    4,500   4,800   18,300   2.9%
         Rent     2,000    2,000    2,000   2,000    8,000   1.3%
     Supplies     2,000    1,800    1,900   2,100    7,800   1.2%
    Telephone     1,800    1,900    2,100   2,300    8,100   1.3%
               -------------------------------------------------
Total Expenses   62,050   62,950   62,750  63,450  251,200  40.1%
               -------------------------------------------------
Net Income       87,950   77,050  119,250  91,550  375,800  59.9%
               =================================================
```

Figure 3.5: Budget spreadsheet

Creating a Spreadsheet

If you are not yet in 1-2-3, bring it up now, so that you have a blank spreadsheet on the screen. A1 appears in the top-left corner of the screen, as shown in Figure 3.6. 1-2-3 is prompting you to begin your spreadsheet by entering something in cell A1.

ENTERING LABELS

In 1-2-3, *labels* are the titles you type in for the various columns and rows. You can put a label in any cell on the spreadsheet. The label is usually a word, like TOTAL.

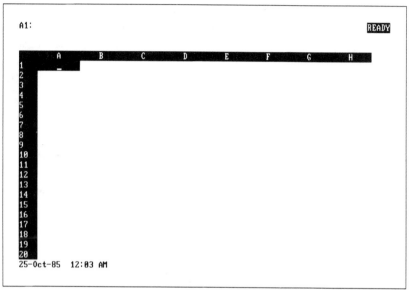

Figure 3.6: The spreadsheet startup screen

You will start your spreadsheet by entering as labels the titles for the columns and rows of the budget.

1. With the cursor in cell A1, type

   MTCT Corporation

   and press ←.

When you press ←, the words *MTCT Corporation* move from the entry line into cell A1 and the edit line at the top of the spreadsheet.

CORRECTING MISTAKES: THE F2 (EDIT) KEY

If you make a typing mistake, make sure the cursor is in the cell with the mistake. In this case, your cursor is still in cell A1, where you entered the MTCT Corporation label. Press the F2 (Edit) key on the left side of the keyboard. The contents of the cell A1 appear again at the entry line at the top of the screen. Use ← to move the cursor until it is on top of any incorrect character. Press the Del key, and the incorrect character will disappear. Type any missing characters. Press ←┘ when you finish editing. The corrected label disappears from the top of the screen and moves into cell A1.

ALIGNING LABELS

When you enter a label, 1-2-3 automatically left-aligns it unless you give it different instructions. To tell 1-2-3 to right-align a label, type " before the label. To center a label, type ^ before the label.

2. Using Figure 3.7 as a guide, enter the remaining labels, including the proper alignment codes. (You will not be able to see the alignment in some cells until later in the tutorial, when you increase the column widths.)

When you have finished, check the spreadsheet and correct any errors you find. Remember that the cursor must be located in the cell you want to edit. Use the arrow keys to move to the cell you are going to edit, press the F2 (Edit) key, and make the correction.

Hint: If you want to erase a label entirely, move your cursor to the cell you want to erase, press the space bar once, and then press ←┘.

SCROLLING

A spreadsheet can be, and often is, much larger than the part you can see on the screen. You can change the part of the spreadsheet you are viewing by scrolling the spreadsheet up and down and from side to side.

To examine the bottom portion of the spreadsheet, put the cursor at cell A1 by pressing the Home key. Now press the PgDn key located on the right side of the numeric keypad. The PgDn key moves the cursor 20 lines down. PgUp moves the cursor up 20 lines. Try moving up and down the spreadsheet a few times, pressing the PgDn, PgUp, and Home keys.

Now return to the Home position by pressing the Home key. You are returned to cell A1.

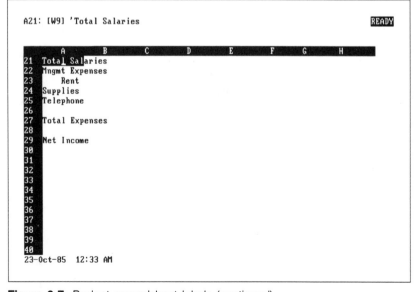

Figure 3.7: Budget spreadsheet labels

Figure 3.7: Budget spreadsheet labels (continued)

SAVING YOUR WORK

What you have typed into the spreadsheet thus far is only stored temporarily in memory. If your system were to lose power, you would lose all of your work. To permanently record the work you have done, you will use a command that will save this spreadsheet either on a floppy or on the hard disk.

3. To access the Command Menu, press the slash (/) key.

4. Press → to move the cursor to the option FILE.

When you move the cursor to FILE, more menu options related to file handling appear on the second line. Notice that one of these options is SAVE. You will tell 1-2-3 to select FILE and go through the steps necessary to name and save your spreadsheet file.

5. Select the FILE option by pressing ←. Notice that the FILE option moves up to display on the first line.

6. Move the cursor to the SAVE option and press ←.

Now 1-2-3 will ask you to name this spreadsheet. The name must have fewer than eight characters and may not begin with a number, but may have a number in any other position.

7. To call this spreadsheet file INCOME, type

   INCOME

   and press ←.

LISTING THE FILES ON YOUR DISK

Notice that the disk drive light comes on as your spreadsheet is being saved. To make sure you have saved the file, you can request that 1-2-3 display a list of the files on your disk.

Rather than use → to move to the LIST option, use the shortcut way: when you come to that part of the command, type the first letter of the option you want, in this case L for List.

8. Type

   / F L W

   to select the Command Menu, *F*ile, *L*ist, and *W*orksheet.

The names of your data files (that is, any spreadsheets you have saved on your disk) will appear on your screen. If the name INCOME does not appear, repeat the saving procedure outlined above. Press ◄┘ to remove the list of files from your screen.

CANCELING A COMMAND

If you choose an option you don't want to perform, you can cancel it by pressing the Esc (escape) key (located on the upper-left corner of the keyboard). Try this now.

9. Type

   / F

The file options appear. Press the Esc key once, and you are returned to the Main Menu. Press Esc again, and you are returned to your spreadsheet.

Now that you have saved the spreadsheet in a permanent file, you are ready to do some more work with it, starting with underlining some of the labels you have already entered.

ENTERING REPEATING LABELS

Most spreadsheets use underlines to make totals, subtotals, and other types of information stand out. 1-2-3 simplifies this task by allowing you to enter only once the underline character you want to repeat across a cell. 1-2-3 then fills the entire cell with this character. Most often you will separate information on a spreadsheet with the dash (—) or the equal sign (=), but you can use any character you want.

Look again at Figure 3.5. Notice where the designer planned for the underlines to be placed.

To tell 1-2-3 to repeat a character, type a backslash (\ ) and then the character you wish to repeat.

10. To create the repeating label in Figure 3.5, move the cursor to cell A10, type

   \=

   and press ⏎.

The cell now contains = = = = = = = = = = =.

11. Repeat this step for each of the remaining columns in row 10. Then move the cursor to cell A30 and enter repeating equals in each cell of that row as well.

12. For rows 20, 26, and 28, type

   \-

   and press ⏎ in each cell.

13. For cells B5 and D5, type

   \~

   and press ⏎.

Your spreadsheet should now look like Figure 3.8.

ENTERING VALUES

Now that the income and expense categories have been labeled, you are ready to start entering the numbers themselves.

The spreadsheet you are setting up will actually have two kinds of numbers in it: the "raw" data, called *values,* that you enter directly, and data that 1-2-3 will calculate for you using formulas you specify. The raw data you are going to enter now is shown in Figure 3.9.

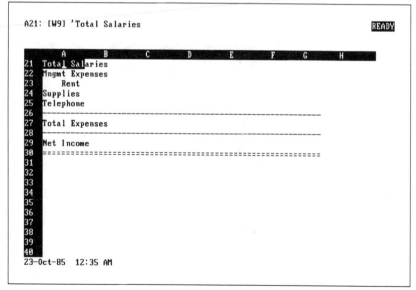

```
A1: [W9] 'MTCT Corporation                                        READY

          A        B        C        D        E        F        G        H
1    MTCT_Corporation              TODAY'S DATE:
2    PROJECTED INCOME STATEMENT TODAY'S TIME:
3    FOR THE YEAR 1986
4
5               ~~~~~~~~ ACTUAL ~~~~~~~~   EST     Y-T-D   %
6    Income:     QTR 1    QTR 2    QTR 3   QTR 4   TOTAL INCOME
7       Sales
8    Rental Property
9    Securities
10   ================================================================
11   Total Income
12
13   Expenses:
14   Salaries:
15   Partner 1
16   Partner 2
17   Associates
18   Administrative
19   Clerical
20   ----------------------------------------------------------------
23-Oct-85  12:35 AM
```

Figure 3.8: Budget with repeating labels

```
A21: [W9] 'Total Salaries                                        READY

          A        B        C        D        E        F        G        H
21   Total Salaries
22   Mngmt Expenses
23       Rent
24   Supplies
25   Telephone
26   ----------------------------------------------------------------
27   Total Expenses
28   ----------------------------------------------------------------
29   Net Income
30   ================================================================
31
32
33
34
35
36
37
38
39
40
23-Oct-85  12:35 AM
```

Figure 3.8: Budget with repeating labels (continued)

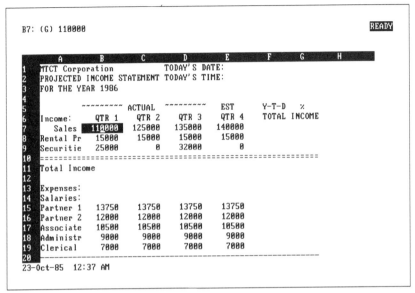

Figure 3.9: Budget with data values

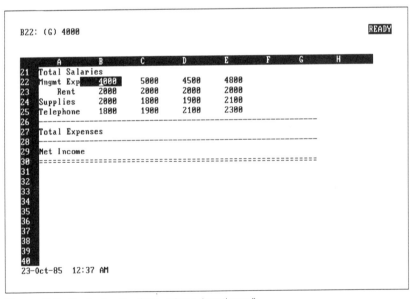

Figure 3.9: Budget with data values (continued)

14. Using that figure as a guide, enter the values in the appropriate cells. Begin in cell B7 by typing the QTR 1 Sales value **110000** and pressing ⏎. Enter all the other values in the same way. Press the Home key when you have finished entering all of the values.

15. To save your work again, enter

/ F S ⏎ R

The R(eplace) command tells the program to replace the old version of your spreadsheet with this updated version.

You have now completed the first part of this lesson, creating a spreadsheet. So far, you have learned or reviewed:

- Entering labels
- Aligning labels
- Correcting mistakes
- Saving your work
- Canceling menu commands
- Entering repeating characters
- Entering data values

Improving the Appearance of Your Spreadsheet

One of the biggest mistakes you may make when you begin to use spreadsheets is to pay insufficient attention to the spreadsheet's appearance. The point of using a spreadsheet is lost if the information cannot be read in the most useful form, at a glance, and without the need for interpretation.

Lotus 1-2-3 allows you to display information in various formats, placing dollar signs with money, percent signs with percentages, and changing column widths, for example. The next sections introduce you to several of the formatting possibilities available.

ADJUSTING COLUMN WIDTHS

Notice that column A in your spreadsheet is too narrow to display the entire label RENTAL PROPERTY. Move your cursor to that label, in cell A8.

1. To increase column A's width, enter

   / W C S

   and press → 6 times. Then press ◄┘.

Hint: You can type the width as a number rather than pressing the arrow key. In this example, you would type

   / W C S 15 ◄┘

2. The same procedure decreases column width. Move the cursor to column G, which is too wide for the percentages that will display there. Adjust it to a width of 6 characters by entering

   / W C S 6 ◄┘

FORMATTING LARGE NUMBERS

Placing a comma in 120000 makes the number much easier to read: 120,000. Placing dollar signs in front of money values and choosing the proper number of decimal places for different kinds of numbers also improves their legibility.

To format the numbers already entered in your spreadsheet, you will use the Worksheet command again, this time selecting the Global Format options to insert commas in all the values that are 1,000 or greater. Because most of the numbers are integers and have no decimal places, you will also choose to display no decimal places.

3. Enter

   / W G F , 0 ◄┘

Column G, where percentages will be displayed, will need a decimal display format. You will change column G's format later. Your spreadsheet should now look like Figure 3.10.

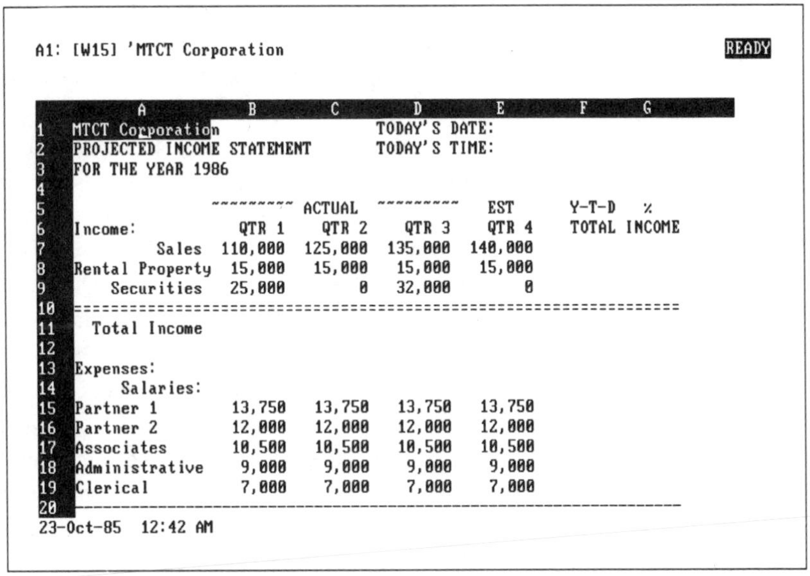

```
A1: [W15] 'MTCT Corporation                                    READY

         A          B       C       D       E       F       G
1  MTCT Corporation                  TODAY'S DATE:
2  PROJECTED INCOME STATEMENT        TODAY'S TIME:
3  FOR THE YEAR 1986
4
5                 ~~~~~~~~~ ACTUAL ~~~~~~~~~  EST     Y-T-D   %
6  Income:         QTR 1   QTR 2   QTR 3   QTR 4  TOTAL INCOME
7        Sales    110,000 125,000 135,000 140,000
8  Rental Property 15,000  15,000  15,000  15,000
9     Securities   25,000       0  32,000       0
10 =====================================================================
11    Total Income
12
13 Expenses:
14    Salaries:
15 Partner 1       13,750  13,750  13,750  13,750
16 Partner 2       12,000  12,000  12,000  12,000
17 Associates      10,500  10,500  10,500  10,500
18 Administrative   9,000   9,000   9,000   9,000
19 Clerical         7,000   7,000   7,000   7,000
20 ---------------------------------------------------------------------
23-Oct-85  12:42 AM
```

Figure 3.10: Formatted budget

4. To save your work again, enter

   / F S ↩ R

In this section, you have learned or reviewed:

- Adjusting column widths
- Formatting large numbers

Computing Values

One of the basic advantages of using 1-2-3 instead of paper and pencil is that the electronic spreadsheet does most of the work for you: it takes care of the adding, subtracting, multiplying, and dividing that are almost always necessary in working with numbers. Calculators provide this same service, but 1-2-3 takes it one step further. Because most of these operations appear in many places in a spreadsheet, 1-2-3 allows you to enter them only once and then simply copy them into all the other cells that are doing the same chore.

In the next sections you will see how to instruct 1-2-3 to perform arithmetic operations and how to copy those instructions that apply to more than one cell.

To give 1-2-3 instructions to add, subtract, multiply, or divide values, you have to supply two kinds of information: the operation you want performed, using the symbols +, −, *, and /, respectively, and the numbers or cells on which you want the operation performed. These instructions are called *formulas*. In the budget you are creating, 1-2-3 needs formulas for Total Income, Total Expenses, and Net Income for each quarter, the total for each row in the Y-T-D (year-to-date) TOTAL column, and the comparison of each line's total against the TOTAL INCOME for the year. You will input each formula only once and then use the Copy command to copy it into other cells where it will be used. You will also learn another shortcut: 1-2-3 allows you to build formulas by pointing to the cells that are referenced in the formula rather than typing each cell address.

ADDITION: USING THE + SIGN

Begin by entering the formula for Qtr 1 Total Income in cell B11. The cells that make up the Total Income are Sales, Rental Property, and Securities, or B7, B8, and B9, respectively.

To tell 1-2-3 that you are about to enter a formula, you type a plus (+) sign before typing anything else. This first plus sign doesn't denote addition or any other particular arithmetic operation. It simply signals to 1-2-3 that what follows is a formula to be performed, not a value or label.

1. With the cursor in cell B11, enter

+

and press ↑ 4 times. This tells 1-2-3 you are beginning a formula, points to Qtr 1 sales, and instructs 1-2-3 to add Sales.

2. Then enter

+

and press ↑ 3 times to instruct 1-2-3 to add Rental Property.

3. Enter

+

and press ↑ 2 times to instruct 1-2-3 to add Securities. Press ◄┘ to enter the complete formula.

Your screen should look like Figure 3.11, with the formula located in cell B11.

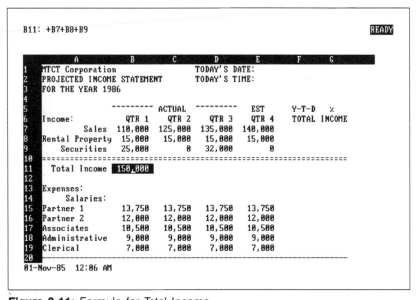

Figure 3.11: Formula for Total Income

Notice that what appears in the cell is the result of the formula, not the formula itself, and that what appears at the top of the screen (as long as your cursor is located in B11) is the formula, not the result of the formula.

Hint: Especially while you are developing and testing a new spreadsheet, you will want to use the option that allows you to print the spreadsheet with the formulas themselves, not their results, displayed in the cells. The command is /Print Printer Options Other Cell-Formulas.

ADDITION: USING THE @SUM FUNCTION

Lotus 1-2-3 has a special set of instructions called the @ functions that speed up formula input. These functions perform special operations (such as summing, averaging, or counting) on the cells you specify. The @SUM function looks like this:

@SUM(*first cell to add..last cell to add*)

Enter this function for Total Salaries in column B, row 21 (cell B21).

4. In cell B21, enter

   @SUM(

   and press ↑ 6 times. This points to the first cell to include in the sum, Partner 1. Type a period.
5. Then press ↓ 4 times to point to the last cell you wish to include in the sum.
6. Enter

) ⏎

   to complete the function.

Your cell should now contain the @SUM function displayed in Figure 3.12.

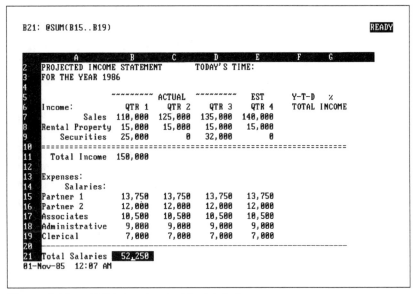

Figure 3.12: @SUM function for Total Salaries

Now enter the @SUM function for Total Expenses in cell B27. In the example above, you pointed to the series of cells to include in the sum. You can also type this range directly into the formula as **@SUM(B21.B26).** 1-2-3 interprets B21.B26 as "start at cell B21 and sum each cell up to and including cell B26."

Hint: If you insert more expense rows between rows 25 and 26, the @SUM function above automatically adjusts to include the new cells. Also notice that the range B21 through B26 includes cell B26, which contains the label ---------. Because the @SUM function interprets all labels as the value 0, the sum is not affected by the inclusion of B26.

For further discussion about @SUM and other 1-2-3 functions, turn to Chapter 4, "Using @ Functions."

SUBTRACTION: USING THE – SIGN

Now you will set up the formula to compute Net Income in cell B29.

7. Move your cursor to cell B29 and enter

+ B11 – B27

using whichever method you feel most comfortable with.

Your net income formula should be calculated as 87,950 for Qtr 1.

COPYING FORMULAS AND FUNCTIONS

Now you will copy all of the formulas and functions you set up for the first quarter to quarters 2, 3 and 4, using the Copy command.

8. Enter

/ C B11 ⏎

Note that the program prompts you for the cells you wish to copy from and to.

9. Enter

C11.E11 ⏎

Your total Net Income should now be completely filled out for all four quarters, as shown in Figure 3.13.

Now repeat this copy procedure for Total Salaries, Total Expenses, and Net Income.

10. Copy the contents of cell B21 into C21.E21, B27 into C27.E27, and B29 into C29.E29.

Your budget is almost complete. In column F, you will enter another @SUM formula.

11. In cell F7, enter

@SUM(B7.E7) ⏎

and copy the function to the remaining cells F8 through F29.

12. This procedure will write over the repeating labels in cells F10, F20, F26, and F28. Re-input them by moving the cursor to each cell and typing \ – ↵ or \ = ↵ as necessary.

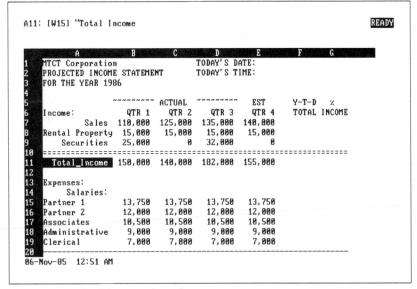

Figure 3.13: Total Income formulas

ERASING UNNECESSARY CELLS

You will also need to erase a few cells: F12, F13, and F14.

13. With the cursor in cell F12, enter

    / R E ↵

14. Repeat the procedure for cells F13 and F14.

Your spreadsheet should look like Figure 3.14.

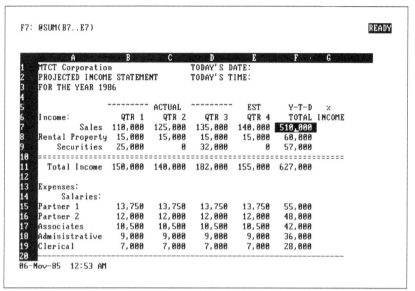

Figure 3.14: Completed Y-T-D totals

Figure 3.14: Completed Y-T-D totals (continued)

Hint: You could also erase the entire range—F12 through F14—all at once by typing

/ R E F12.F14 ↵

DIVISION: USING THE / SIGN

The only remaining formula for you to enter is the percent of Total Income calculation for each line item in column G, which will divide each Y-T-D Total (column F) by Total Income (cell F11).

15. In cell G7, enter

+F7/F11 ↵

FORMATTING CELLS WITH PERCENTAGES

To display values in your spreadsheet as percentages, you need to reformat the range of cells in column G.

16. Enter

/ R F P 1 ↵ G7.G30 ↵

The value displayed should be 81.3%.

Now copy the formula to the cell beneath it to calculate % Rental Property to Total Income.

17. Enter

/ C G7 ↵ G8 ↵

THE ERR MESSAGE

Notice that the result in cell G8 is ERR. Because 1-2-3 relatively adjusted the row number, the formula divides by cell F12, which 1-2-3 interprets as zero because it has no value. When you divide or multiply by zero, the ERR message is displayed. In the next section you will learn how to "freeze" a cell reference in a formula so that it does not adjust when the formula is copied.

FREEZING CONSTANTS WITH ABSOLUTE REFERENCES: THE F4 (ABSOLUTE) KEY

The adjustment 1-2-3 made to the row number, from F7 to F8, works as intended, but you want to keep F11 constant as the denominator. You can enter a "freeze" instruction to any cell reference that is to remain constant, or *absolute,* in a formula. In this case, you want F11 to remain absolute. To do this, you enter the "freeze" symbol ($) in the formula preceding the column location to keep that column number from being adjusted when the formula is copied to another cell. Enter the $ symbol preceding the row reference to keep the row number the same.

18. In cell G7, press the F2 (Edit) key. Position the cursor under the F of F11. Press the F4 (Absolute) key to make that reference absolute; then press ◄━┛.

Your formula should read + F7/ + $F$11, which instructs 1-2-3 to keep Total Income as the denominator for any duplicate formula. If the $ you entered replaced the F, your formula is incorrect because the insert mode was off. Press the Ins key once to turn insert on and then re-edit the formula, this time inserting the $ in front of the F. Now copy the formula to each row in column G.

19. Enter

   / C G7 ◄━┛ G8.G29 ◄━┛

Review the formula in cell G8 and notice that now only the first cell designation has changed.

CLEANING UP AFTER THE COPY COMMAND

To erase the unnecessary cell formulas in G12 through G14, use the Range Erase command.

20. Enter

     / R E G12.G14 ↵

Re-input the repeating underlines where ERR appears (cells G10, G20, G26, G28, and G30).

21. Enter

     \ - ↵

for a single underline or

     \ = ↵

for a double underline.

Your spreadsheet should now look like Figure 3.15.

```
            A          B        C         D        E         F       G
 1 MTCT Corporation              TODAY'S DATE:      10/01/86
 2 PROJECTED INCOME STATEMENT    TODAY'S TIME:      10:30 AM
 3 FOR THE YEAR 1986
 4
 5                ~~~~~~~~~ ACTUAL ~~~~~~~~~   EST      Y-T-D    %
 6 Income:          QTR 1    QTR 2    QTR 3    QTR 4    TOTAL  INCOME
 7        Sales    110,000  125,000  135,000  140,000  510,000  81.3%
 8 Rental Property  15,000   15,000   15,000   15,000   60,000   9.6%
 9     Securities   25,000        0   32,000        0   57,000   9.1%
10 ===================================================================
11   Total Income  150,000  140,000  182,000  155,000  627,000 100.0%
12
13 Expenses
14     Saleries:
15 Partner 1        13,750   13,750   13,750   13,750   55,000   8.8%
16 Partner 2        12,000   12,000   12,000   12,000   48,000   7.7%
17 Associates       10,500   10,500   10,500   10,500   42,000   6.7%
18 Administrative    9,000    9,000    9,000    9,000   36,000   5.7%
19 Clerical          7,000    7,000    7,000    7,000   28,000   4.5%
20 -----------------------------------------------------------------
21 Total Salaries   52,250   52,250   52,250   52,250  209,000  33.3%
22 Mngmt Expenses    4,000    5,000    4,500    4,800   18,300   2.9%
23        Rent       2,000    2,000    2,000    2,000    8,000   1.3%
24     Supplies      2,000    1,800    1,900    2,100    7,800   1.2%
25    Telephone      1,800    1,900    2,100    2,300    8,100   1.3%
26 -----------------------------------------------------------------
27 Total Expenses   62,050   62,950   62,750   63,450  251,200  40.1%
28 -----------------------------------------------------------------
29 Net Income       87,950   77,050  119,250   91,550  375,800  59.9%
30 ===================================================================
```

Figure 3.15: Completed budget

22. To save your work again, enter

/ F S ↤ R

In this section you have learned or reviewed:

- Entering formulas by pointing
- Addition using the + sign
- Addition using the @SUM function
- Subtraction using the − sign
- Copying formulas and functions
- Erasing unnecessary cells
- Division using the / sign
- ERR messages
- Freezing constants with the F4 (Absolute) key
- Cleaning up after the Copy command

Dating Your Work

It is a good practice to display the current date on each spreadsheet you create, so that you will later know when the file was last updated. This is called *date-stamping* your work. After you have entered the date, you can display it in any of several formats.

The following sections discuss some of the date functions available in 1-2-3 and the format options available with those functions.

DATE STAMPING WITH @DATE AND @TIME

To record a date that will not change every time you update the spreadsheet, use the formula @DATE(YY,MM,DD) (where, for example, YY is 86, MM is 10, and DD is 1). For time specifications that will not change, use @TIME(hr,min,sec) to specify the exact time.

1. In cell F1, enter

   @DATE(85,10,23)

2. In cell F2, enter

   @TIME(0,57,0)

CHOOSING DISPLAY FORMATS
FOR DATES AND TIMES

Notice that the value displayed is a very large number—the number of days since January 1, 1900. 1-2-3 stores all dates and times (except those entered as text labels) as a calculation from 1900, so that dates can be treated as numbers. Using this conversion, 1-2-3 can, for example, subtract one date from another. September 5, 1986 subtracted from September 10, 1986 yields the value 5. 1-2-3 accomplishes this by converting both dates into single numbers, performing the arithmetic required, and then converting them back to whatever format you have specified for the date to display.

Normally you will want dates to appear in standard day-month-year format, and times to appear in standard hour:minute format.

3. Reformat cell F1 using the Range Format Date 4 command. Reformat cell F2 using the Range Format Date Time 2 command. Cell F1 will now display the number as a date and cell F2 will now display the number as a time, as shown in Figure 3.16.

Hint: You can type @NOW in a cell to display your computer's internal clock. When you use @NOW, you can display the current date and time, according to your clock. Each time you use the spreadsheet, @NOW updates the date and time. This feature can be useful for managing regular input and changes to the spreadsheet as well as for keeping track of printouts.

For further details about how you can use date functions, see Chapter 4, "Using @ Functions."

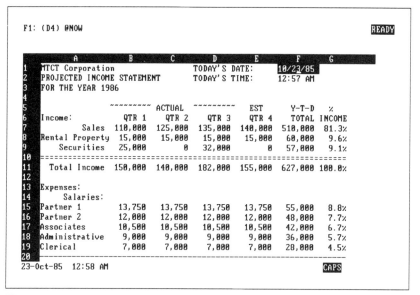

Figure 3.16: Date and time format

In this section you have learned or reviewed:

- Date stamping your work with @DATE and @TIME
- Formatting dates and times

Composing Text Notes

It is often necessary in financial analysis to summarize results briefly in a memo. Let's compose a short memo that reports the Total Income, Total Expenses, Net Income, and some key values from the spreadsheet.

To create a memo, you type directly into cells, just like you enter values, labels, and formulas. 1-2-3 allows you to enter up to 240 characters in a single cell.

Retrieve the INCOME spreadsheet if it is not already on your screen.

1. Enter

    / F R INCOME ⟵

ENTERING TEXT

To input the following text in the memo, move your cursor to cell A41. Press the Caps Lock key to capitalize the letters you will type in row 41 and 42.

2. Enter the memo as shown in each of the cells in Figure 3.17.

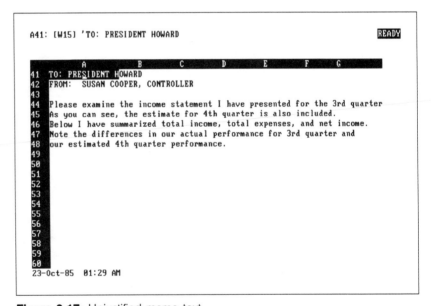

```
A41: [W15] 'TO: PRESIDENT HOWARD                                    READY

              A          B          C        D        E        F        G
41  TO: PRESIDENT HOWARD
42  FROM:   SUSAN COOPER, CONTROLLER
43
44  Please examine the income statement I have presented for the 3rd quarter
45  As you can see, the estimate for 4th quarter is also included.
46  Below I have summarized total income, total expenses, and net income.
47  Note the differences in our actual performance for 3rd quarter and
48  our estimated 4th quarter performance.
49
50
51
52
53
54
55
56
57
58
59
60
23-Oct-85  01:29 AM
```

Figure 3.17: Unjustified memo text

ALIGNING TEXT

Now tell 1-2-3 to justify the text so that it neatly fits, aligned between columns A and G, using the command Range Justify.

3. In cell A44 enter

/ R J A44.G44 ↵

Your text should look like Figure 3.18, which displays the justified text.

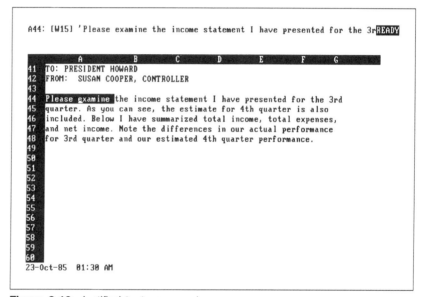

Figure 3.18: Justified text paragraph

INCLUDING SPREADSHEET VALUES IN MEMO TEXT

You can also include some of the values from your budget in the memo without having to type them in. The first time you type a memo, this may not appear to be much of a time-saver, but if you change any of the values in your spreadsheet later, the memo will automatically be updated.

Having 1-2-3 copy the contents of a cell that contains a label or value into another cell is called *referencing*. To reference Total Income, Expenses, and Net Income for each quarter, put the cursor in the destination cell, enter a + sign, enter the cell location of the label or value you want to reference, and press ↵. Whenever you then update or change the value in your budget, it will change in your memo automatically.

4. To reference Total Income in cell A52, move the cursor to cell A52 and enter

   +A11 ⬅

The label Total Income appears below the paragraph you typed.

5. Repeat this procedure using the cell references shown in Figure 3.19.

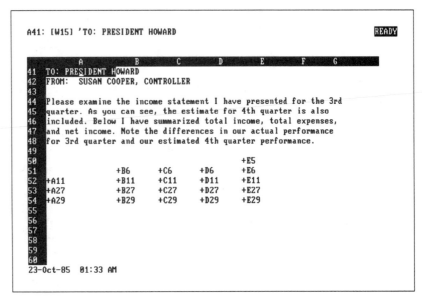

A41: [W15] 'TO: PRESIDENT HOWARD   READY

```
           A           B         C         D         E        F        G
41  TO: PRESIDENT HOWARD
42  FROM:  SUSAN COOPER, CONTROLLER
43
44  Please examine the income statement I have presented for the 3rd
45  quarter. As you can see, the estimate for 4th quarter is also
46  included. Below I have summarized total income, total expenses,
47  and net income. Note the differences in our actual performance
48  for 3rd quarter and our estimated 4th quarter performance.
49
50                                                    +E5
51                     +B6       +C6       +D6       +E6
52  +A11               +B11      +C11      +D11      +E11
53  +A27               +B27      +C27      +D27      +E27
54  +A29               +B29      +C29      +D29      +E29
55
56
57
58
59
60
23-Oct-85  01:33 AM
```

Figure 3.19: Cell reference formulas

Your memo should look like Figure 3.20 once you have correctly entered the closing sentence in cell A56.

6. To save your work, enter

   / F S ⬅ **R**

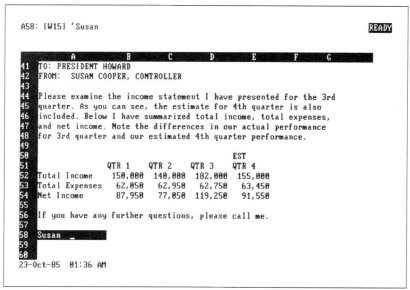

Figure 3.20: Completed memo

In this section you have learned or reviewed:

- Composing text notes
- Aligning text notes
- Including in text notes spreadsheet values that change automatically when the spreadsheet value changes

Changing Spreadsheet Values: Using What-If

Whenever you change a data value, the result of any formula or function that depends on that value changes automatically.

Changing values to see what would happen to other values is called playing "what-if." It takes 1-2-3 only a few seconds to recalculate all the cells affected by a change in one cell.

However, there are times, especially when you are making many changes to spreadsheet values, when you do not want 1-2-3 to recalculate automatically after every change. In the sections that follow, you will learn how to change values using both automatic and manual recalculation.

CHANGING A VALUE

To see automatic recalculation at work, change the Qtr 4 estimate for Sales from 140,000 to 150,000.

1. Press the Home key and move your cursor to cell E7, Qtr 4 Sales. Enter

    150000 ←

Notice that the Total Income increases by 10,000; so do the Y-T-D total and Net Income. The cell containing % INCOME also adjusts to reflect the change. Now take a look at the memo. Press the Home key; then press the PgDn key twice.

Notice that the memo has also been updated to reflect the change in Qtr 4 Total Income. This ability to *integrate,* or include, values from a spreadsheet with text is one of the great features of 1-2-3. Your updated memo should look like Figure 3.21.

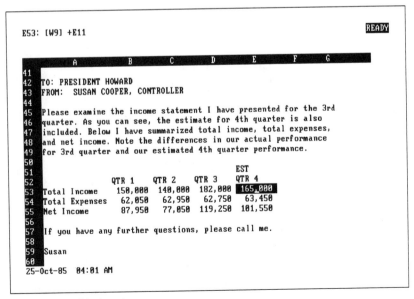

Figure 3.21: Updated memo

SETTING RECALCULATION TO MANUAL

When you are going to be changing a lot of values, you may want to turn off 1-2-3's automatic recalculation feature. To do this, you would enter

/ W G R M ⏎

When you have turned off automatic recalculation, you can instruct 1-2-3 to recalculate as described in the following section.

RECALCULATING SPREADSHEET VALUES: THE F9 (CALC) KEY

When you have set recalculation to Manual and want 1-2-3 to recalculate the formulas and functions dependent on values you changed, simply press the F9 (Calc) key.

To turn automatic recalculation back on, enter

/ W G R A ⏎

After playing what-if, where you change values just to see what might happen, you will often want to return to the spreadsheet that has the real data in it. Rather than save this version, retrieve the last saved version of the INCOME spreadsheet. Enter

/ F R INCOME ⏎

The spreadsheet before you appears just as it did before you last saved it. It's generally a good idea to save a spreadsheet before you play what-if, so that you can retrieve the unaltered data later.

In this section you have learned or reviewed:

- Changing spreadsheet values
- Setting recalculation to manual
- Manual recalculation using the F9 (Calc) key

Working with Spreadsheets Larger Than the Screen

Some spreadsheets are very wide—that is, they contain information in more columns than will fit on the screen. If you have a spreadsheet with 36 columns and 50 rows of sales items, expense, and net income data, it is difficult to see what happens when you change a value in the outer rows and columns. In the following sections you will see how to direct 1-2-3 to look at different sections of the spreadsheet by splitting the screen into "windows." Each window is a view of a different portion of the spreadsheet.

Another problem that arises with larger spreadsheets is not being able to view the descriptive row titles in column A or the column titles (usually in one of the top rows) when viewing the sections in far-off columns or distant rows. The following sections also discuss how to set titles.

SETTING ROW TITLES

You can't see the row titles when you are looking at the twentieth column of a spreadsheet because 1-2-3 can display only a limited amount of columns on the screen at one time. To display the row labels (or *titles*) on the left side of the screen at all times, use the Worksheet Titles Vertical command. Tell 1-2-3 where the titles should end by first moving your cursor to the column immediately following the titles. Everything to the left of the cursor will become a vertical title, as shown in Figure 3.22.

If the spreadsheet is very long, use the Worksheet Titles Horizontal command to fix horizontal column titles above the cursor. You can set both vertical and horizontal titles using the Worksheet Titles Both command, fixing titles to the left and above the cursor (Figure 3.23).

Hint: Once titles are set, the cursor won't move beyond them. Use the F5 (Goto) key to move the cursor into the title cells after they have been set. To cancel the Titles settings completely, use the Worksheet Titles Clear command.

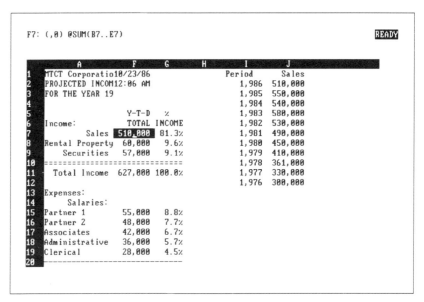

```
F7: (,0) @SUM(B7..E7)                                              READY

          A          F      G      H      I        J
1   MTCT Corporatio10/23/86                    Period    Sales
2   PROJECTED INCOM12:06 AM                     1,986   510,000
3   FOR THE YEAR 19                             1,985   550,000
4                                               1,984   540,000
5                    Y-T-D    %                 1,983   580,000
6   Income:        TOTAL INCOME                 1,982   530,000
7        Sales    510,000  81.3%               1,981   490,000
8   Rental Property 60,000   9.6%              1,980   450,000
9      Securities   57,000   9.1%              1,979   410,000
10  ==============================             1,978   361,000
11    Total Income 627,000 100.0%             1,977   330,000
12                                              1,976   300,000
13  Expenses:
14      Salaries:
15  Partner 1        55,000   8.8%
16  Partner 2        48,000   7.7%
17  Associates       42,000   6.7%
18  Administrative   36,000   5.7%
19  Clerical         28,000   4.5%
20  ------------------------------
```

Figure 3.22: Row titles set to view columns H–K

```
B14:                                                              READY

         A          B         C         D        E         F        G
1   MTCT Corporation           TODAY'S DATE:      10/23/86
2   PROJECTED INCOME STATEMENT  TODAY'S TIME:     12:06 AM
3   FOR THE YEAR 1986
4
5                   ~~~~~~~~~  ACTUAL ~~~~~~~~~~   EST    Y-T-D    %
6   Income:         QTR 1     QTR 2     QTR 3    QTR 4   TOTAL INCOME
14      Salaries:
15  Partner 1        13,750    13,750    13,750   13,750  55,000   8.8%
16  Partner 2        12,000    12,000    12,000   12,000  48,000   7.7%
17  Associates       10,500    10,500    10,500   10,500  42,000   6.7%
18  Administrative    9,000     9,000     9,000    9,000  36,000   5.7%
19  Clerical          7,000     7,000     7,000    7,000  28,000   4.5%
20  -------------------------------------------------------------------
21  Total Salaries   52,250    52,250    52,250   52,250 209,000  33.3%
22  Mngmt Expenses    4,000     5,000     4,500    4,800  18,300   2.9%
23         Rent       2,000     2,000     2,000    2,000   8,000   1.3%
24     Supplies       2,000     1,800     1,900    2,100   7,800   1.2%
25    Telephone       1,800     1,900     2,100    2,300   8,100   1.3%
26  -------------------------------------------------------------------
27  Total Expenses   62,050    62,950    62,750   63,450 251,200  40.1%
```

Figure 3.23: Row and column titles set to view columns H–K and row 25

CREATING WINDOWS

You can temporarily split your screen into two separate sections, or windows, by using the Worksheet Window command to view widely separated columns or rows at the same time. You can split the screen horizontally (top and bottom halves) for long spreadsheets (Figure 3.24) or vertically (left and right halves) for wide spreadsheets.

```
B29: (,0) +B11-B27                                              READY

         A          B          C          D          E        F        G
1  MTCT Corporation                    TODAY'S DATE:       10/23/86
2  PROJECTED INCOME STATEMENT          TODAY'S TIME:       12:06 AM
3  FOR THE YEAR 1986
4
5              ~~~~~~~~~   ACTUAL  ~~~~~~~~~~~~   EST      Y-T-D    %
6  Income:       QTR 1      QTR 2      QTR 3     QTR 4    TOTAL  INCOME
14     Salaries:
15  Partner 1     13,750     13,750     13,750    13,750   55,000   8.8%
16  Partner 2     12,000     12,000     12,000    12,000   48,000   7.7%
17  Associates    10,500     10,500     10,500    10,500   42,000   6.7%
18  Administrative  9,000      9,000      9,000     9,000   36,000   5.7%
         A          B          C          D          E        F        G
24       Supplies   2,000      1,800      1,900     2,100    7,800   1.2%
25       Telephone  1,800      1,900      2,100     2,300    8,100   1.3%
26  -----------------------------------------------------------------
27  Total Expenses  62,050     62,950     62,750    63,450  251,200  40.1%
28  -----------------------------------------------------------------
29  Net Income      87,950     77,050    119,250    91,550  375,800  59.9%
30  =================================================================
31
```

Figure 3.24: Horizontal windows in a spreadsheet

MOVING BETWEEN WINDOWS

Using the F6 (Window) key, you can jump back and forth between the windows you have created. Notice that when the cursor moves in one window, the other window moves as well, in synchronized movement.

You can turn off the synchronized (sync) feature by using the Worksheet Window Unsync option. When sync is turned off, moving the cursor in one window does not cause movement in the other.

To clear the windows from the screen, use the Worksheet Window Clear command.

Hint: You can use the Worksheet Window command with the Worksheet Titles command to fix titles within a particular window.

In this section, you have learned to:

- Fix column and row labels using the Worksheet Titles command
- Split the screen into two separate windows
- Move between windows using the F6 (Window) key

Printing Spreadsheets

The printing options in 1-2-3 are versatile, flexible, and easy to use. The 1-2-3 Print menu allows you to specify different kinds of printers, enter headers and footers for each page, select all or part of the spreadsheet to print, change the margins and page length, and choose to print either on the printer itself or into a file (where you could add finishing touches with a word processing program).

At the same time, the print options are set up so that most of the time you need specify nothing more than the range of the spreadsheet you want printed.

To see how to print a range in your spreadsheet, first make sure your printer is turned on and is on-line. Follow the prompts on the screen as you enter the following:

/ P P R A1.G56 ◄─┘ A G Q

Your printed report should look like Figure 3.25.

For further details about using 1-2-3's printing possibilities, see Chapter 7, "Formatting, Printing, and File Handling."

In this section you have learned or reviewed:

- Selecting the range for a printed report
- Printing the spreadsheet

```
MTCT Corporation                 TODAY'S DATE:     10/23/85
PROJECTED INCOME STATEMENT       TODAY'S TIME:     12:57 AM
FOR THE YEAR 1986

               ~~~~~~~~ ACTUAL ~~~~~~~~    EST      Y-T-D    %
Income:         QTR 1    QTR 2    QTR 3    QTR 4    TOTAL  INCOME
       Sales  110,000  125,000  135,000  140,000  510,000   81.3%
Rental Property 15,000   15,000   15,000   15,000   60,000    9.6%
    Securities  25,000        0   32,000        0   57,000    9.1%
===============================================================
  Total Income 150,000  140,000  182,000  155,000  627,000  100.0%

Expenses:
    Salaries:
Partner 1        13,750   13,750   13,750   13,750   55,000    8.8%
Partner 2        12,000   12,000   12,000   12,000   48,000    7.7%
Associates       10,500   10,500   10,500   10,500   42,000    6.7%
Administrative    9,000    9,000    9,000    9,000   36,000    5.7%
Clerical          7,000    7,000    7,000    7,000   28,000    4.5%
---------------------------------------------------------------
Total Salaries   52,250   52,250   52,250   52,250  209,000   33.3%
Mngmt Expenses    4,000    5,000    4,500    4,800   18,300    2.9%
         Rent     2,000    2,000    2,000    2,000    8,000    1.3%
     Supplies     2,000    1,800    1,900    2,100    7,800    1.2%
    Telephone     1,800    1,900    2,100    2,300    8,100    1.3%
---------------------------------------------------------------
Total Expenses   62,050   62,950   62,750   63,450  251,200   40.1%
---------------------------------------------------------------
Net Income       87,950   77,050  119,250   91,550  375,800   59.9%
===============================================================


TO:   PRESIDENT HOWARD
FROM: SUSAN COOPER, CONTROLLER

Please examine the income statement I have presented for the 3rd
quarter. As you can see, the estimate for 4th quarter is also
included. Below I have summarized total income, total expenses,
and net income. Note the differences in our actual performance
for 3rd quarter and our estimated 4th quarter performance.

                                          EST
                QTR 1    QTR 2    QTR 3    QTR 4
Total Income   150,000  140,000  182,000  155,000
Total Expenses  62,050   62,950   62,750   63,450
Net Income      87,950   77,050  119,250   91,550
```

Figure 3.25: Printed report

Summary

This is the end of the spreadsheet tutorial. You now have the basic skills to begin making 1-2-3 spreadsheets on your own. You might want to start by experimenting with the budget spreadsheet you have just created. The budget spreadsheet will reappear in other chapters of this book, so don't delete it from your files.

The next chapter explains and gives practical examples of using 1-2-3's built-in functions. Seeing specific problems from various professional fields will give you a good foundation for applying them in your own work.

Chapter 4

Using @ Functions

In this chapter, you will learn to:

- Use statistical @ functions: @SUM, @COUNT, @AVG, @MIN, @MAX, @VAR, and @STD
- Use financial @ functions: @DDB, @SLN, @SYD, @IRR, @NPV, @FV, @PV, @PMT, @RATE, @TERM, and @CTERM
- Use date @ functions: @NOW, @DATE, @TIME, @DATEVALUE, @TIMEVALUE, and @SECOND, @MINUTE, @HOUR, @DAY, @MONTH, and @YEAR
- Use logical @ functions: @IF, @TRUE, and @FALSE
- Use special @ functions: @VLOOKUP, @HLOOKUP, @INDEX, @CHOOSE, @CELL, @CELLPOINTER, @COLS and @ROWS, @ERR, @NA, @ISERR, and @ISNA
- Use mathematical @ functions: @ABS, @INT, @ROUND, @INT
- Use engineering @ functions: @ACOS, @ASIN, @ATAN, @COS, @LN, @LOG, @MOD, @SIN, @SQRT, @TAN

A *function* is a time-saving formula that has been abbreviated to a single word. Most functions operate on numbers—add them, subtract them, find out if they equal one another—and record the result.

In 1-2-3, all functions start with the symbol @. Most take action on a particular cell or group of cells, which are specified in parentheses after the function name, along with any other information the function needs to do its job. This information is called the *arguments* of the function. Arguments must be separated by commas, and the last argument is always followed by a parenthesis. As you read about each function in this chapter, you will be given the function's *syntax*, which consists of the name of the function followed by the arguments it requires.

One very useful feature of 1-2-3 functions is that they can be nested: that is, a function can be performed on another function. For example, using @SQRT (the square root function), you could take the square root of the sum of a group of numbers derived with the @SUM function. The complete function would look like this:

@SQRT(@SUM(A1..A4))

If cells A1 to A4 contain 1, 4, 5, and 6, then the sum is 16; the square root of 16 is 4, so the result of this function is 4.

This chapter will teach you how to set up @ functions in several different contexts. The sample problems and examples are designed to help you understand how to solve other problems so that you can widen the applicability of your expertise with 1-2-3. You learn not just which buttons to push but also examine some fundamental theoretical distinctions behind financial, logical, statistical, and mathematical analysis. Most of the examples in this chapter are designed to be of particular value to people who are already familiar with the problems themselves and want to learn to do them with 1-2-3. You need not do the problems that don't concern you, though you might find them interesting anyway.

If you have never used functions before, start by reading the first section, "Using Statistical Functions," which starts with @SUM, the function that adds a group of cells together. You will then be better prepared to tackle later sections that address the more advanced functions—mathematical, financial, engineering, and logical formulas.

If you already know how to use functions with statistical analysis, be sure to look at the sample problem in this section, which shows how to set up an ANOVA spreadsheet to analyze variance. This model is taken from the book *Statistics for Social Sciences* by William Hayes (Holt, Rinehart and Winston, Inc., 1974). This text is considered by students and professionals alike to be a classic in the field of statistical analysis. It can be used as an excellent reference for building models and offers step-by-step instructions as well as invaluable theoretical background.

Financial users should review the new 1-2-3 financial functions that compute depreciation, rates, and terms of investments.

The logical functions offer a powerful means of generating alternate values in one cell, based on the value found in another cell or cells. These functions are useful for anyone working with relatively complex relationships among numbers.

The special functions offer simple ways of indexing tables and lists of values so that you can make choices among values on the basis of another value. Using special functions also enables you to build sophisticated error-checking methods into your spreadsheets.

Mathematical problem solvers and engineers should turn to the section "Using Engineering Functions," which shows how to use mathematical functions in applied engineering applications.

This chapter can teach you to use a variety of time-saving functions. Regardless of your profession or level of experience with 1-2-3, you will learn to make your spreadsheets more efficient by using these functions. Basic statistical functions and their uses are described in the next section, starting with @SUM.

Using Statistical Functions

Lotus 1-2-3's statistical functions can compute the sum, average, count, standard deviation, minimum, maximum, and the variance of a series of values.

The @SUM, @COUNT and @AVG functions have a wide variety of applications outside the world of statistical analysis. Basically, they simplify tedious repetitions of adding, counting, and averaging numbers.

@MIN and @MAX find the minimum and maximum values in a series of numbers, which is often useful in such jobs as managing sales and estimating production quotas.

@STD and @VAR are invaluable statistical functions that are commonly used within a structured analysis of groups of data for revealing trends and specifying relationships, which are the foundations of statistical and financial prediction.

@SUM: ADDING A SERIES OF VALUES

@SUM(*first cell of series..last cell of series*)
or
@SUM(*x1,x2,...xn*)

Returns the sum of values included in the range, where each *x* is a number, cell reference, or arithmetic expression, separated by commas.

Example: @SUM(A1..A10,4,6,3 + 2)

One of the most common tasks you do with numbers—and the most open to the possibility of making mistakes on a calculator—is adding groups of numbers together. To do almost any job involving numbers, like setting up a budget, balancing an account, or estimating taxes, you spend much of your time simply adding numbers. @SUM is the 1-2-3 function that automatically calculates the sum of a range of values for you.

The range you specify to be summed can be part of a column or row, a block of cells and columns, or discontinuous groups of cells. Let's look at examples of each.

For example, @SUM(D3..D8) adds cells D3 through D8, which is part of a column. In this case, using @SUM is only a little faster than typing

+ D3 + D4 + D5 + D6 + D7 + D8

But if you want to sum a very long range of numbers, this function can save time.

Another advantage to using @SUM is that you can insert or delete a new row or column between the range referenced by @SUM, and the program will automatically adjust the range in the function. For example, assume you deleted row 5 from your worksheet. If you had entered the formula as   + D3 + D4 + D5 + D6 + D7 + D8, you would get an ERROR message in the new formula cell:

+ D3 + D4 + ERR + D5 + D6 + D7

If you had entered the @SUM function as @SUM(D3.D8), however, the new function would look like this:

@SUM(D3..D8)

Note that although you need to type only one period to enter a function, as in @SUM(D3.D8), the program always displays two periods (D3..D8) after you press ◄─┘.

Hint: Whenever possible, define a sum range to include an extra cell at the end of the function. Some people use an underline to mark this cell. Because the underline has no mathematical value, it does not affect the sum of the range. Then you can always add an extra cell at the end of the list by inserting a row between the underline and the last value of the range. Otherwise, you have to edit the @SUM function itself to contain the new cell.

You can use @SUM to add a block of rows and columns.

@SUM(D3..C5)

adds all the cells in column D starting at D3 *and* all the cells in column C through row 5.

You can also use @SUM to add discontinuous groups of cells.

@SUM(D3..D8,D10,C1..C10)

adds the cells D3 through D8, then skips cell D9, adds cell D10, and adds cells C1 through C10.

@COUNT: COUNTING THE NUMBER OF VALUES IN A SERIES

@COUNT(*first cell of series..last cell of series*)
or
@COUNT(*x1,x2,...xn*)

Returns a count of the number of values in a series, where each *x* is a number, cell reference, or arithmetic expression, separated by commas.

Example: @COUNT(A1..A10,4,6,3 + 2)

@COUNT is one of the building blocks in several more complex functions, such as @AVG, which averages a group of cells, and @STD, which calculates standard deviation.

@COUNT can be used for many nonstatistical housekeeping chores in your spreadsheet. With it, you can keep tabs on the weeks in a quarter or year by counting the number of lines in your weekly cash report. You can also use @COUNT to keep a running total of the records in your database.

@COUNT ignores blank cells, but it does count labels, so for most uses of this function, you will want exclude labels from the range specification.

Like @SUM, the range you specify to count entries in can refer to part of a column or row, a block of columns and rows, or a discontinuous group of cells.

	- - A - -	- - B - -	- - C - -	- - D - -
1	24	25	26	

In the above example

@COUNT(A1..D1)

produces the result 3, because only three cells of the four cells in the range contain values or labels.

@COUNT can also count cells in a block of rows and columns or in discontinuous groups of cells.

@AVG: AVERAGING A SERIES OF VALUES

@AVG(*first cell of series..last cell of series*)
or
@AVG(*x1,x2,...xn*)

Returns the average of values included in a series, where each x is a number, cell reference, or arithmetic expression, separated by commas.

Example: @AVG(A1..A10,4,6,3 + 2)

@AVG, the average function, is a combination of two other functions: it SUMS the values in the range specified and divides by the COUNT of the number of cells in the range. @AVG is a important element in many complicated statistical analyses.

@AVG ignores blank cells, so be sure all zero values in your range have been entered as zeros, not blanks. If all the cells in the range are blank, @AVG returns an ERROR message.

The range you specify to average entries like @SUM can refer to part of a column or row:

	- -A- -	- -B- -	- -C- -	- -D- -
1	32	33	35	

In the above example

@AVG(A1..D1)

produces the result 33.33, because the sum of the four cells is 100, but the count of the range is 3 as only three of the four cells in the range contain values. @AVG divides 100 by 3 instead of by 4.

@AVG can also count cells in a block of rows and columns or in discontinuous groups of cells.

@MIN AND @MAX: FINDING THE MINIMUM AND MAXIMUM VALUES IN A SERIES

@MIN(*first cell of series..last cell of series*)
@MAX(*first cell of series..last cell of series*)
or
@MIN(*x1,x2,...xn*)
@MAX(*x1,x2,...xn*)

Returns the minimum or maximum value found in a series, respectively, where each *x* is a number, cell reference, or arithmetic expression, separated by commas.

Example: @MIN(A1..A10,50,C10 + 50)

@MIN finds the minimum (that is, the smallest value) in a range of cells. @MAX finds the maximum value in the range. Both functions ignore blank cells, but because they do count labels as zeros, be sure to exclude text labels from your range specification when you're looking for the minimum value in a range of numbers.

Like @SUM, the range you specify to find the minimum or maximum entries in a range can refer to part of a column or row.

	- -A- -	- -B- -	- -C- -	- -D- -
1	32	33	35	

In the above example

@MIN(A1..C1)

produces the result 32, because the lowest value in the three cells is 32.

@MAX(A1..C1)

produces the result 35, because the highest value in the three cells is 35.

@MIN and @MAX can also find the minimum or maximum in cells in a block of rows and columns or in discontinuous groups of cells.

@VAR AND @STD: FINDING THE VARIANCE AND STANDARD DEVIATION OF A SERIES

@VAR(*first cell of series..last cell of series*)
@STD(*first cell of series..last cell of series*)
or
@VAR(*x1,x2,...xn*)
@STD(*x1,x2,...xn*)

Returns the standard deviation (@STD) or variance (@VAR) of a series, where each *x* is a number, cell reference, or arithmetic expression, separated by commas.

Example: @VAR(A1..A10,12,14,C10−4)

The statistical functions examined thus far—@SUM, @COUNT, @AVG, @MIN, and @MAX—are relatively straightforward arithmetic formulas that are useful in many nonstatistical applications. These are statistics used for assessing current conditions of a range of numbers; they are often called "descriptive" statistics. When most people think of statistics, it is descriptive statistics they have in mind: those that organize data.

With the @VAR function, we begin to move into a different area of statistics, called "predictive" or "inferential" statistics. By analyzing relatively small sample groups of numbers, the analyst makes predictions about the probable condition of the larger group from which the numbers came, based on strict rules of experimental design and probability theory. The Nielsen ratings are an example of this second group of statistics: the pollers attempt to predict the television preferences of a vast audience by examining the actual viewing habits of a small sample of people.

In this section, you will learn how to calculate the variance and standard deviation of a series of numbers. You will then learn to combine these functions with the functions @SUM, @AVG, and @COUNT.

In statistics, the *variance* is a description of how widely the numbers in a range deviate from the average, or *mean,* of the range. The range (0,50,100) varies much more from the mean than the range (49,50,51), although they both have the same mean, 50. The formula for variance is the average of the squared deviations from the mean: S^2.

Because the variance uses the square of the deviations, it is always an expression of variability of the squared units of measurement. The *standard deviation* of this squared expression allows you to talk about a distribution in terms of its original unsquared units of measurement. The standard deviation is simply the square root of the variance.

To find the variance of a range, you need only specify the range, and 1-2-3 does the rest of the work. 1-2-3 first calculates the variance and then reports the square root of the calculation.

Problem: You want to compare the distributions for two groups of students who took the same test. One group had breakfast; the other did not. You set up your data so that you can analyze the two groups with various statistical procedures and make predictions about the population from which the two groups came (students in general who do eat breakfast and students in general who don't eat breakfast). Determine the mean, variance, and standard deviation for group A and group B:

Group A	*Group B*
94	90
87	81

Group A	Group B
75	75
92	87
88	88
99	95
80	87
85	66
77	75
89	80

Solution: Enter the scores for group A in cells A1 through A10 and for group B in cells B1 through B10. In cell A12, enter the mean or average of group A as

@AVG(A1.A10)

In cell B12, do the same for group B. Enter

@AVG(B1.B10)

In cell A13, calculate the standard deviation for group A by entering

@STD(A1.A10)

In cell B13, do the same for group B. Enter

@STD(B1.B10)

Finally, calculate the variance for groups A and B. In cell A14, enter

@VAR(A1.A10)

In cell B14, enter

@VAR(B1.B10)

For your purposes, these may be the only statistics you need for your analysis. If you wanted to perform more advanced analyses, you now have the raw material you need. You could, for example, easily perform a t-test or chi-squared test from the data now available.

@VAR allows you to calculate the variance of an entire population. It can be used either as a descriptive statistic or in a formula to analyze a sample, producing inferential statistics that will allow you to make assumptions about the larger population. A more realistic and widely used technique of analyzing variance is the ANOVA method. How to construct an ANOVA spreadsheet that can be reused is demonstrated in the following section.

SAMPLE PROBLEM: CALCULATING ANALYSIS OF VARIANCE

Even using a pocket calculator, doing an analysis of variance (ANOVA) is a painstaking and difficult chore that those of us who do statistical analysis often face.

If you often do a particular statistical procedure such as the ANOVA, you can set up the sample spreadsheet that follows as a blank master spreadsheet named ANOVA. Setting up this spreadsheet may take a little time, but you will never have to set up another one, and you will never have the attendant fear that you have left a step out of the analysis or summed before you squared where you should have squared before you summed.

After you have created the master spreadsheet ANOVA, test it with data from an ANOVA you have already performed to make sure that the formulas you have set up are accurate. Then erase the test data. Whenever you need to do an analysis of variance, just retrieve the spreadsheet ANOVA, enter your raw data, and adjust the formulas for any changes in the sample size from the master shell. If you want to save the results, you can save the spreadsheet in a file using a new name, which keeps the original copy of ANOVA intact. For more on 1-2-3 file handling, see Chapter 7.

For additional explanations of the formulas presented in the following problem, see *Statistics for the Social Sciences* by William Hayes (Holt, Rinehart and Winston, Inc., 1974).

Problem: Set up an analysis of variance between the two sets of test scores in Figure 4.1, using the Fixed Effects model (Model I).

Each set contains 15 test scores. (In this example the sample size is unrealistically small, for the sake of convenience. If you are setting up a master shell, you will probably want to allow for greater sample sizes.)

```
A1: [W12] "QTY A                                                        READY

        A            B            C           D          E         F
1      _QTY A       QTY B        QTY C        SST        SSB       SSW
2
3   E RAW A ^/N E RAW B ^/N                 MS BETW MS WITHIN    F RATIO
4
5       RAW A        RAW B       RAW A^2    RAW B^2
6         7            8
7         9.5          8
8        11           11
9        12.5         13
10       16.5         21
11       17.5         25
12       18           25
13       19.5         26
14       20.5         28
15       23.5         29
16       27           35
17       27.5         38
18       28.5         40
19       29           41
20       30           42
```

Figure 4.1: Raw data for ANOVA

Solution: First, set all columns to a width of 12 using the Worksheet Global Column-Width 12 command. Now set all labels to be right-aligned by using the Worksheet Global Label-Prefix Right command. Starting in row 6 of columns A and B, enter the raw scores for each group and the labels as shown in Figure 4.1.

In cell C6, compute the square of each score in column A, entering the formula once and copying it to the other cells. Enter

+A6^2

In cell D6, compute the square of each score in column B, entering the formula once and copying it to the other cells. Enter

+B6^2

Your spreadsheet should look like Figure 4.2.

```
A1: [W12] "QTY A                                              READY

         A           B          C           D         E          F
1     _QTY A       QTY B      QTY C         SST       SSB        SSW
2
3  E RAW A ^/N E RAW B ^/N               MS BETW  MS WITHIN   F RATIO
4
5     RAW A       RAW B      RAW A^2     RAW B^2
6       7           8          49          64
7      9.5          8         90.25        64
8      11          11         121         121
9      12.5        13        156.25       169
10     16.5        21        272.25       441
11     17.5        25        306.25       625
12     18          25         324         625
13     19.5        26        380.25       676
14     20.5        28        420.25       784
15     23.5        29        552.25       841
16     27          35         729        1225
17     27.5        38        756.25      1444
18     28.5        40        812.25      1600
19     29          41         841        1681
20     30          42         900        1764
```

Figure 4.2: Raw data with squares computed

In cell A2, sum all the squares of scores. This is QTY A. Enter

@SUM(C6.D20)

In cell B2, sum all the raw scores. This is QTY B. Enter

@SUM(A6.B20)

In cell A4, sum all the raw scores in column A, square the result, and divide the result by @COUNT for that column. Enter

(@SUM(A6.A20)^/@COUNT(A6.A20)

In cell B4, sum all the raw scores in column B, square the result, and divide the result by @COUNT for column B. Enter

(@SUM(B6.B20)^2)/@COUNT(B6.B20)

In cell C2, sum A4 and B4. Enter

@SUM(A4.B4)

Even though you're only adding two numbers, use the @SUM function rather than the formula +A4+B4. When you use this spreadsheet as a master, changes will be easier to manage. Call the sum in cell C2 QTY C. Your spreadsheet should look like Figure 4.3.

```
C2: [W12] @SUM(A4..B4)                                          READY

        A            B            C           D         E          F
1      QTY A        QTY B        QTY C        SST       SSB       SSW
2    18834.25       687.5    16040.41666
3  E RAW A ^/N  E RAW B ^/N                 MS BETW  MS WITHIN  F RATIO
4   5900.416666    10140
5      RAW A        RAW B        RAW A^2    RAW B^2
6        7            8           49          64
7        9.5          8           90.25       64
8       11           11          121         121
9       12.5         13          156.25      169
10      16.5         21          272.25      441
11      17.5         25          306.25      625
12      18           25          324         625
13      19.5         26          380.25      676
14      20.5         28          420.25      784
15      23.5         29          552.25      841
16      27           35          729        1225
17      27.5         38          756.25     1444
18      28.5         40          812.25     1600
19      29           41          841        1681
20      30           42          900        1764
```

Figure 4.3: Quantity A,B,C computed

In cell D2, calculate the sum of squares total (SST):

$$A - (B^2 / N)$$

where N is the count of all raw scores. To do this, enter

+A2−(B2^2/@COUNT(A6.B20))

The result should be 3079.041666.

In cell E2, calculate the sum of squares between (SSB):

$$C - (B^2 / N)$$

Enter

$$+C2-(B2\char`\^2/@COUNT(A6.B20))$$

The result should be 285.2083333.

In cell F2, calculate the sum of squares within (SSW):

$$A - C$$

Enter

$$+A2-C2$$

The result should be 2793.833333.

In cell D4, calculate the mean square between (MS between):

$$SSB / J - 1$$

where J is the number of samples. Enter

$$+E2/(@COUNT(A6.B6) - 1)$$

The result should be 285.2083333.

In cell E4, calculate the mean square within (MS within):

$$SSW / N - J.$$

Enter

$$+F2/(@COUNT(A6.B20) - @COUNT(A6.B6))$$

The result should be 99.77976190.

In cell F4, calculate the F ratio:

MS between / MS within

Enter

+D4/E4

The result should be 2.858378571.

Now look up the F in a standard F distribution table, with $J - 1$ and $N - J$ degrees of freedom. The result is significant.

The final step is to protect all formulas by using the Range Protect command on cells A1 through F20. Then use Range Unprotect to unprotect the raw scores in cells A6 through B20. Note that the unprotected cells are of a higher intensity. Turn protection on by using the Worksheet Global Protection Enable command (for more on 1-2-3 protection, see Chapter 7).

Your completed spreadsheet should now look like Figure 4.4.

```
A1: [W12] "QTY A                                                          READY

        A           B           C           D           E           F
1     QTY A       QTY B       QTY C        SST         SSB         SSW
2    18834.25     687.5    16040.41666  3079.041666 285.2083333 2793.833333
3  E RAW A ^/N E RAW B ^/N              MS BETW    MS WITHIN    F RATIO
4  5900.416666   10140                 285.2083333 99.77976190 2.858378571
5     RAW A       RAW B       RAW A^2     RAW B^2
6        7           8          49          64
7        9.5         8          90.25       64
8       11          11         121         121
9       12.5        13         156.25      169
10      16.5        21         272.25      441
11      17.5        25         306.25      625
12      18          25         324         625
13      19.5        26         380.25      676
14      20.5        28         420.25      784
15      23.5        29         552.25      841
16      27          35         729        1225
17      27.5        38         756.25     1444
18      28.5        40         812.25     1600
19      29          41         841        1681
20      30          42         900        1764
```

Figure 4.4: Completed ANOVA spreadsheet

The ANOVA spreadsheet you have just created can be modified to include more rows for larger sample sizes. To insert rows, place the cursor in row 7 and use the Worksheet Insert Row command to insert the desired number of rows (to designate the number of rows, just press ↓ once for each row). The formulas you entered will adjust automatically to include new rows as long as you insert them properly, using the above sequence.

To erase the raw data in this example, use the Range Erase command in cells A6 through B20. Save the spreadsheet under the name ANOVA. If you wish, you can use this spreadsheet, with minor changes and additions to the formulas, for the other standard variance analyses.

In this section, you have learned to use:

- @SUM to add a range of values
- @COUNT to count values or labels in a range
- @AVG to compute the average for a range of values
- @MIN and @MAX to find the minimum or maximum in a range of values
- @VAR and @STD to compute variance and a standard deviation

Using Financial Functions

Lotus 1-2-3's @ functions simplify methods of financial analysis that are often time consuming and complicated. This section uses the 1-2-3 financial functions to look at depreciation computations, present-value analysis, and investment evaluations. Experienced 1-2-3 users take note: several of the functions described here are new with Release 2 of 1-2-3.

If you have been using a sophisticated pocket calculator to compute internal rate of return, net present, future, and present values, you will be happy to learn that 1-2-3 derives these variables much more quickly and easily, using @IRR for internal rate of return, @NPV for net present value, @FV for future value, and @PV for present value.

We will also examine several functions that help to analyze investments: @RATE, @TERM, and @CTERM.

The first problem—depreciation—is a standard and often unpleasant business analysis made workable by three new 1-2-3 functions: @DDB (double-declining balance), @SLN (straight line), and @SYD (sum of the year's digits), which allow depreciation to be calculated according to these three popular accounting techniques. Each method, the functions each uses, and the differences among them are discussed.

DEPRECIATION

Depreciation is a method used by accountants to allocate the original cost of a capital asset over each time period in which the asset is used to produce revenue. Depreciation stops in the year that the asset is assumed to be no longer useful and is generally sold for its salvage value.

Different methods of depreciation are used in different situations—for example, when computing taxable income over the period involving the asset. The three methods 1-2-3 offers in computing depreciation—double-declining balance, straight line, and sum of the year's digits—are illustrated in the next three sections. A typical business depreciation problem is used to demonstrate the difference between these three methods.

@DDB: Computing Double-Declining Balances

@DDB(*cost, salvage value, life, period*)

Returns depreciation based on the double-declining balance method, where the arguments are numbers, cell references, or arithmetic expressions.

Example: @DDB(A1,A2,A3,A4)

The double-declining balance method of depreciation (DDB) sets the rate of depreciation for each period such that a greater amount of depreciation occurs in earlier periods. The equation for DDB for a period is:

$$(bv * 2) \: / \: n$$

where *bv* is the book value in that period or the cost minus the sum of depreciation to date, and *n* is the life of the asset.

To set up the depreciation calculation, you reference the cells that contain the cost, salvage value, life, and period as you enter the

@DDB function. Because the DDB method computes depreciation for each period differently, make sure to double-check the period number used in the function.

@SLN: Computing Straight-Line Depreciation

@SLN(*cost, salvage, life*)

Returns depreciation using the straight-line method, where the arguments are numbers, cell references, or arithmetic expressions.

Example: @SLN(A1,A2,A3)

The straight-line method (SLN) computes the asset's depreciation evenly for each period of the life of the asset. The equation used is:

$$(c - s) / n$$

where c is the cost of the asset, s is its salvage value, and n is its useful life.

As you enter the @SLN function, you reference the cells that contain the cost, salvage value, and life of the asset. Because the SLN function computes the amount for depreciation that is equal for all periods, use the Range Value command to copy the value from the original function to the other year's value for depreciation.

@SYD: Computing Sum of the Year's Digits

@SYD(*cost, salvage, life, period*)

Returns depreciation based on the sum of the year's digits, where the arguments are numbers, cell references, or arithmetic expressions.

Example: @SYD(2000,A1,A2,A3)

The sum-of-the-year's-digit method (SYD) is another method that sets the rate such that the asset's depreciation is greater in earlier periods. The equation used is:

$$\frac{(c-s)(n-p+1)}{n\,(n+1)\,/\,2}$$

where c is the cost of the asset, s is its salvage value, n is its useful life, and p is the current period.

As you enter the @SYD function, you reference the cells that represent the cost, salvage value, life, and period of the asset. As with the DDB method, double-check the period, as the function's result for depreciation depends on it.

Sample Problem:
Analyzing the Effect of Depreciation on Net Income

Problem: You purchased a copying machine for $20,000 in 1985. Your office manager reports that the useful life of this machine is five years, and at the end of that time it will sell for about $3,000. Compute the depreciation using three methods and decide which method best affects taxable income.

For each method you will use, you need the following information:

- Cost: The amount paid for the asset—$20,000
- Salvage value: The amount the asset is worth at the end of the useful period—$3,000
- Life: The number of periods the machine will be useful—5
- Period: The time period you want to find the depreciation for—1985–1989

Solution: Construct a spreadsheet for looking at the three methods. Enter the labels and data values using Figure 4.5.

Column A has a width of 9, which causes the last E in NET INCOME to be truncated. Use the Worksheet Column Set-Width 15 command to set the width to 15.

Format the spreadsheet using the Range Format Currency 0 command for the range B3 through B4 and Range Format, 0 for the range B10 through B20.

You next enter the three functions for the DDB, SLN, and SYD methods (Figure 4.6). Move your cursor to cell B12 and enter

@DDB(B3,B4,B5,B8)

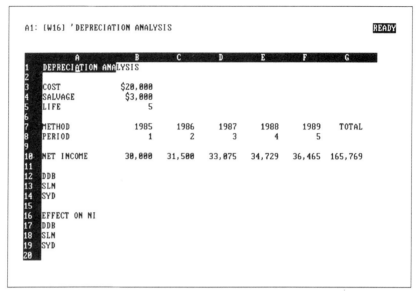

Figure 4.5: Depreciation analysis spreadsheet labels and values

In cell B13 enter

@SLN(B3,B4,B5)

In cell B14 enter

@SYD(B3,B4,B5,B8)

In the above functions, cell B8 refers to the period cell whose column position will change relatively as the period changes. The other cell references must remain constant or absolute, so freeze the constants before copying the functions to the remaining periods. For example, to edit the function for DDB in cell B12:

1. Press the F2 (Edit) key once.
2. Move the cursor to the first cell reference in the function, B3.
3. Press the F4 (Abs) key once.

Notice that $ signs are placed around the cell reference. This makes

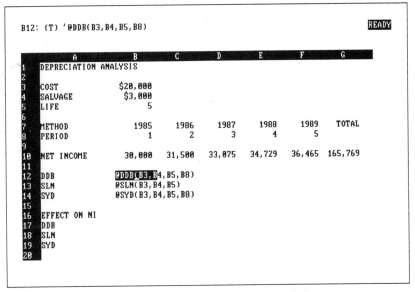

Figure 4.6: Functions for DDB, SLN, and SYD depreciation

the location reference of COST absolute. The formula will always reference cell B3.

4. Move the cursor to the second cell in the function, B4.

5. Press the F4 (Abs) key once.

Notice that $ signs are placed around the cell. This makes the location referenced for SALVAGE absolute. The formula will always reference cell B4.

6. Move the cursor to the third cell in the function, B5.

7. Press the F4 (Abs) key once.

Notice that $ signs are placed around the cell. This makes the location referenced for LIFE absolute. The formula will always reference cell B5.

8. Press ◄— to complete the edit of the cell as shown in Figure 4.7.

Edit cells B3, B4, and B5 for the SLN and SYD function using the F2 key to begin the edit. Press the F4 key with the cursor positioned on the cell to add the $ signs, and press ◄┘ to complete the edit.

Now use the Copy command to copy the formulas in cells B12 to B14 to the remaining periods in cells C12 to F14. Next, enter the function that computes the total for DDB. In cell G12, enter

@SUM(B12.F12)

Finally, copy this formula to the remaining cells G13 through G15. Your half-completed spreadsheet should look like Figure 4.8.

Depreciation is subtracted from net income as a non-cash expense. If you subtract the depreciation amounts calculated by each depreciation method from net income one at a time, you can see clearly the differences in net income. Net income varies, reflecting a higher value for less depreciation and a lower value for more depreciation. Enter the formula in cell B17 that subtracts DDB from net income and displays the effect of the first method of depreciation:

+B10-B12

In cell B18, enter

+B10-B13

for the SLN effect, and in cell B19 enter

+B10-B14

for the SYD effect. Now copy the formula to the remaining four periods in cells C17 through F19 for each method. Finally, enter a function to compute the total for DDB in cell G17. Type

@SUM(B17.F17)

and then copy this formula to the remaining cells G18 through G19. Your spreadsheet should look like Figure 4.9.

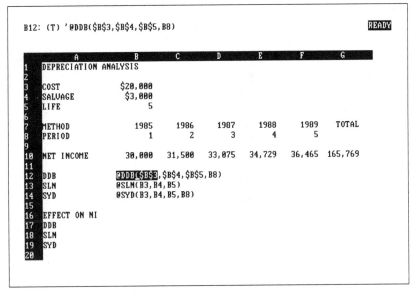

Figure 4.7: Formula for DDB using absolute signs

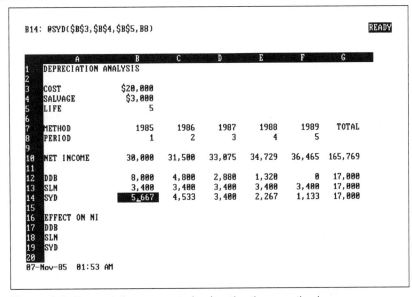

Figure 4.8: Depreciation computed using the three methods

```
B17: +B10-B12                                                    READY

         A        B        C        D        E        F        G
 1  DEPRECIATION ANALYSIS
 2
 3  COST     $20,000
 4  SALVAGE   $3,000
 5  LIFE          5
 6
 7  METHOD     1985     1986     1987     1988     1989    TOTAL
 8  PERIOD        1        2        3        4        5
 9
10  NET INCOME 30,000   31,500   33,075   34,729   36,465  165,769
11
12  DDB       8,000    4,800    2,880    1,320        0   17,000
13  SLN       3,400    3,400    3,400    3,400    3,400   17,000
14  SYD       5,667    4,533    3,400    2,267    1,133   17,000
15
16  EFFECT ON NI
17  DDB      22,000   26,700   30,195   33,409   36,465  148,769
18  SLN      26,600   28,100   29,675   31,329   33,065  148,769
19  SYD      24,333   26,967   29,675   32,462   35,332  148,769
20
28-Oct-85  01:56 AM                                             CAPS
```

Figure 4.9: Completed depreciation analysis formulas

Save your new spreadsheet in a file called DEPREC. This spreadsheet will be used to create a graph in Chapter 6.

CASH FLOW ANALYSIS

The most widely used financial and investment analysis is cash flow analysis. Although not all experts agree that the Internal Rate of Return, or IRR, is the most important measurement of an investment, they invariably use it as part of their analysis nevertheless.

Present value, or PV, a close relative of IRR, is a more accepted ruler for investment and financial performance, because it takes into consideration the time value of money.

Besides @IRR and @PV, 1-2-3 also offers two other cash flow analysis functions commonly used in accounting applications: Net Present Value (@NPV) and Future Value (@FV), which are also discussed in this section.

@IRR: Finding Internal Rate of Return

@IRR(*initial guess, net cash flow*)

Returns the internal rate of return, where the initial guess is a number, cell reference, or arithmetic expression, and the net cash flow is either a list of numbers entered as function arguments or a range of cells in the spreadsheet.

Example: @IRR(A1,A2..A10)

The rate that discounts an investment's cash benefits over time to zero, including the initial cash cost of that investment, is known as the internal rate of return or the IRR. It assumes you can reinvest the proceeds at that IRR.

Financial analysts use this value to measure the profitability of a project as well as to rank different projects, such as real estate investments, oil and gas investments, and joint ventures. The IRR is also used to make capital asset budget decisions.

The IRR needs two inputs, the initial guess for the IRR and net cash flow. The initial guess must be a value between 0 and 1. It is used to start the mathematical routine used by 1-2-3. This example will use 0.10 as the initial guess.

The net cash flow is the amount of money the investment generates. The example will demonstrate how to use 1-2-3 to apply this function to the asset used in the depreciation spreadsheet.

Problem: Suppose that a machine costing $20,000 will generate a savings in production of $3,000, $4,500, $6,000, $5,000, and $3,000, respectively, in its five-year life. At the end of this period you will sell it for $3,000. What is the IRR of this investment?

Solution: Set up your spreadsheet model like Figure 4.10, with the labels and values shown.

The net cash flow is simply the annual savings or cash inflows plus the salvage price of the asset less the initial cost, as shown in our spreadsheet model. Enter the formula for cash flow in cell B25 as

@SUM(B22.B24)

Now copy the formula in B25 to the remaining cells C25 through F25.

Finally, format cells B21 through F60 for commas and cells B27 through C28 as percentages, using the Range Format command.

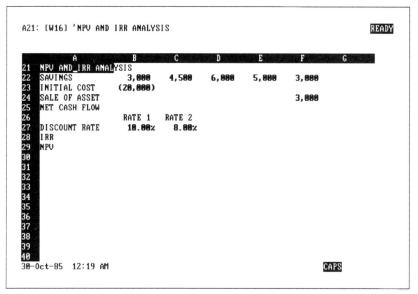

Figure 4.10: IRR and NPV analysis labels and values

(Cells B21 through F60 are formatted now because this range will be used for several accounting examples.) Enter the function for IRR in cell B28:

    @IRR(B27,B25.F25)

Your result should be 9.75%, as shown in Figure 4.11. Save this spreadsheet to use in the next examples.

@NPV: Finding Net Present Value

> @NPV(*discount rate,net cash flow*)
>
> Returns the net present value, where the discount rate is a number, cell reference, or arithmetic expression, and the net cash flow is either a list of equal or unequal numbers entered as function arguments, or a range of cells in the spreadsheet.
>
> *Example:* @NPV(.8,A1.A10)

The net cash flow of a project can be discounted at a certain rate to determine the net present value, or NPV. If the NPV is positive

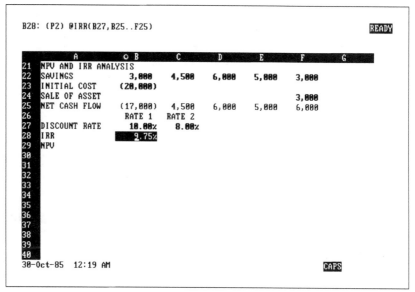

Figure 4.11: IRR analysis

for the project, it is generally acceptable if the rate used is an acceptable rate of return. The NPV can also be used to test the IRR computed by 1-2-3.

Remember, this function assumes that outflows occur at the end of a period. If cash flows occur at the beginning of a period, you can adjust the discount rate as follows, using the @NPV function:

$$@NPV(\textit{discount rate} * (1 + \textit{discount rate}), \textit{cash flow})$$

Problem: Determine whether the IRR is correct by evaluating the NPV using a discount rate higher than the IRR value and evaluating the NPV using a discount rate lower than the IRR value.

Solution: In cell B29, enter the function for the NPV using the 10% discount rate in cell B27 and the same net cash flow series used in the IRR problem·

$$@NPV(B27,B25.F25)$$

The resulting NPV is (87), or − 87. The discount rate is too high, so you should decrease it. Enter another NPV formula in cell

C29 using the 8% discount rate in cell C27 and the same series of cash flows:

@NPV(C27,B25.F25)

The resulting NPV is 639, which means the discount rate is too low. This confirms that the IRR is between 10% and 8%. Your screen should look like Figure 4.12.

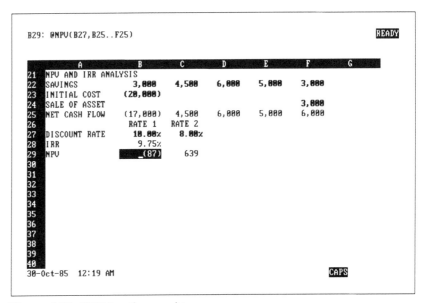

Figure 4.12: NPV function results

Save this spreadsheet, as it will be used to illustrate further examples.

You might want to experiment now by entering different discount rates in cells B27 and C27.

@FV: Computing Future Value

@FV(*periodic payment, fixed interest rate, term*)

Returns the future value, where the arguments are numbers, cell references, or arithmetic expressions.

Example: @FV(C1,C2,C3)

This function computes the future value, or FV, of an investment made as a payment over a number of periods earning a fixed interest rate. The equation for FV is:

$$PMT * \frac{(1 + int)^n - 1}{int}$$

where *PMT* is the periodic payment, *int* is the periodic interest, and *n* is the number of periods.

Problem: You want to deposit $2,000 each year to a retirement plan on December 31, beginning at age 25 and continuing for 35 years. Your bank offers a fixed 10.2% interest rate. The account representative suggests that you would be better off depositing the money on January 1 of each year. What is the difference in the amount you will receive after 35 years if: (a) you deposit on December 31 each year, and (b) you deposit on January 1 each year?

Solution: Beginning in cell A31, enter the labels and values for the FV and PV analysis section of your spreadsheet using Figure 4.13 as a guide. Then format the rate cells B33 and F33 as percentages.

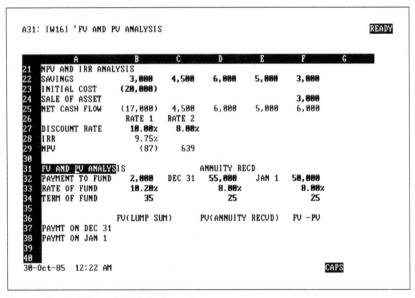

Figure 4.13: FV and PV labels and values

Next, enter the first formula for FV in cell B37 to compute the FV of the deposits made at the end of the year:

@FV(B32,B33,B34)

Now enter the second formula for FV in cell B38 to compute the FV of the deposits made at the beginning of the year:

@FV(B32,B33,B34)*(1 + B33)

Your results should look like Figure 4.14, which shows the future value of the accounts for both options. Depositing at the beginning of the period accumulates more money. You will continue with this spreadsheet in the next section.

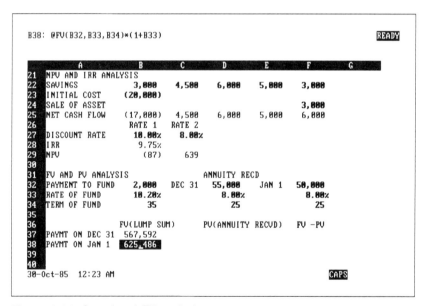

Figure 4.14: Completed FV analysis

@PV: Computing Present Value

@PV(*periodic payment, fixed interest rate, term*)

Returns the present value, where the arguments are numbers, cell references, or arithmetic expressions.

Example: @PV(C1,C2,C3)

The present value (PV) method determines the current value of a future payment or series of future payments. The equation for PV is:

$$PMT * \quad \frac{1-(1+int)^{-n}}{int}$$

where *PMT* is the periodic payment, *int* is the periodic interest, and *n* is the number of periods.

This function differs from the @NPV in that the cash flows or payments for @PV must be equal or even. @NPV is used to compute present value for uneven cash flows.

Problem: In the retirement program outlined above, you elect either to receive your proceeds in a lump-sum payment at the end of the 35 years or in the form of an annuity (a series of payments) to be paid either: (a) the amount of $55,000 each December 31 for 25 years or (b) the amount of $50,000 each January 1 for 25 years. Assume you can deposit the money received in a savings account earning 8% interest. Among all the options, which is the best?

Solution: Enter the formula for PV in cell D37 to compute the PV of receiving $55,000 for 25 years earning 8% interest at the end of the year:

@PV(D32,D33,D34)

Next, enter the formula for PV in cell D38 to compute the PV of receiving $50,000 for 25 years earning 8% interest at the beginning of the year:

@PV(F32,F33,F34)*(1 + F33)

Finally, compare the FV to the PV in cell F37 for the option of making payments at the end of the year and receiving payments at the end of the year by subtracting the FV from the PV. Enter the formula

+ D37 – B37

Copy this formula to cell F38. The results in Figure 4.15 show that the PV of receiving the $55,000 at the end of each year is greater than the lump-sum payment. However, if you elected to make your payment on January 1, you are better off choosing the lump-sum option instead of annual payments at the beginning of each year, because of the negative net present value.

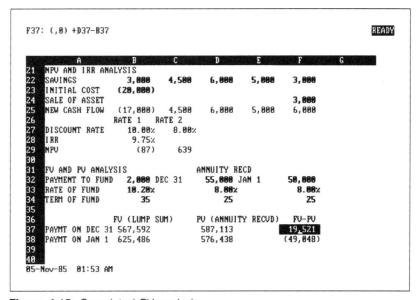

Figure 4.15: Completed PV analysis

MORTGAGE ANALYSIS

With the cost of real estate on the rise and competition among banks for your business stiffening, it is becoming more important to shop around for interest rates and terms of mortages before you buy. If you want to make a fixed monthly payment, you should compute the payments at various interest rates and terms to know what you can best afford. The 1-2-3 @PMT function can help you negotiate loan terms.

You can also use @PMT to compute the loan constant (k) for more sophisticated real estate analyses, such as analyzing the payment of loan balances. The formula for k is:

$$k = Loan\ amount\ /\ payment$$

The functions @TERM and @CTERM, described in the section following this, derive the term of a loan, given other parameters such as the present and future value.

These functions, along with the other financial functions described in this chapter, allow you to examine all the possibilities open to you in negotiating a mortgage or loan so that you can arrive at the optimum terms for your personal or business needs.

The next section illustrates the use of the @PMT function in a real estate context.

@PMT: Finding Payment per Period

@PMT*(principal of loan, fixed interest rate, term)*

Returns the payment amount for fixed interest rate at the given term, where the arguments are numbers, cell references, or arithmetic expressions.

Example: @PMT(5000,A1/12,A3)

The payment or PMT amount for a loan is frequently computed when examining the affordability of property or an investment. The interest rate is assumed fixed and the number of years needed to repay the loan is considered the term. The equation for PMT is:

$$Prin * \frac{int}{1 - (int + 1)^{-n}}$$

where *Prin* is the principal amount, *int* is a fixed interest rate, and n is the term of the loan in years.

Problem: There is an investment opportunity in a 3-unit building that is selling for $250,000. The term of the loan needed to finance this project is 30 years with a fixed interest rate of 12.5%. Assuming no down payment, what will be the minimum monthly payment for this investment?

Solution: Beginning in cell A41, enter the labels and values as shown in Figure 4.16. Then format cell A43 using the Percent format.

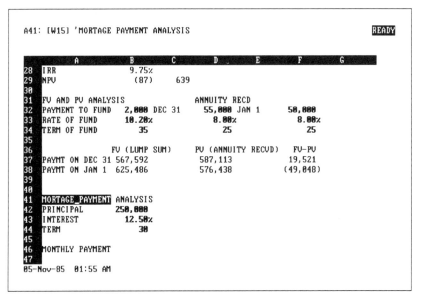

Figure 4.16: Mortgage analysis labels and values

Now enter the @PMT formula in cell B46. You are adjusting the annual interest rate to a monthly rate by dividing by 12 and adjusting the term to reflect 12 payments per year. Enter

@PMT(B42,B43/12,B44*12)

The monthly payment that results is $2,668, as shown in Figure 4.17.

INVESTMENT ANALYSIS

When you invest your money well, you can reach your financial goals quickly and with greater certainty. To do that, you have to be

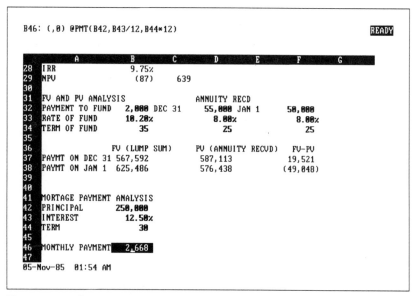

```
B46: (,0) @PMT(B42,B43/12,B44*12)                                    READY

                  A         B         C        D         E        F        G
28  IRR                   9.75%
29  NPV                    (87)      639
30
31  FV AND PV ANALYSIS                     ANNUITY RECD
32  PAYMENT TO FUND      2,000 DEC 31        55,000 JAN 1      50,000
33  RATE OF FUND        10.20%               8.00%            8.00%
34  TERM OF FUND           35                 25               25
35
36                      FV (LUMP SUM)     PV (ANNUITY RECVD)   FV-PV
37  PAYMT ON DEC 31  567,592                587,113         19,521
38  PAYMT ON JAN 1   625,486                576,438        (49,048)
39
40
41  MORTAGE PAYMENT ANALYSIS
42  PRINCIPAL          250,000
43  INTEREST           12.50%
44  TERM                  30
45
46  MONTHLY PAYMENT     2,668
47
05-Nov-85  01:54 AM
```

Figure 4.17: Completed PMT function

able to analyze investments precisely, and 1-2-3's investment analysis functions are just the tools you need.

Whether you analyze investments professionally, dabble in stocks on the side, or want to choose a better savings account, you will find the @RATE and the @TERM functions invaluable in examining and selecting investment opportunities.

The first problem discussed is an analysis of two kinds of fixed interest accounts, using the function @RATE.

@*RATE: Calculating the Rate*

@RATE(*fv,pv,term*)

Returns the required rate to earn the future value specified from the present value, given the term, where the arguments are numbers, cell references, or arithmetic expressions.

Example: @RATE(A1,B1,B10*12)

An initial amount of money can be deposited earning a fixed interest rate for a term until a certain future value is accumulated.

The rate that is required to earn the future value may be a monthly compounded rate or an annually compounded rate. Lotus 1-2-3 will determine the lowest rate needed for both methods of compounding to earn the desired future value.

Problem: What rate must an initial deposit of $4,000 earn over five years to accumulate $8,000: (a) compounded annually or (b) compounded monthly?

Solution: Beginning in cell A48, enter the labels and values for the Investment Rate Required and Term Required section of the spreadsheet, using Figure 4.18 as a guide. Then format cells B53 through C56 using the Percent format.

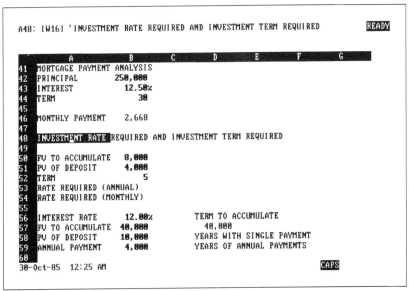

Figure 4.18: Required rate and term labels and values

Next, enter the @RATE formula for annual compounding in cell C53:

@RATE(B50,B51,B52)

Now enter the @RATE formula for monthly compounding in cell C54:

@RATE(B50,B51,B52∗12)∗12

The results appear as shown in Figure 4.19. The required rate is slightly lower for monthly compounding.

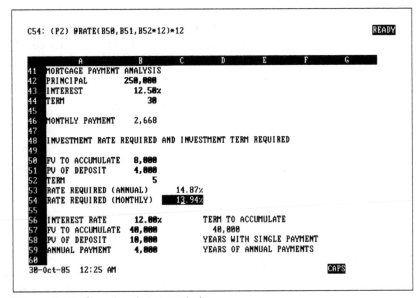

Figure 4.19: Completed rate analysis

Save this spreadsheet to use in the following example.

@TERM and @CTERM: Calculating Terms for Single and Multiple Deposits

@**TERM**(*payment, interest rate, future value*)

@**CTERM**(*interest rate, future value, present value*)

Return the term in years, where the respective arguments are numbers, cell references, or arithmetic expressions.

Example: @TERM(A1,B1,C1)

These functions both compute the term in years to accumulate a future value. CTERM assumes a single deposit at the beginning of a period at a fixed interest rate, and TERM assumes a series of deposits over a period at a fixed interest rate.

Problem: You want to accumulate $40,000 either by purchasing a $10,000 certificate of deposit (CD) that earns an interest rate of 12% now or by purchasing a series of $4,000 CDs that are guaranteed to earn 12% interest over the next few years. Should you purchase the $10,000 CD now or the series of CDs over time?

Solution: You have to determine which option requires a lesser term to accumulate the $40,000. In cell C58, enter the CTERM formula as

@CTERM(B56,B57,B58)

This formula computes the number of years the deposit will have to remain to earn the future value. In cell C59, enter the TERM formula:

@TERM(B59,B56,B57)

The result appears as in Figure 4.20. The shorter required term is seven years, using the option to make annual deposits of $4,000.

In this section, you have learned to use:

- Depreciation analysis with @DDB, @SLN, and @SYD
- Three depreciation methods to calculate the impact of depreciation on net income
- Cash flow analysis with @IRR, @NPV, @FV, and @PV functions
- Mortgage analysis with the @PMT function
- Investment analysis with @RATE, @TERM, and @CTERM functions

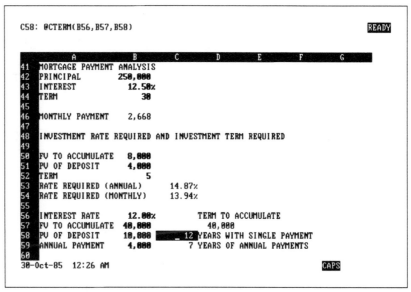

Figure 4.20: Completed term analysis

Using Date Functions

You will often want to display the current date on the spreadsheet so that when you read printouts later, you will know when the file was last updated. You will want to keep other dates constant—for example, as references to specific dates or as labels for time periods. Lotus 1-2-3 offers several @DATE functions that record dates and times in different ways for different purposes.

@NOW replaces @TODAY from Release 1A. This date function is used to record the current date and time. Each time a 1-2-3 spreadsheet is retrieved, 1-2-3 automatically updates any date entered with @NOW.

@DATE and @TIME are used to enter dates and times that will not change.

Because these dates are all stored as single numbers, they can be manipulated just like any other number. They can be added and subtracted to and from one another, formatted into other date forms without manual editing, and broken into their component time units (like hours, days, minutes, or seconds).

@DATEVALUE and @TIMEVALUE convert dates entered as plain text labels into date values that can be manipulated, like the dates originally entered with @DATE, @TIME, and @NOW.

@SECOND, @MINUTE, @HOUR, @DAY, @MONTH, and @YEAR are the functions that can extract the second, minute, hour, day, month, or year components from dates and times in 1-2-3 (except plain textual dates).

The sections that follow illustrate each of the date functions and their practical uses.

@NOW: USING THE INTERNAL CLOCK

@NOW

Returns the date and time.

1-2-3 has an automatic clock called @NOW that you can access. By entering @NOW, 1-2-3 will look at its internal clock and count the number of days to the nearest second since January 1, 1900 to the current date and time. This number will be stored in any cell that contains @NOW. The cell can be formatted to display a variety of day, month, year and time combinations. To enter the date/time function in a cell, type @NOW and press ←┘.

The value displayed is a very large number—the number of days to the nearest second since 1900. Because you don't normally think of years and months in terms of such numbers, this date format is not very useful. You can change the date into standard year, month, and day formats by using the Range Format Date command and choosing one of the options offered. You may display a date using date formats or a time using HH:MM or HH:MM:SS.

The date format options are:

Menu item	Description	Example
1	DD-MMM-YY	01-Oct-86
2	DD-MMM	01-Oct
3	MMM-YY	Oct-86

Menu Item	Description	Example
4	MM/DD/YY	10/1/86
5	MM/DD	10/01

The time format options are:

Menu item	Description	Example
1	HH:MM:SS AM/PM	02:30:14 PM
2	HH:MM AM/PM	02:30 PM
3	HH:MM:SS 24 Hr Long Intl	14:30:14
4	HH:MM 24 Hr Short Intl	14:30

The spreadsheet in Figure 4.21 shows an example of the @NOW function formatted to display a date and time.

@DATE AND @TIME: SETTING A FIXED DATE

@DATE(*YR,MO,DA*)
@TIME(*HR,MIN,SEC*)

@DATE returns the date as the number of days since January 1, 1900, to the nearest second, and @TIME returns the time as the fraction of a day to the nearest second.

Example: @DATE(86,11,23)
@TIME(10,30,3)

To record a date that will not change every time you update your spreadsheet, use the formula @DATE(YY,MM,DD). For example: @DATE(86,10,01), where YY is 86, MM is 10, and DD is 1.

To enter a year greater than 1999, type all four digits of the year. For example: @DATE(2000,10,1).

For time specifications that will not change, use @TIME(HR-,MIN,SEC). For example, @TIME(10,30,5) enters the time 10:30 AM, which will be stored unaltered until you edit it.

Just as with the dates and times specified with @NOW, you must format these cells with either the Range Format Date

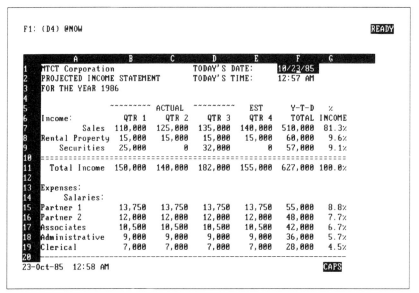

Figure 4.21: @NOW displaying date and time format

command or the Range Format Date Time command. Otherwise, the dates and times will be displayed as very large numbers.

@DATEVALUE AND @TIMEVALUE: EXTRACTING DATE VALUES FROM TEXT DATES

@DATEVALUE(*text date*)
@TIMEVALUE(*text time*)
or
@DATEVALUE(*text date location*)
@TIMEVALUE(*text time location*)

Returns the date or time as a number from textual date or time labels.

Example: @DATEVALUE(G1)

It's easier to enter dates and times as labels than it is to use the @DATE and @TIME functions. The labels can then be converted to the equivalent of the @DATE or @TIME functions by using the @DATEVALUE or @TIMEVALUE functions. The date and time can then be formatted and used in formulas, just as if you had used the @DATE and @TIME functions in the first place.

For example, you can type the label ''10/7/86 in cell G1 and convert it to a date value in cell F1 by typing

@DATEVALUE(G1)

and converting the label to the value that represents the number of days from January 1, 1900 to October 7, 1986. Then format the value in cell F1 using the Range Format Date command.

OTHER DATE AND TIME FUNCTIONS: EXTRACTING DATE AND TIME ELEMENTS FROM DATE VALUES

You can extract the day, hour, minute, month, second, or year from any date or time that was generated by @NOW, @DATE, @TIME, and from text label dates that have been converted with @DATEVALUE or @TIMEVALUE. For each function, specify the cell location of the date or time you wish to extract and the specific time period you want extracted.

Function	Result
@DAY(*date location*)	Day number (1-31)
@MONTH(*date location*)	Month number (1-12)
@YEAR(*date location*)	Year number (1900-2100)
@SECOND(*time location*)	Second number (1-60)
@MINUTE(*time location*)	Minute number (1-60)
@HOUR(*time location*)	Hour number (1-24)

USING DATE ARITHMETIC

With date arithmetic, you can subtract the number of days from one date from another to calculate the number of days between them. For example, if you want to compute the number of days between 8/21/86 and 8/31/86, you subtract the date @DATE(86,8,21) from the date @DATE(86,8,31), and the result is 10 days. Because 1-2-3 stores the number of days for @DATE(86,8,21) as 31645 and for @DATE(86,8,31) as 31655, 31645 is simply subtracted from 31655.

You can also determine the number of weeks, months, and years between dates. By dividing the result by 7 you obtain weeks, by 30 you obtain months, or by 365 you obtain years. You can also determine time units such as hours, minutes, or seconds. You multiply the number of days by 24 to obtain hours, by 144 to obtain minutes, or by 8640 (144 × 60) to obtain seconds.

Remember, when you use date functions you are interested in the relative difference between dates. For example, you may want to award a raise for all employees who have not received a raise in six months. You could compute the number of days between today's date and their last raise date. This type of calculation involves using the logical @IF function introduced in the next section to test for the presence of dates or times.

You can use these functions with databases to select database records based on time or date differences. Chapter 9, "Using a Database," will discuss how to do this.

In this section, you have learned to use:

- @NOW, @DATE, and @TIME functions to record dates
- @DATEVALUE and @TIMEVALUE functions for converting plain text dates to numerically stored dates
- @DAY, @MONTH, @YEAR, @SECOND, @MINUTE, and @HOUR to extract date and time elements from numerically stored dates
- Date arithmetic

Using Logical Functions

Very often the operation you want to perform on a value in one cell depends on the value in another cell. 1-2-3 can perform this kind of test with the @IF function. Experienced 1-2-3 users should note that @IF can now be performed on text as well as on values and formulas.

The 1-2-3 @IF, @TRUE, and @FALSE functions perform the same kind of logical decision making as the IF statements programmers use in languages such as BASIC or FORTRAN to test values. You may not learn to become a sophisticated programmer by reading this section, but you will learn how to set up many of the same kinds of procedures that are integral to good programming, simply by making 1-2-3 test values for you and compute values based on the results of the tests.

You can use the @IF function to perform very simple tests or extremely complicated ones, depending solely on your own needs and inclinations. You might, for example, build a spreadsheet that keeps track of the interest you earn in an account, given that the interest rates change as the balance in the account grows: 8% for balances less than $1000, 10% for balances greater than $1000.

Using logical functions, you can build a conditional formula that performs different actions, depending on the value—the condition—found in the cell, instead of manually changing the interest rates when the balances change. In this example, you would reformulate your interest problem as a conditional statement:

IF the balance is less than $1000, THEN calculate the interest at 8%; OTHERWISE calculate the interest at 10%.

If the condition "less than $1000" is true, then the rate used to calculate the interest is 8%; if the condition "less than $1000" is false, then the rate used is 10%.

In the section that follows, you will see how to translate such a statement into an @IF function that will carry out a useful test and take the actions you want under the conditions you specify as a result of the test.

@IF: TESTING THE TRUTH OF CONDITIONS IN CELLS

@IF(*condition, TRUE instruction, FALSE instruction*)

Returns (and executes, if applicable) the first instruction if the condition evaluated is true, and the second instruction if the condition evaluated is false. The instruction can be a number, formula, function, label, or cell reference. If the instruction is a formula, function, or cell reference, the result, not the instruction itself, will be displayed.

Example: @IF(B6 > = 275,1,0)

When you test a cell using the @IF function, you must supply @IF with:

1. A condition or conditions to test
2. The instruction to perform if the condition is TRUE
3. The instruction to perform if the condition is FALSE

To specify a condition to test for, use any one of the logical operators listed below.

Operator	*Definition*
=	equals
>	greater than
<	less than
> =	greater than or equal to
< =	less than or equal to
< >	not equal to

The condition being evaluated can be an equation that compares values or a check for the existence of a particular label, value, or date:

Equation	*Condition*
C8 = "8%"	Is the value in cell C8 equal to 8%?
D14 = @DATE(1,1,86)	Is the value in cell D4 equal to the date January 1, 1986?
A3 = 5	Is the value in cell A3 equal to 5?
D4 > 1000	Is the value in cell D4 greater than 1000?
(E7*.1) < 200	Is 10% of the value in cell E7 less than 200?
B3 = "Yes"	Is the value in cell B3 equal to Yes?

If the condition tests TRUE, the result of carrying out the TRUE instruction is displayed in the cell. If the condition tests FALSE, the result of carrying out the FALSE instruction is displayed in the cell.

Some of the instructions 1-2-3 might carry out are:

Instruction	*Result*
.4∗A3	Multiplies A3 by .4
D4/1000	Divides D4 by 1000
0	Enters a zero

After stating your condition as a formula, determine the instruction to be placed in the cell if the condition tests TRUE and the instruction to be placed in the cell if the condition tests FALSE.

@IF can test for one condition or several conditions. Let's look at a simple example of a single condition.

Testing for a Single Condition

A single @IF condition is very useful when there are at least two ways of calculating a formula based on another cell's information. In calculating costs, a different ratio is frequently used to compute the cost, depending on the amount of another cell.

Problem: Assume that you have determined that costs are 15% of sales for sales less than 100,000 and 12% of sales for sales greater than 100,000. Construct an @IF function that computes cost, using the data in Figure 4.22.

Solution: Enter the @IF formula in cell B3 that will calculate 1985 costs:

@IF(B2<100000,B2∗.15,B2∗.12)

This is the formula as it you would actually type it in. It might be easier to make sense of it with a little translation:

IF cell B2 is less than 100000 multiply cell B2 by .15.
Otherwise, multiply cell B2 by .12.

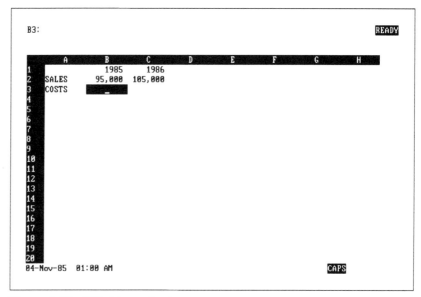

Figure 4.22: @IF data and values

In this example, the condition B2<100000 is TRUE because 95,000 is less than 100,000, so the value 95,000 is multiplied by 0.15, yielding the value 14,250.

Now enter the @IF formula in cell C3 that will calculate 1986 costs:

@IF(C2<100000,C2*.15,C2*.12)

Again, a translation:

IF cell C2 is less than 100000 multiply cell C2 by .15.
Otherwise, multiply cell C2 by .12.

The condition C2<100000 is FALSE, because 105,000 is greater than 100,000, so the value 105,000 is multiplied by .12, yielding the value 12,600.

Hint: @IF functions can be copied just like regular formulas and can reference absolute constants just as regular formulas can.

Testing for Multiple Conditions

You can test for more than one condition at a time with the @IF function by using the logical operators #AND#, #OR#, and #NOT#.

When a formula uses AND, both conditions must test TRUE for the whole formula to test TRUE. If just one of the conditions tests FALSE, the whole formula tests FALSE. For example, you might invent a formula to decide whether or not to buy a car: if the price is under $12,000 AND if the model is in stock, you will buy the car. You will not buy the car if just one of the conditions is true; they must both be true.

When using the OR operator, only one condition needs to test TRUE for the whole formula to test TRUE. Therefore, both conditions must test FALSE for the whole formula to test FALSE.

When a formula uses NOT, then the condition must test FALSE for the statement as a whole to test TRUE. For example, if the value in cell B2 is NOT equal to ten, then multiply B2 by 1400, otherwise, put nothing in the cell:

@IF(#NOT#B2 = 10,B2*1400," ")

The condition tests TRUE when B2 is NOT 10, and the result B2 is multiplied by 1400. When B2 is 10, the condition tests FALSE, and the result is " ".

Problem: Salaries are 10% of sales if sales minus costs are less than 80,000 OR if sales are less than 100,000. Otherwise, salaries are 11% of sales.

Solution: Enter the @IF function in cell B4 that will calculate salaries:

@IF(B2 – B3<80000#OR#B2<100000,B2*.10,B2*.11)

which translates into:

IF B2 minus B3 is less than 80,000 #OR# B2 is less than 100,000, multiply B2 by .10. Otherwise, multiply B2 by .11.

The condition tests TRUE for 1985 salaries because sales (95,000) were less than 100,000, so 95,000 is multiplied by .10, yielding the value 9,500.

The condition tests FALSE for 1986 salaries because sales were greater than 100,000, and sales minus costs were greater than 80,000, so the value 105,000 (sales) is multiplied by .11, yielding 11,550.

Testing for Labels

One of the new features included in Release 2 is that @IF can check cells with labels for certain conditions (that is, text instead of numbers and formulas). You can enter text codes such as Y or N, which are easier to read than numeric codes such as 1 or 0.

Problem: Using the spreadsheet in Figure 4.23, compute 6% sales tax in column D for clients who have a Y in column C.

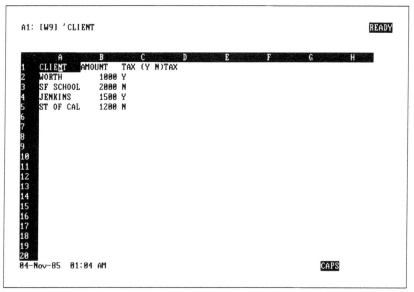

Figure 4.23: Using @IF to check for labels

Solution: Enter the formula for the tax in cell D2:

@IF(C2 = "Y",B2*.06,0)

Now copy this @IF function to cells D3 through D4. Notice that the sales tax calculated for two of the clients is 0, and that they are the clients who do not have a Y in column C, as shown in Figure 4.24.

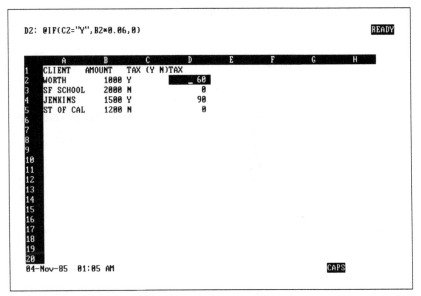

Figure 4.24: Results of label check

Hint: You can use the Worksheet Global Zero command to suppress the zeros, or you can change the @IF function's FALSE instruction result from "0" to " ", which will print a blank:

@IF(C2 = "Y",B2*.06," ")

Just as you can test labels, you can now tell 1-2-3 to print a label if you have Release 2.

Printing Conditional Text Messages

It is often faster and easier to read a descriptive printed message instead of a value. The @IF function allows for a result to be a message, as illustrated in the next example.

Problem: Print a message in column E that reads TAX-EXEMPT for all clients with an N in column C and a message that reads TAXABLE for clients with a Y in column C.

Solution: Enter the @IF function in cell E2:

@IF(C2 = "N","TAX-EXEMPT","TAXABLE")

Copy the function to cells E3 through E4. Your spreadsheet should look like Figure 4.25.

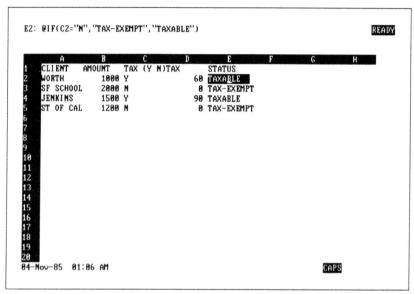

Figure 4.25: Using @IF to print messages

Testing Dates for Values

You can use @IF to extract the day, month, or year from a date and use that portion of the date as a condition, unless the date is entered as a plain text label. If it is plain text, you first have to convert it with @DATEVALUE or @TIMEVALUE.

Problem: You need to know which employees were hired in March in order to evaluate them for annual raises. Use the @IF function to print the message RAISE EVALUATION THIS MONTH for all employees hired in March.

Solution: Enter the @DATE formulas shown in the spreadsheet in Figure 4.26. Then enter the following @IF function in cell C2:

    @IF(@MONTH(B2)=3,
    "RAISE EVALUATION THIS MONTH"," ")

Copy this function to cells C3 to C5 using the Copy command. Your results should appear as the messages shown in Figure 4.27.

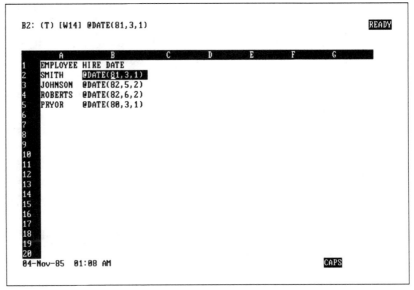

Figure 4.26: @DATE formulas for hire date

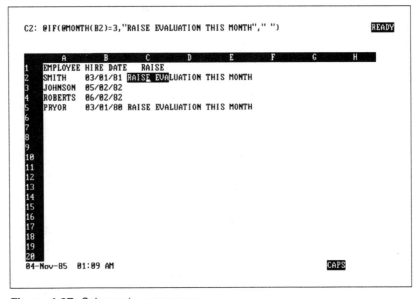

Figure 4.27: Salary raise messages

Problem: Determine the holding period of a stock. When you purchase a stock and keep it for more than six months, its gain or loss is considered to be long term when you sell it.

Solution: Enter the @DATE formulas shown in the spreadsheet in Figure 4.28. Then enter an @IF function that tests the number of months between the purchase date and the sale date in cell C2:

@IF(B2 – A2 > 180,"LONG-TERM","SHORT-TERM")

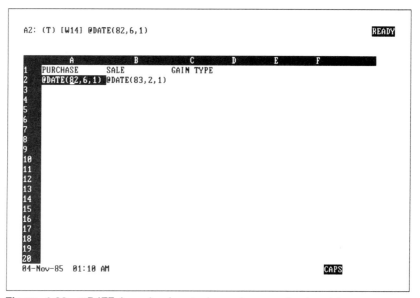

Figure 4.28: @DATE formulas for stock purchase and sales dates

Notice that the formula actually tests for 180—the number of days in six months—rather than for the number of months per se. Your results should appear as shown in the spreadsheet in Figure 4.29.

@IF functions can be constructed to carry out complex instructions. The logical functions @TRUE and @FALSE are used to verify which instruction—TRUE or FALSE—will be performed as a result of an @IF function.

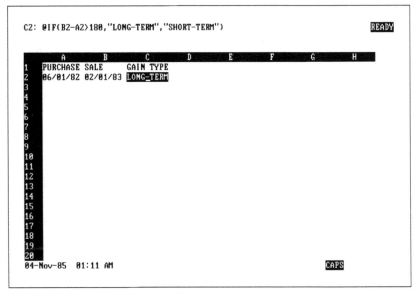

Figure 4.29: Completed stock gain/loss analysis

USING @TRUE AND @FALSE: EXTRACTING TRUTH STATUS USING NESTED @IFS

@TRUE
@FALSE

Used primarily within an @IF function, these functions return the value of 1 for TRUE or 0 for FALSE, depending on the truth value of the condition specified.

Example: @IF(A1>10,@TRUE,@FALSE)

When you test a condition with the @IF function, the result is either TRUE or FALSE, and what displays in the cell is the result of the instruction @IF performed. You will often want to see not only the result but also which instruction was performed to obtain it—the TRUE or FALSE instruction.

Lotus 1-2-3 now offers a sure way to verify whether the result of the @IF condition is TRUE or FALSE, so you know which instruction was carried out without working backward from the result displayed. These functions are @TRUE and @FALSE. @TRUE returns a value of 1 when the condition is TRUE; @FALSE returns a value of 0 when the condition is FALSE.

Another very useful feature of 1-2-3's @IF function is that you can use IFs within IFs, or nested IF functions. That is, you can have one IF statement dependent on the truth value returned by another IF statement. The following example should help clarify this idea.

Problem: Test values in cells C1, D1, and E1 using multiple @IF statements and determine if the condition is TRUE or FALSE:

@IF(C1>100,@IF(D1>50,.10,0),@IF(E1>40,.15,0))

The logic of this @IF can be translated as:

IF C1 is greater than 100, then test D1. IF D1 is greater than 50, then the result is .10. Otherwise, the result is 0.

IF C1 is not greater than 100, then test E1. IF E1 is greater than 40, then the result is .15. Otherwise, the result is 0.

It is almost impossible to figure out, just from looking at the results you obtain—.15, .10, or 0—whether the logic of the formula is producing TRUE and FALSE under the circumstances you want.

Solution: Add to the @IF statement the @TRUE and @FALSE flags to have them display 1 for TRUE or 0 for FALSE.

@IF(C1>100,@TRUE,@FALSE)

The value returned by @IF function above is 1 if the value in C1 is greater than 100. The logic of the function is verified and the original two @IF statements can be substituted back into the function.

In this section, you have learned to use:

- @NOW, @DATE, and @TIME functions
- Simple @IF functions
- Complex @IF functions

- @IF functions to test for labels
- @IF functions to test for dates
- @TRUE and @FALSE to verify logic of @IF functions

Using Special Functions

This section examines 1-2-3's special functions, which allow you to take advantage of the organization of your spreadsheet and select information in one cell according to the information in another cell, much like the @IF function. The special functions allow you to establish and use simple and complex relationships among values, using:

- @VLOOKUP to look up values indexed by column
- @HLOOKUP to look up values indexed by row
- @INDEX to look up values indexed by rows and columns
- @CHOOSE to choose values from a sort list

Following the discussion of these selection functions is a section on special functions that deliver information about the cells themselves. These functions, which are used primarily for spreadsheet housekeeping and testing, include:

- @COLS and @ROWS to count rows or columns
- @CELL and @CELLPOINTER to give information about a cell
- @NA, @ERR, @ISERR, and @ISNA to trap errors

SELECTING INFORMATION FROM A SPREADSHEET

The section on @IF considered building a spreadsheet that keeps track of the interest earned on an account, given that the interest rate changes as the balance in the account grows.

In that example only two possibilities were proposed: a rate of 8% when the balances is less than $1000, and a rate of 10% when the balance is greater than $1000.

In a more realistic example, the account would have many rate gradations as the balance grows. You could specify those changes in the form of a table:

Balance	Rate
0–500	7 3/4%
500–1000	8 %
1000–5000	8 1/4%
5000–10,000	10 %

It would be possible to determine which rate to apply, given a particular balance value using @IF, but the number and complexity of the @IF functions would be a challenge in logic for even the best 1-2-3 users. Constructing a table is a much simpler way to achieve the same results.

In this example, you build a table similar to the one above. Then, given the balance in your account, 1-2-3 can first look up the balance and then the rate in your table. The program can then apply the proper rate to the original balance, calculating the interest you would be earning.

The @1-2-3 functions @VLOOKUP, @HLOOKUP, and @INDEX were developed for precisely this kind of problem: extracting information from a table, given a particular key value.

Lotus 1-2-3 can use either a label or a number as the key value. The *key* is the cell reference 1-2-3 looks for in the table. When it finds the key, it looks for the value associated with it, and returns it as the result of the lookup function.

The table can be set up so that the keys and the values associated with them are organized either by rows, columns, or both.

@VLOOKUP is vertical lookup. It is used when the table is set up so that all the keys are in one column, and the values associated with them are in the same row, one column over, as in the balance-rate table discussed above.

@HLOOKUP is horizontal lookup. It is used when the table is set up so that all the keys are in one row, and the values associated with them are in the same column, one row below.

@INDEX is both horizontal lookup and vertical lookup. It is used when the table is set up so that keys are in both a row and a column, and the values associated with them are indexed in the columns below and in the rows beneath the columns.

@CHOOSE is one-way lookup. It is used when a short list is set up so that an offset is the key used to choose the value from the list. The list is entered directly into the function as an argument instead of in a table elsewhere on the spreadsheet.

@VLOOKUP and @HLOOKUP are examined first in more detail in the sections that follow.

@VLOOKUP: Looking Up Values Indexed by Columns

@VLOOKUP(*key, table range, offset*)

Returns the value from the table range specified, on the same row as the key, in the column counted to the right by the offset. The key is a text label, number, cell reference, or arithmetic expression; the table range is a range of cell references (or the name of the range); the offset is a number, cell reference, or arithmetic expression.

Example: @VLOOKUP(B1,C1.D10,2)

In vertical lookup, the left column of the table contains the key values. The column of keys is the *index*. The adjacent columns store the data associated with each key.

To look up a value associated with a particular key, @VLOOKUP needs to know the key value, the location of the table, and the number of the column containing the information you want to retrieve, called the *offset*. The offset is the count of the number of columns that the information you want to retrieve is from the index (the key column).

An example of a vertically organized table is the tax lookup table in Figure 4.30. Income both for single and for married taxpayers is shown, and either can be used as the key column by which tax is looked up.

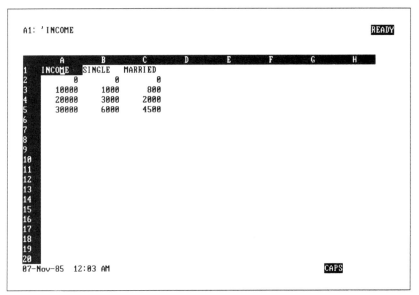

Figure 4.30: Tax @VLOOKUP table

The key numeric values must always be in ascending order. In column A you find the index of key values ranging from 0 to 30000 in ascending order. Suppose you want to look up the amount of tax for a single person in column B. The offset position of that column is 1 because column B is one position to the right of the index located in column A. If you want to look up the amount of tax for a married couple in column C, the offset position of that column is 2 because column C is two positions to the right of the index located in column A.

Problem: Bob Smith is a single taxpayer with total income of $15,000, and Frank and Mary Jones are married taxpayers with total income of $28,000. Use the **@VLOOKUP** function to compute their tax.

Solution: Enter the lookup table in Figure 4.30 into a spreadsheet. Next, enter Bob Smith's name in cell A7 and his income in cell

B7. Lotus 1-2-3 will calculate his tax by scanning the index values in column A for the greatest index value that is less than or equal to the income of 15,000. In this case, 10,000 is the greatest value less than 15,000 in the table, and the single tax amount is offset by one column from the index column A. Bob lucks out; he owes only $1,000 in tax. In cell C7 enter the @VLOOKUP function that will do this calculation:

@VLOOKUP(B7,A2.C5,1)

Enter F/M Jones in cell A8 and their income in cell B8. Their tax is calculated by scanning the index for 28,000, which is the key value in this case. The greatest value less than 28,000 in the table is 20,000, and the married tax amount is offset by two columns from the index column A. The Joneses must pay $2,000 in tax. In cell C8 enter the @VLOOKUP function that will do this calculation:

@VLOOKUP(B8,A2.C5,2)

The @HLOOKUP function is related to the @VLOOKUP function.

@HLOOKUP: Looking Up Values Indexed by Row

@HLOOKUP(*key, table range, offset*)

Returns the value from the table range specified, on the same column as the key, in the row counted down by the offset. The key is a text label, number, cell reference, or arithmetic expression; the table range is a range of cell references (or the name of the range); the offset is a number, cell reference, or arithmetic expression.

Example: @HLOOKUP(B1,C1.D10,2)

@HLOOKUP, or horizontal lookup, is similar to @VLOOKUP, except the index is a row of key values instead of a column. Release 2 now allows @VLOOKUP or @HLOOKUP to use text labels as key values. For example, you can construct a table of product prices for varying regional prices as shown in Figure 4.31.

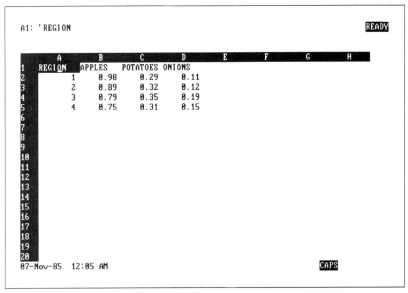

Figure 4.31: Product price @HLOOKUP table

Problem: You are a produce broker and your sales in pounds for apples, potatoes, and onions for this week are as follows:

Region	Volume	Product
1	2100	Apples
1	2500	Potatoes
2	2700	Onions
2	2800	Potatoes
3	1700	Apples
4	1800	Apples

You want to know the total revenue (price × quantity) for each product in each region. Use the @HLOOKUP function to compute revenue by region and product.

Solution: Construct the table for the price data as shown in Figure 4.31. Beginning in cell A7, enter the label REGION, in cell B7 VOLUME, in cell C7 PRODUCT, and in cell D7 REVENUE, and the data shown for sales. Your spreadsheet should appear as shown in Figure 4.32.

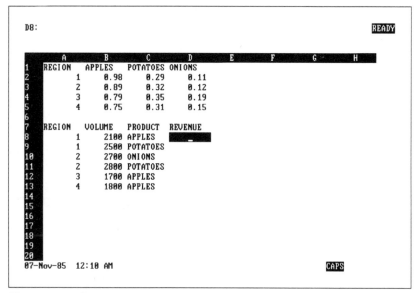

Figure 4.32: Price and revenue section

Now you are ready to enter the first @HLOOKUP function in cell D8 for computing revenue from the first Region 1 Apples sale. You must first look up the price and then multiply by the sales volume. Enter

@HLOOKUP(C8,A1.D5,A8)*B8

1-2-3 looks up "Apples" in the index in row 1 of the table and selects the price for region 1 (.98) from the offset row 1. It multiplies the value by 2100, yielding a resulting revenue of 2058. It would be tedious to enter @HLOOKUP for the remaining five sales. Before copying the formula, check to see if there are any absolute constants that should not change. The location of the table should remain constant and the other cells should change. To adjust the table range for the formula in cell B15:

1. Press the F2 (Edit) key.
2. Move the cursor to cell A1.
3. Press the F4 (Abs) key once.
4. Press the Enter key.

Notice that 1-2-3 has made the entire range A1 through D5 absolute. Your formula should now read:

@HLOOKUP(C8,$A$1.$D$5,A8)＊B8

Use the Copy command to copy the formula in cell D8 to cells D9 through D13 now. Your results should look like Figure 4.33.

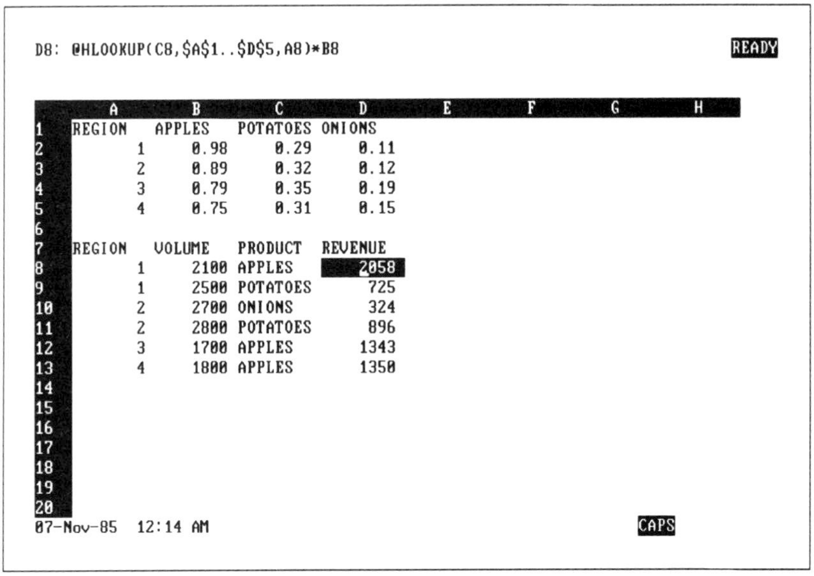

```
D8:  @HLOOKUP(C8,$A$1..$D$5,A8)*B8                                    READY

        A        B        C        D        E        F        G        H
1   REGION    APPLES   POTATOES ONIONS
2            1        0.98     0.29     0.11
3            2        0.89     0.32     0.12
4            3        0.79     0.35     0.19
5            4        0.75     0.31     0.15
6
7   REGION    VOLUME   PRODUCT  REVENUE
8            1        2100 APPLES     2058
9            1        2500 POTATOES    725
10           2        2700 ONIONS      324
11           2        2800 POTATOES    896
12           3        1700 APPLES     1343
13           4        1800 APPLES     1350
14
15
16
17
18
19
20
07-Nov-85  12:14 AM                                                  CAPS
```

Figure 4.33: Completed @HLOOKUP formulas

@INDEX: Looking Up Values Indexed by Both Rows and Columns

@INDEX(*table range, column, row*)

Returns the value in the cell location in the table range specified by column key and row key specified, where table range is a range specification or range name and column key and row key are either the column and row locations of the sought value or the cell locations where the column and row locations can be found.

Example: @INDEX(A1.B10,A3,B4)

The @INDEX function is useful when you must select a value from a table based on two key values. *Table range* is the location of the values in the table; *column* represents the first key value to find in the *horizontal index,* or which column of the table to look in; and *row* represents the first key value to find in the *vertical index,* or which row of the table to look in. Thus, the value located in the intersection of the table's row and column is the result of the @INDEX function and may be used in a formula.

You may use numbers or values as key values and nonintegers are rounded to the integer part (2.4 is 2). If a negative number is used as a key value, an ERR results.

Problem: You must compute shipping costs for sending merchandise from various zones for various weights. You compute the shipping cost by multiplying the cost per pound from a table by the weight of the merchandise. Plants are located in zones 1, 2, 3, and 4, and orders may be filled from any plant and shipped to any zone, because some merchandise is not available at some plants.

Solution: Construct a spreadsheet that uses a table of costs per zone and enter the data shown in Figure 4.34. (You may recognize this table from the U.S. Postal Service or UPS rate structures, which group zip codes into zones.)

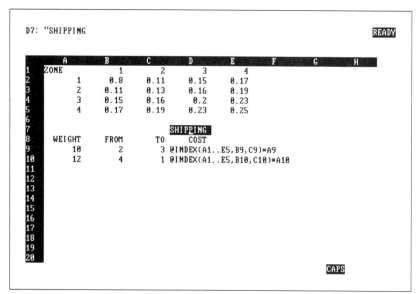

Figure 4.34: @INDEX spreadsheet data and functions

The function in D9 selects the value from the intersection of the second column and the third row from the table, .16, and multiplies it by the weight in cell A9, 10, and the cost is $1.60. The function in D10 selects the value from the intersection of the fourth column and the first row of the table, .17, and multiplies it by the weight in cell A10, 12, and the cost is $2.04. (See Figure 4.35.)

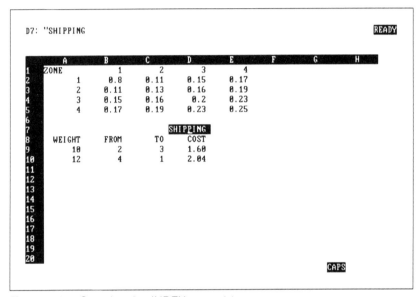

Figure 4.35: Completed @INDEX spreadsheet

You can also use this function to construct an ACRS (Accelerated Cost Recovery Schedule) schedule that requires the month the asset was placed in service as a key as well as the useful life of the asset as a key.

@CHOOSE: Choosing Values from a List

@CHOOSE(*offset, item 0, item 1,...item n*)

Returns the value of the item in the list entered in the function, according to the offset specified. The offset can be a number, a cell reference that contains the offset, or an arithmetic expression.

Example: @CHOOSE(A1,0,50,100,200)

@CHOOSE is similar to @HLOOKUP and @VLOOKUP in that it selects a value from a list of values, or *items*. However, instead of using an exact key value as the selection criteria, it uses an offset or a positional number to choose the item from a list. Lists of values may be labels or numbers and must be listed in descending order, like @HLOOKUP and @VLOOKUP.

The list of values must be entered into the @CHOOSE function, not in a separate table. This makes working with the @CHOOSE a little cumbersome, because you must enter the list several times or copy the function instead of entering the list once in one table and then referencing it.

The offset specifies the position of the item to choose from the list. You must therefore make your key values range from 0, which chooses the first item in the list, to *n* where *n* is the position of the last item in the list. This means you may have to construct formulas that reduce your key values to 0, 1, and so on, so that they can be used as offset references. All key values must be numbers and are interpreted as integers (1.3 becomes 1). Blanks are interpreted as 0.

This function can replace complex @IF statements because it allows you to test for many distinct key values and include many values in the list. You can also use this function to construct ACRS depreciation schedules, which base depreciation on the expected useful life of an asset. You include the years of useful life as a key value and the various rates used for each useful life as the list of values to choose from, according to the following formula:

@CHOOSE(*key value location of useful life, rate for 3-year life, rate for 5-year life, ... rate for n-year life*)

Problem: Your firm charges customers a fixed percent for computer usage based on the status of the type of work performed. If microcomputer service is required, the status is 0 and the rate is .05; for a minicomputer, status is 1 and the rate is .07; for a time-sharing mainframe, status is 2 and the rate is .10; for mainframe programming, status is 3 and the rate is .12.

Solution: Enter the data shown in Figure 4.36 and the @CHOOSE function to select the correct billing rate for computer usage based on status.

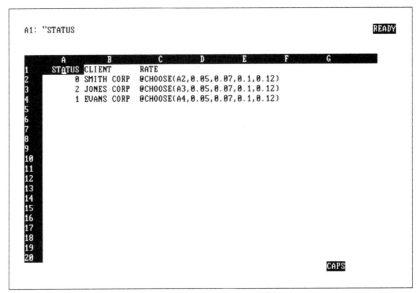

Figure 4.36: @CHOOSE data and functions

Figure 4.37 shows the result of the @CHOOSE functions. On the first line, @CHOOSE looks in cell A2 for the offset, finds 0, and therefore selects the first rate in its list—.05. On the second line, @CHOOSE looks in cell A3 for the offset, finds that it is 2, and selects the third rate in its list—.10. On the third line, @CHOOSE looks in cell A4, finds an offset of 1, and chooses the second rate in its list—.07.

The structure of @CHOOSE can be somewhat confusing. When the offset is 0, the first item is selected. When it is 1, the second item is selected. When it is 2, the third item is selected, and so on. Remember that the offset is not the position of the item on the list, but its position relative to the cell containing the offset.

When you have large amounts of data to manage or complicated relationships among the data, you may find that the selection functions reviewed here become cumbersome or insufficient. At that point, turn to the chapters on data management and setting up databases, beginning with Chapter 8. There you will find special database functions designed specifically to simplify and organize the information in your spreadsheets.

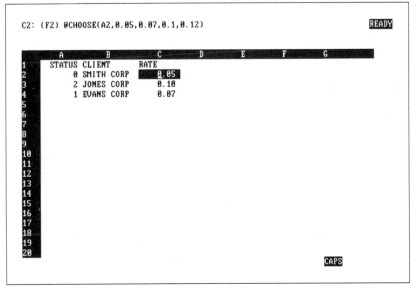

Figure 4.37: Completed @CHOOSE spreadsheet

MAKING SURE YOUR SPREADSHEET DOES WHAT YOU WANT

There is an old saying about computers: they do only what you tell them to do, not necessarily what you want them to do. You need to make sure that what you told your spreadsheet to do is also what you want it do. That is not always possible just from looking at the result the spreadsheet produces. Lotus 1-2-3 offers several functions designed specifically to assist you in checking the structure of your spreadsheet and the formulas it contains. The functions examined in this section are:

- @COLS and @ROWS: Count columns and rows
- @CELL and @CELLPOINTER: Get information about a cell
- @ERR, @NA, @ISERR, and @ISNA: Trap errors

We will first look at using @COLS and @ROWS to check and manage spreadsheet structure.

@COLS AND @ROWS:
Counting Columns and Rows

@COLS(*range*)
@ROWS(*range*)

Return the number of rows or columns contained in the specified range.

Example: @COLS(A14..BY45)
@ROWS(A14..BY45)

@ROWS finds that there are 31 rows in the range. The process is equivalent to setting up the formula +45−14. @COLS finds that there are 77 columns in the range, the equivalent of adding 26 (for the A–Z columns) + 25 (for the AA–AZ columns), + 25 (for the BA–BY columns).

These two functions are often used as part of a formula that divides the sum of a row or column by the number of items in the column. They are similar to the statistical function @COUNT, except that they do not ignore blank or label cells.

When you create a named range, you assign a name to a group of cells. This same range, A14 through BY45, could be a tax table. You could name it TAXTABLE and enter the @ROWS function as:

@ROWS(TAXTABLE)
@COLS(TAXTABLE)

Although the name TAXTABLE is easier to remember than the range A14..BY45, it is no longer obvious how many rows or columns are in the range.

You may want to find out how many columns are in a named range, to measure how many columns and rows of the range will fit on a printed page, to verify how many key values are in a table (to assure none are left out), or to measure how many values there are in a table (@COLS × @ROWS).

@CELL and @CELLPOINTER:
Getting Information about a Cell

@CELL(*attribute, range*)

Returns the attributes specified for the cell or range of cells specified. The attributes that can be requested are address, row, col, contents, type, prefix protect, width, and format.

Example: @CELL("column",BY1)

@CELLPOINTER(*attribute*)

Returns the information requested to the current cursor location.

Example: @CELLPOINTER("column")

@CELL and @CELLPOINTER provide information about a cell's contents, format, and location. These functions are useful in macros (the routines that help you save keystrokes) and in identifying the column, address, or row of a cell (or other attributes and information) and then performing routines based on that information.

@CELL requires you to enter the location of the cell you want information about; @CELLPOINTER delivers the information requested about the cell where the cursor or cell pointer is currently located.

To use @CELL or @CELLPOINTER, enter the attributes you request about a cell as a code enclosed in quotation marks (" "), in either upper- or lowercase letters.

A range may be one cell or the beginning of a range (such as a named range). Enter an ! (exclamation mark) in front of the range name or at the beginning of the range you want information about. !TAXTABLE is the range beginning at A14. It may also be entered as !A14.

Table 4.1 lists the attributes and information you can find about a cell using @CELL or @CELLPOINTER.

These functions are useful for testing macros, especially for determining whether the user has entered the correct information in the correct location.

@NA and ERR: Trapping Errors

@NA

Returns the message NA in a cell where data is missing.

Example: @NA

Attribute	Displays
"address"	Current cell address
"row"	Current row number
"col"	Current column number
"contents"	Current cell contents
"type"	Current cell contents TYPE
	b for a blank cell
	v for a numeric value or formula
	l for a label or string-value formula
"prefix"	Current cell label prefix
	' for left-aligned label
	" for right-aligned label
	^ for center-aligned label
"protect"	1 for protection status, 0 for nonprotected status
"width"	Current column width
"format"	Current numeric format
	F0 to F15; Fixed, 0 to 15 decimal places
	S0 to S15; Scientific, 0 to 15 decimal places
	C0 to C15; Currency, 0 to 15 decimal places
	G for General
	P0 to P15; Punctuated, 0 to 15 decimal places
	D1 to D5 for date and D6 to D9 for time
	T for text
	H for hidden
	A blank if the cell contains an empty string

Further examples

@CELL("column",J9) = 10   *J is the tenth column*

@CELL("format",J9) = C0   *Format is currency 0 places*

@CELL("protect",J9) = 1   *The cell is protected*

@CELLPOINTER("address") = A1   *The cursor is at HOME*

@CELLPOINTER("row") = 1   *The cursor is at HOME*

Table 4.1: Information displayed by @CELL and @CELLPOINTER

@ERR

Returns the message ERR when an error condition is present in the cell.

Example: @IF(C4<0,@ERR,1)

Trapping errors is the process of finding errors in a spreadsheet and stopping them dead in their tracks. If you don't, errors can occur all over your spreadsheet, causing results to display incorrectly without your being aware of it.

@NA displays where data is missing, @ERR flags an error as an error, and @ISERR and @ISNA (discussed in the next section) test for the presence of the first two error conditions.

You often have cells in which values ought to go, but for which information is not available. You may not want to leave a cell blank because formulas may reference it. You want those cells to read NA—which means the result is Not Available. Enter @NA in the cell for which the information is missing. Lotus 1-2-3 then displays NA in the cell and any cell that depends on it.

When using @IF, you have to check cells for values less than or equal to 0 before you can multiply or divide that cell by another value. To set up this check, enter @ERR as the true instruction when the condition "less than or equal to 0" exists. @ERR will then print the message ERR when the condition is true. The @IF statement looks like this:

@IF(C4< = 0,@ERR,C4*.48)

This @IF checks to see if C4 is less than or equal to 0. If this condition is true, the message ERR is displayed; if false, the value in cell C4 is safely multiplied by .48 and the result is displayed.

Lotus 1-2-3 displays ERR for a formula that has been incorrectly defined. If this occurs in many cells, you should check to see if there is division or multiplication by zero.

@ISERR, @ISNA: Testing for Error Conditions

@ISERR(x)

Returns 1 (true) if a specified condition exists in a cell and 0 (false) if it does not, where x is the condition specified.

Example: @ISERR(0)

@ISNA(*x*)

Returns 1 (true) if NA appears in the cell, and 0 (false) if it does not, where *x* is the specified cell.

Example: @IF(@ISNA(C4),14,0)

These two functions are used in conjunction with the @ERR and @NA functions. They are similar to @TRUE and @FALSE in that they are logical operators—that is, they are always either true or false. When true, a 1 displays. When false, a 0 displays. ISERR asks "IS it true that this cell contains ERR"?, and delivers the answer 1 (true) or 0 (false). ISNA asks "IS it true that this cell contains NA?" and delivers the answer 1 (true) or 0 (false).

@ISERR is used to keep unwanted ERR messages from appearing all over a spreadsheet. It tests to see if a formula will produce the ERR message.

For example

.48/C4

can be rewritten using @ISERR as:

@IF(@ISERR(.48/C4),0,.48/C4)

ISERR asks "will .48 divided by C4 produce an ERR?" It is much simpler to create the formula that is the true instruction and use @ISERR to test for an error rather than try to make a test that tests for all values that could cause an error.

@ISNA looks at a cell in the same fashion as @ISERR looks at a formula. For example:

@IF(@ISNA(C4),0,C4)

tests cell C4 for NA, which may be @NA or the result of a formula that depends on a cell with @NA and is therefore NA. If the cell C4 is NA, then @IF displays a 0. If it is **not** a NA, @IF displays the value C4. This type of trapping keeps NAs from appearing all over a spreadsheet.

In this section, you have learned how to use:

- @VLOOKUP with values
- @HLOOKUP with labels
- @CHOOSE and @INDEX with lists of data
- @COLS and @ROWS to count columns and rows
- @CELL and @CELLPOINTER to discover information about a cell
- @ERR, @NA, @ISERR, and @ISNA for trapping errors

Using Mathematical Functions

Lotus 1-2-3 offers a thorough variety of mathematical functions. These are divided into two groups—simple mathematical functions and advanced functions. ("Simple" here does not necessarily mean the complexity of the function itself, but of the problems in which the use of the function arises.)

The simple mathematical functions are widely used in all types of spreadsheet formulas. These include rounding numbers with @ROUND, generating random numbers with @RAND, truncating real numbers to integer numbers with @INT, and converting numbers to their absolute values with @ABS. This section defines and explains only these simpler functions.

The more complex mathematical functions, including trigonometric functions (such as deriving sines, cosines, and tangents), logarithmic functions (such as deriving logs and lns) and the remainder (or modulo) function, which are more specifically used in engineering problems, are examined in a separate section, using actual applied engineering problems developed and written by an engineer.

The discussion of the simpler mathematical functions begins with @ABS, finding the absolute value of a number.

@ABS: FINDING THE ABSOLUTE VALUE OF A NUMBER

@ABS(x)

Returns the absolute value of a number or expression, changing the value to its absolute or positive value where x is the value, cell reference, or arithmetic expression.

Example: @ABS(− 29.489)

@ABS, or the absolute value function, returns the number in its argument stripped of its plus or minus sign. This is useful, for example, if you need to take the square root of a negative number. You can use @ABS to make sure that the number returned is not negative. The absolute value of a positive number is always positive. For example:

```
@ABS( − 4500)  = 4500
@ABS(1.456)    = 1.456
```

@INT: TRUNCATING TO AN INTEGER VALUE

@INT(x)

Returns the truncated integer value, where x is the value, cell reference, or arithmetic expression.

Example: @INT(2.4)

@INT, or the integer part function, truncates the decimal values of a number. This is useful, for example, when you are calculating the date in whole days with @NOW, rather than displaying the seconds with which @NOW originally stores the time/date. For more information about the @NOW function, see the section "Using Date Functions" in this chapter.

```
@INT(96.8)   = 96
@INT( − 96.8)= − 96
```

Note that the integer part of a number is not the rounded value.

@ROUND: ROUNDING A NUMBER

@ROUND(*x*, *n*)

Returns the rounded value of a number, where *x* is the value, cell reference, or arithmetic expression and *m* is the decimal interval, separated by commas.

Example: @ROUND(1.2,1)

The most widely used mathematical function is @ROUND, the rounding function, which rounds numbers and/or formulas to the nearest division by ten specified. For example, the function can round to the nearest thousand or to a decimal place you specify.

@ROUND requires two arguments: *x*, or the number/formula to round, and *n*, the number of places to round to, which can be up to 15 places on either side of the decimal point. Values of *n* between 1 through 15 round to the right of the decimal place. For example:

@ROUND(123.456,2) = 123.46   *.456 is rounded up to .46*
@ROUND(123.456,1) = 123.4   *.45 is rounded down to .4*
@ROUND(123.456,0) = 123   *0 rounds to the nearest integer*

Values of *n* from −1 through −15 round to the left of the decimal place:

@ROUND(123.456, −1)   = 120   *123 is rounded down to 120*
@ROUND(123.456, −2)   = 100   *123 is rounded down to 100*
@ROUND(1123.456, −3) = 1000   *1123 is rounded down to 1000*

A problem with using 1-2-3's format features (such as Currency, Fixed, Punctuated, and Percent—two decimal places) is that a value that has not been rounded appears rounded. When you add the values that appear on a report printed from such a spreadsheet problem, they appear to have the wrong total.

Before @ROUND:

Value Displayed	Value Stored
(fixed format, two decimal places)	
123.03	123.025
123.03	123.025
246.05	246.05

The @ROUND function makes certain that what is displayed is what is stored.

After @ROUND:

Value Displayed	Value Stored	@ROUND function
(fixed format, two decimal places)		
− −A− −		
1 123.03	123.025	
2 123.03	123.025	
3 _____	_____	
4 246.06	246.05	@ROUND(@SUM(A1.A2),2)

Because you don't want to change the actual data values, you can round the sum of the values so that the values are rounded for computation but not for storage.

If you want to round a value and store the new rounded value, you must round the original value in another column and use the Range Values command to copy the rounded value to the original column.

@RAND: GENERATING A RANDOM NUMBER

@RAND

Returns a random number between 0 and 1. It requires no arguments or parameters.

@RAND, the random variable function, is often used in statistics, probability, and risk analysis. @RAND generates a random number between 0 and 1. When you recalculate your spreadsheet, the number changes. If you want to keep a particular number generated with @RAND constant, store the permanent value of the @RAND number using the Range Value command, copying the value into the cell where the @RAND function was originally.

To generate a larger random number, multiply the upper limit of the interval by the @RAND function and add the lower limit of the interval.

Random Number Value Desired	*@RAND formula*
0–1	@RAND
1–10	@RAND*9 + 1
1–100	@RAND*99 + 1
100–1000	@RAND*900 + 100
1000–10,000	@RAND*9000 + 1000
5000–7000	@RAND*2000 + 5000

@RAND generates real numbers; that is, numbers with decimals. If you want to generate an integer value, use the @INT function to transform the real number into an integer.

20–75	@INT(@RAND*55) + 20
30–100	@INT(@RAND*70) + 30

In this section, you have learned to use:

- @ABS to find the absolute value
- @INT to truncate an integer
- @ROUND to round a number
- @RAND to generate a random number

Using Engineering Functions

The discussion of each function in this section assumes you understand the theoretical distinctions involved in the use of these mathematical functions. The functions covered are:

@PI:	Using the Pi constant
@TAN:	Deriving a tangent
@EXP:	Using the constant e (inverse function of LN)
@SIN:	Deriving a sine
@COS:	Deriving a cosine
@MOD:	Deriving a remainder (modulo)
@SQRT:	Computing a square root
@ATAN:	Deriving an arc tangent
@ATAN2:	Deriving a four-quadrant arc tangent
@ASIN:	Deriving an arc sine
@ACOS:	Deriving an arc cosine
@LOG:	Computing a logarithm
@LN:	Computing a natural log

Each function is examined in relation to a fitting sample problem in applied engineering, which highlights not only the problem but also how best to use 1-2-3 to solve it. If you need a reference text, a good one is Irving Drooyan, et al., *Essentials of Trigonometry* (Macmillan, 1981).

@PI: USING THE CONSTANT PI

@PI

Pi is the ratio of the circumference of a circle to its diameter. In Lotus 1-2-3 it is stored as 3.1415926. @PI requires no arguments or parameters and is normally used as part of an expression.

Example: @PI*D3

In Lotus 1-2-3, angles used in trigonometric functions (such as @SIN, @COS, @TAN, @ATAN, @ASIN, @ACOS) must be expressed in radians. Data concerning angles is commonly expressed in degrees. You must convert degrees to radians to use 1-2-3's trigonometric functions.

Problem: Convert a 42-degree angle to radians using @PI.

Solution: Degrees can be easily converted into radians by using the @PI function. If an angle value (x) is 42 degrees, the conversion can be done as follows:

$$x \text{ degrees} * (@PI/180) = 42 * (@PI/180) = 0.733038 \text{ radians}$$

@TAN: DERIVING A TANGENT

@TAN(x)

Returns the tangent of x, where x is either a number, a cell address, or an arithmetic expression.

Example: @TAN(C10/C12)

Problem: You must calculate the height of trees in the J&K Logging company's woodlot to determine the value of the timber. The height can be determined by standing the distance (a) away from the tree and determining the angle (x) between the ground and the top of the tree.

Solution: You have measured the angle (x) to be 42 degrees. Before you can use the 1-2-3 @TAN function, you must convert that measurement into radians. (To convert degrees into radians, see the example given for the @PI function.)

When you convert 42 degrees to radians, the result is 0.733038. If you were standing a distance of 20 feet from the base of the tree when the measurement of 42 degrees was taken, then the tree's height can be derived as follows:

TAN(x) = b/a = height of tree/distance from tree
a * TAN(x) = b
(20 ft) * TAN(0.733038) = b = 18.00808 ft

To convert this formula using 1-2-3, enter

20*@TAN(.733038)

@EXP: USING THE CONSTANT e (INVERSE FUNCTION OF LN)

@EXP(x)

Returns the e constant raised to the power of x, where x is a number, cell address, or arithmetic expression.

Example: @EXP(C10*C12)

Problem: During inventory at L&M Bioengineering, Inc., you have to determine the amount of bacteria in stock. The present number of bacteria can be calculated from the number of bacteria recorded at the last count, if the rate of bacteria growth is known. The number of bacteria in a certain culture increases continuously at a rate per hour that is always 2 percent of the number present at the last inventory. If the original number of bacteria was 5000, and the last inventory was thirty days ago (720 hours), then the present number of bacteria can be calculated using the formula for natural growth:

$$N_{new} = N_{old} * EXP(r * t)$$

Solution: N_{new} is the present number of bacteria, N_{old} is the number of bacteria recorded at the last inventory, r is the rate of growth, t is the amount of time since the last inventory (in hours), and e is a value of approximately 2.718282.

To convert this formula using 1-2-3, enter

5000*@EXP(.02*720)

9.0E+09 is the amount of bacteria in stock.

@SIN: DERIVING A SINE

@SIN(x)

Returns the sine of x, where x is interpreted as an angle in radians, and x is a number, cell address, or arithmetic expression.

Example: @SIN(C10*C12)

Problem: Determining the instantaneous current. The instantaneous current (i) is an alternating current circuit that can be determined by using the equation:

$$i = I_{max} * \text{Sin } (w * t)$$

where (i) is expressed in amperes, (t) is expressed in seconds, and I_{max} and w are constants.

Solution: If I_{max} = 0.02 A, w = 377 and t = 1 s, then the instantaneous current (i) can be determined by entering

0.02*@SIN(377*(@PI/180))

The instantaneous current is 0.005847 A.

Note: w = 377 for an alternating current of 60 Hz (w = 2(PI $*$ f) where f is the frequency).

@COS: DERIVING A COSINE

@COS(x)

Returns the cosine of x, where x is interpreted as an angle expressed in radians, and where x is either a number, cell address, or arithmetic expression.

Example: @COS(A10)

Problem: You have to calculate the square footage of a square storage area. Unfortunately, it is filled with boxes, so you cannot accurately measure the length of the walls. There is, however, a cleared walkway that diagonally crosses the room from one corner to the other.

Solution: By measuring the length of the diagonal (a) and the angle between the diagonal and the adjacent wall (x), you can determine the length of the adjacent wall (b) by using the @COS function. The length of the adjacent wall (and consequently the other walls, because the room is square) can be found by using the following formula:

$$COS(x) = b/c = \text{adjacent wall/diagonal}$$
$$c * COS(x) = b$$

The diagonal is measured to be 20 feet and the angle is known to be 45 degrees (or 0.785398 radians).

To convert this formula using 1-2-3, enter

20*@COS(.785398)

The length of the wall is 14.14213 feet.

The square footage of the square room is then the length of the wall squared. You must now edit the formula to include the ^ that will square your result. Enter

(20*@COS(.785398))^2

The room is 200 square feet.

@MOD: DERIVING A REMAINDER (MODULO)

@MOD(x,y)

Returns the remainder left after division, where x is the number, cell address, or arithmetic expression to be divided, and y is the number, cell address, or arithmetic expression by which x is to be divided.

Example: @MOD(10,6) = 4

Problem: Your computer system uses a paged memory allocation system. In such a system, memory is allocated in fixed-size blocks called *pages*. The smallest memory size that can be allocated is the size of the page. If your program does not fill the block completely, RAM is wasted.

For example, if your program is 600 bytes long and the page size of your computer's RAM is 1,000 bytes, the operating system will allocate 1,000 bytes of memory to your program, and 400 bytes of RAM will be wasted.

Solution: The amount of wasted RAM can be determined using the @MOD function. If the length of the program (*x*) is 2,256 bytes and the page size (*y*) is 1,000 bytes, then the number of bytes used in the last page of your program can be determined by:

$$MOD(x,y) = MOD(2256,1000) = 256 \text{ bytes}$$

The number of unused bytes = (page size) − (number of used bytes).

To convert this formula using 1-2-3, enter

1000 − @MOD(2256,1000)

744 bytes are unused in the last page of your program.

@SQRT: COMPUTING A SQUARE ROOT

@SQRT(*x*)

Returns the square root of *x*, where *x* is a number, cell reference, or arithmetic expression.

Example: @SQRT(16) = 4

Problem: A new fence is needed along one side of a square playground. You know the area of the playground and can determine the length of fence required by using the @SQRT function.

Solution: If the area of the playground (*x*) is 144 square feet, then the length of one side of the square playground area can be determined as follows:

$$SQRT(x) = \text{the length of one side}$$

To convert this formula using 1-2-3, enter

@SQRT(144)

The side of the playground is 12 feet.

@ATAN: DERIVING AN ARC TANGENT

@ATAN(*x*)

Returns the arc tangent of *x*, (the angle in radians whose tangent is *x*), where *x* is a number, cell reference, or arithmetic expression.

Example: @ATAN(C10/14)

Problem: J&K Solar Panel, Inc., has a contract to install a solar panel on the roof of a house. The solar panel has to be positioned so that during the hours of peak sunlight the panel is at an angle approximately 90 degrees to the direction of the sun. You have determined that the pitch of the roof is too steep to fulfill this requirement, and that the panel should be raised at an angle of 7.1 degrees (0.123918 radians) from the roof line. You want to determine if a particular solar panel that is in stock is suitable for the task. You know that you can determine the angle at which the panel will sit on the roof by measuring the height of the solar panel (*h*) and the length of the offset leg (*a*) that protrudes from the base of the panel at a 90-degree angle.

Solution: If the height of the panel is 8 feet and the length of the offset leg is 1 foot, the angle (*x*) can be determined as follows:

$$x \ = \ \text{ATAN}(a/h)$$

To convert this formula using 1-2-3, enter

@ATAN(1/8)

The result is .124354 radians (about 7.1 degrees); thus the solar panel will be suitable in this case.

@ATAN2: DERIVING A FOUR-QUADRANT ARC TANGENT

@ATAN2(*x, y*)

Returns the arc tangent of *x/y*, the angle in radians whose tangent is *x/y*, where *x* and *y* values are considered separately, such that the arc tangent is returned in the correct quadrant.

Example: @ATAN2(A10,A12)

@ASIN: DERIVING AN ARC SINE

@ASIN(x)

Returns the arc sine, the angle in radians whose sine is *x*, where *x* is a number, cell reference, or arithmetic expression.

Example: @ASIN(29.6/B24)

Problem: A Girl Scout troop has been assigned to install a flagpole. The engineer has told them that to support the pole properly, the angle between the flagpole and the guide wire must be at least 35 degrees (0.610865 radians). They have tied one of the guide wires from the top of the pole to the base of a nearby tree, and now they must determine if the angle (*x*) is at least 35 degrees. They know that the length of wire from the top of the pole to the base of the tree (*a*) is 24.7 feet and that the distance from the flagpole to the tree (*b*) is 14.5 feet.

Solution: They can determine the angle by using the @ASIN function in the following manner:

$$x = \text{ASIN}(b/a)$$

To convert this formula using 1-2-3, enter

@ASIN(14.5/24.7)

The result is 0.627403 radians, or an angle of about 36 degrees. The guide wire is positioned properly.

@ACOS: DERIVING AN ARC COSINE

@ACOS(x)

Returns the arc cosine of *x*, the angle in radians whose cosine is *x*. The value returned is always between 0 and pi. If *x* is not a number, cell reference, or arithmetic expression with a value between −1 and +1, the value returned is ERR.

Example: @ACOS(28/I7)

Problem: A wheelchair access code requires that the access ramps into buildings cannot rise at an angle greater than 15 degrees

(0.261799 radians). The building inspector can determine the rise angle (*x*) of the ramp by measuring the length of the ramp (*a*) and the distance from the building entrance to the end of the ramp (*b*).

Solution: If the length of the ramp is measured to be 10 feet and the distance from the end of the ramp to the entrance is 9.78 feet, the rise angle (*x*) can be determined by using the @ACOS function:

$$x = ACOS(b/a)$$

To convert this formula using 1-2-3, enter

@ACOS(9.78/10)

The result is 0.210148 radians (about 12 degrees), so the ramp meets the housing code.

@LOG: COMPUTING A LOGARITHM

@LOG(*x*)

Returns the logarithm base 10 of *x*, where *x* is a number, cell reference, or arithmetic expression. If *x* is zero or negative, the value ERR is returned.

Example: @LOG(25)

Problem: It is sometimes necessary to know the number of digits in an integer before printing or displaying it, to ensure that it is formatted correctly. If all of the numbers are known to be positive, the @LOG function can be used to determine the number of digits to the left of the decimal point. (The @ROUND function can be used to fix the number of digits to the right or left of the decimal point.)

Solution: If the value (*x*) is 256, the number of digits to the left of the decimal point can be determined by taking the integer value of the result of @LOG(*x*) and adding 1 as shown below:

$$INT(LOG(x)) + 1$$

To convert this formula using 1-2-3, enter

@INT(@LOG(256)) + 1

The number of digits is 3.

@LN: COMPUTING A NATURAL LOG

@LN(x)

Returns the natural logarithm or logarithm base e of x, where x is a number, cell reference, or arithmetic expression. If x is zero or negative, the value ERR is returned.

Example: @LN(A1)

Problem: When you create line or bar graphs, problems can arise if the numeric range of the data is extreme. This is because the Lotus 1-2-3 graphics display adjusts the graph's Y (vertical) axis using the highest and lowest values, and divides this axis into equal intervals. If one or more data values is significantly larger than the rest, the smaller values will shrink nearly out of sight on the graph in order to accommodate the largest values.

Solution: Professional chartmakers avoid this problem by using logarithmic scaling, dividing the Y axis into unequal intervals that become progressively smaller toward the top of the graph. This allows for the display of both the highest and lowest values on the same graph. Although Lotus 1-2-3 does not offer the direct capability of producing logarithmic graphs, its @LN (natural logarithm) function can produce the same effect. Consider the following data in cells A1 through A5 of a spreadsheet:

1
2
3
4
1000

If you attempted to graph this range in 1-2-3, the values 1, 2, 3, and 4 would be barely distinguishable from one another, while the data point for the 1000 value would soar to the top of the graph, as shown in Figure 4.38.

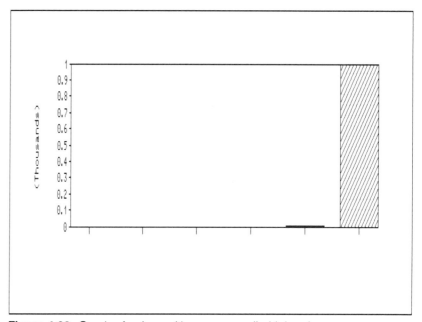

Figure 4.38: Graph of values with one unusually high value

This may be appropriate for some applications, but for others (for example, plotting volatile securities prices over a long period) a more proportionate logarithmic scaling results in better-looking, less deceptive graphs.

If this range were in column A, you would enter the @LN function in column B:

@LN(A1)

Copy it into the other cells in column B opposite the data to be graphed in A. Change the A axis to cells B1 through B6 (in the Graph menu).

The data would now be displayed in such a way that you could distinguish between the lower range of values on the graph, as in Figure 4.39.

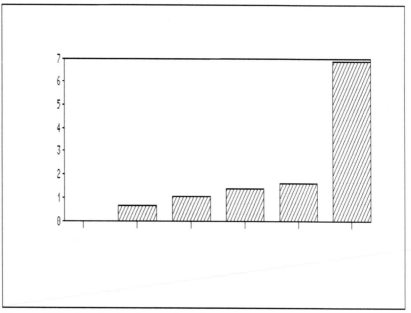

Figure 4.39: Graph of values adjusted using @LN

You can overlay a graph of logarithmic adjusted values using a common scale to approximate the real original values by creating a second graph based on the values in the spreadsheet shown in Figure 4.40. In this example, because the original values range from 10 to 1000, a good scale for the second graph would display the logarithmic values for intervals of 100, as shown in Figure 4.41.

To create the new graph in Figure 4.41, specify the values in column D as the A range. You can then print the graphs on paper, relabel the Y axis using the original values 100–1000 on the overlay, and then photocopy the overlay onto clear plastic. (For instructions and information on printing graphs, see Chapter 6.)

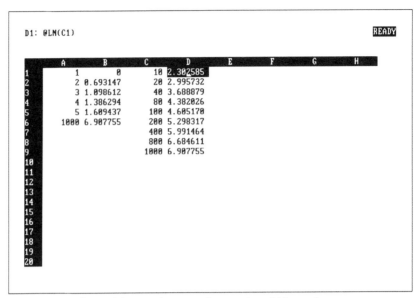

Figure 4.40: Spreadsheet values used to scale @LN graph

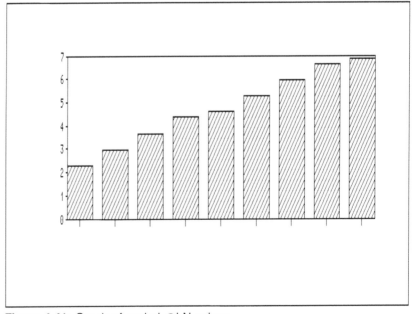

Figure 4.41: Graph of scaled @LN values

In this section, you have learned to use:

- The constants @PI and @EXP
- @TAN, @SIN, @COS to derive a tangent, sine, and cosine
- @ATAN, @ASIN, @ACOS to derive an arc tangent, arc sine, and arc cosine
- @SQRT to compute a square root
- @MOD to derive a remainder
- @LOG to compute logrithms
- @LN to compute a natural log

Summary

In this chapter, you have worked with 1-2-3's functions in both business and scientific applications. Much more can be done with them than was demonstrated here; in fact, most quantifiable problems can be solved using these functions in conjunction with 1-2-3's other commands and features.

In the next chapter, you will begin to apply 1-2-3's commands and functions to some of the more advanced data analysis and decision-making techniques commonly used in business, such as regression and probability analyses. The chapter also introduces setting up and using data tables.

Chapter 5

Data Analysis Techniques

In this chapter, you will learn to:

- Set up data for analysis
- Predict net income, taking inflation into account
- Test the effect of different inflation rates on net income using data tables
- Estimate data using regression analysis
- Multiply a matrix of numbers by another matrix of numbers
- Invert a matrix

Nearly all business decisions require keeping an eye on the future: analyzing risks, making decisions, predicting probable future events. Decisions always involve a degree of uncertainty. Dealing with uncertainty is perhaps the central problem for financial managers. Many decisions require a horizon of analysis that may reach years into the future for predicting business, financial, and economic variables: sales, profit, inflation, competition.

Any of the many methods of measuring risks and uncertainties must still end with a human judgment. The more systematic the approach, the better informed the judgment.

Analyzing risk for decision making involves two central elements: historical data and current data. The result is a prediction about future values. The point is first to discover the relationship between variables and second, to predict a change in one assuming a change occurs in another, based on the established relationship.

The variables might be inflation, product demand growth, cost factors, sales estimates, and the like. Does a change in one factor guarantee a change in the others? If not, how likely is it that a change in one will predict a change in the others? And finally, what are the changes likely to be? The more rigorously these questions are answered, the more the risk of decision making is reduced.

The greater the number of possible forecasts that are tested, the more information a decision maker has to base his or her decisions on. Playing 'what-if'—evaluating present and future business commitments based on possible changes in the business world and company performance—has become a bedrock of financial management, especially since the development of electronic tools such as 1-2-3 that make these once-complicated analyses simple.

It is simple in 1-2-3, for example, to extend a forecast to estimate data based on current values. The other feature of 1-2-3 that becomes enormously useful in this kind of business forecasting is the recalculation speed of the Data Table command, which automatically changes values and displays the results.

Release 2 of 1-2-3 also includes new commands that are useful in two popular methods of forecasting and analyzing data: data regression analysis and data matrix multiplication. We will examine both of them in this chapter.

Regression analysis enables you to forecast—to predict data—by analyzing the relationships among different business variables. The closer the relationship, the more likely a change in one variable can predict a change in the other variable, and can predict what that change will be. Once the degree of relationship between two variables is established (by analyzing how the two have varied together in the past), you can then predict the change that will occur in one variable when the other changes.

For example, once a relationship has been established between the inflation rate and sales for a particular company (by evaluating the degree to which the two changed together in past years), then the variable relationship between the two can be used to forecast future sales, usually in combination with other proven sales predictors. This particular example is, in fact, a frequent use of regression analysis in financial applications. Future inflation is a factor used in predicting sales, which in turn are used to predict costs and profit.

This method of analysis produces predictions from which decisions can be made. To make decisions, however, you also need to know what the risks are—how certain the predictions are.

Probability analysis is the process of establishing the degree of risk involved in making a prediction, based on how strong the relationship between the two variables has been in the past and how large your pool of evidence for the existence of the relationship is. It is possible, after all, that the strong relationship you established between the inflation rate and sales data for last year was a fluke, and that most of the time the two actually have no effect on one another.

Everyone uses probability analysis in everyday life, in less formal language. You bet on the outcome of a game, on winning the lottery, even on getting a raise. You tell yourself, "I have a 50/50 chance of getting the outcome I'm predicting." This same process is used in assessing business risk: determining the chance—the probability—of a certain forecast or prediction. For example, you might establish a best case, worst case, and cases in between for a particular forecast and then assess the probability of each case and compute the most likely forecast.

If you would like to brush up on forecasting techniques, *Financial Management: Theory and Practice* by Eugene Brigham (Dryden, 1985) is an excellent reference. This book also offers a disk with 1-2-3 templates to perform the corresponding text's many examples.

Lotus 1-2-3 uses the option name "Data" for two distinct groups of commands that have little to do with one another and require separate treatment. The first group consists of Data commands that do not require a database: Data Fill, Data Table, Data Regression, and Data Matrix; the second consists of those that do require a database: Data Sort, Data Query, Data Distribution, and Data Parse. This chapter focuses only on the first group of commands, those that are not database related. The database-related commands are discussed in Chapters 8 and 9.

While the data analysis techniques presented in this chapter can be useful in all sorts of applications, they are of special use to people who work with statistical and financial predictions. The examples were designed to suggest uses for 1-2-3's data analysis techniques, especially in these areas.

The first example is a simple one, predicting future net income with inflation taken into account, using 1-2-3's Data Table command. A more intermediate example follows, using regression analysis to predict sales based on changes in inflation. Lotus 1-2-3's new Data Regression command makes this once-complicated analysis a matter of a few keystrokes.

Assessing the risk of estimated inflation is automated using the data matrix multiplication command in the next example. Lotus 1-2-3 automates the computation of forecasts with a process called *matrix multiplication,* which will be examined along with probability in the section "Using Probability Analysis."

Setting Up Data for Analysis

Lotus 1-2-3's data analysis methods require that the data appear in a specific format, which is often different from the format in which the data was originally entered. To save you reentering the data, 1-2-3 offers a variety of time-saving commands with which you can either move or copy the data into the format required.

A common way analysts look at data that ranges over a period of years is the columnar format shown in Figure 5.1.

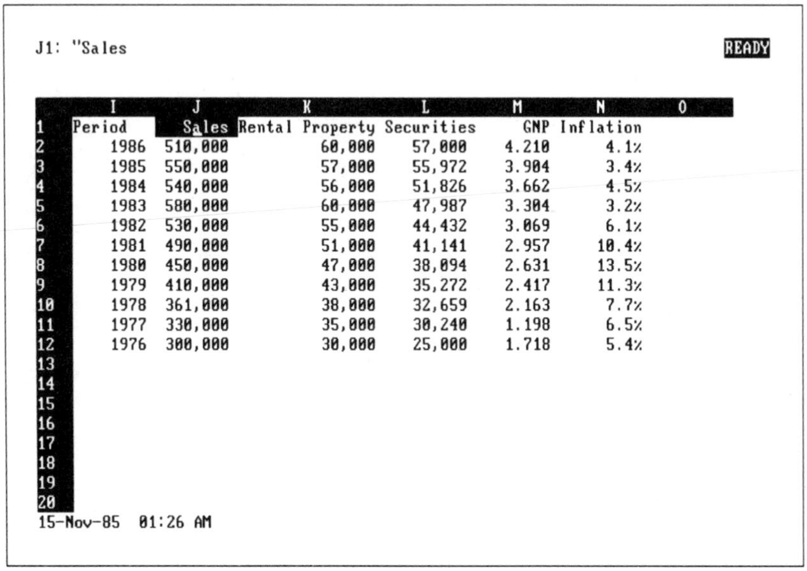

```
J1: "Sales                                                              READY

        I        J       K         L         M       N        O
1  Period       Sales Rental Property Securities    GNP Inflation
2     1986    510,000          60,000    57,000    4.210     4.1%
3     1985    550,000          57,000    55,972    3.904     3.4%
4     1984    540,000          56,000    51,826    3.662     4.5%
5     1983    580,000          60,000    47,987    3.304     3.2%
6     1982    530,000          55,000    44,432    3.069     6.1%
7     1981    490,000          51,000    41,141    2.957    10.4%
8     1980    450,000          47,000    38,094    2.631    13.5%
9     1979    410,000          43,000    35,272    2.417    11.3%
10    1978    361,000          38,000    32,659    2.163     7.7%
11    1977    330,000          35,000    30,240    1.198     6.5%
12    1976    300,000          30,000    25,000    1.718     5.4%
13
14
15
16
17
18
19
20
15-Nov-85  01:26 AM
```

Figure 5.1: Data in columnar format

You will use the INCOME spreadsheet created in Chapter 3 to illustrate how to use Range Transpose, Range Value, and Data Fill commands to reformat data for analysis. If you have not yet created the INCOME spreadsheet, take a few minutes to do so now.

Figure 5.2 shows the data in Figure 5.1, the original spreadsheet from which it came.

```
MTCT Corporation                  TODAY'S DATE:        10/23/86
PROJECTED INCOME STATEMENT        TODAY'S TIME:        06:34 PM
FOR THE YEAR 1986

                 ~~~~~~~~  ACTUAL  ~~~~~~~~~~~   EST    Y-T-D    %
Income:           QTR 1     QTR 2      QTR 3    QTR 4  ' TOTAL INCOME
        Sales    110,000   125,000   135,000  140,000  510,000  81.3%
Rental Property   15,000    15,000    15,000   15,000   60,000   9.6%
     Securities   25,000         0    32,000        0   57,000   9.1%
                 ====================================================
   Total Income  150,000   140,000   182,000  155,000  627,000 100.0%

Expenses:
     Salaries:
Partner 1         13,750    13,750    13,750   13,750   55,000   8.8%
Partner 2         12,000    12,000    12,000   12,000   48,000   7.7%
Associates        10,500    10,500    10,500   10,500   42,000   6.7%
Administrative     9,000     9,000     9,000    9,000   36,000   5.7%
Clerical           7,000     7,000     7,000    7,000   28,000   4.5%
                 ----------------------------------------------------
Total Salaries    52,250    52,250    52,250   52,250  209,000  33.3%
Mngmt Expenses     4,000     5,000     4,500    4,800   18,300   2.9%
         Rent      2,000     2,000     2,000    2,000    8,000   1.3%
     Supplies      2,000     1,800     1,900    2,100    7,800   1.2%
    Telephone      1,800     1,900     2,100    2,300    8,100   1.3%
                 ----------------------------------------------------
Total Expenses    62,050    62,950    62,750   63,450  251,200  40.1%
                 ----------------------------------------------------
Net Income        87,950    77,050   119,250   91,550  375,800  59.9%
                 ====================================================
```

Figure 5.2: Data in income statement format

RANGE COMMANDS

Range commands are used to perform operations on ranges of cells. You saw earlier in Chapter 3 how to use some of the Range menu's underlined options, which are Format, Erase, Label, Justify, Protect, and Unprotect.

The Transpose and Value options are chiefly used to modify the positions and contents of a range of cells. For example, you can use the Range Transpose command to copy FROM row labels TO column labels. The Range Value command copies the contents of a cell or range that contains a formula to a range that contains the value of that formula. Combining Range Transpose with Range Values copies the values from formulas in a column to values in a row. The sample problem will show how to use these two commands to prepare data for regression analysis. First, though, we will review some basic points about each command.

COPYING VALUES FROM FORMULAS

The new Range Value command is the equivalent of pressing the F2 (Edit) F9 (Calc) sequence in Release 1A when you wanted a cell to contain a value permanently or wanted to keep a formula from changing. If you specify the FROM and TO range as the same, you can Edit-Calc a range of cells with the Range Value command.

You can also relocate the value of a formula from one or more cells to one or more cells in another area of the spreadsheet. Specify the FROM range as the formula(s), and the TO range as the new cell(s).

COPYING COLUMNS TO ROWS OR ROWS TO COLUMNS

The values for data are often located in a spreadsheet by column rather than by the row format required by the data analysis commands. In the old 1-2-3, you had to copy each cell from the column to the row. Copying a column into a row is known as *transposing* a range. Now you can copy all of the values (both labels or numbers) to the new cells by using Range Transpose, which saves time and avoids errors.

If you were to transpose the formulas in the spreadsheet, they would be adjusted relatively. Because for data analysis you need the results of the formulas and not the formulas themselves, tell 1-2-3 to copy the values (the results of the formulas) rather than the formulas themselves. First, use the Range Value command to copy the values to a new, temporary column. Then transpose the values from the temporary column into the appropriate row and, finally, delete the temporary column.

Hint: You can edit a cell formula to make it absolute by using the F4 (Absolute) key before using the Range Transpose command to copy a cell with a formula. The transposed value will then remain unchanged.

FILLING DATA VALUES IN EQUAL INTERVALS

To enter numeric data that is in a sequence with equal intervals between each number, the Data Fill command is quite useful. To use the Data Fill command, you specify four types of information.

1. The cell location where you want 1-2-3 to enter the data.
2. The *start value,* the beginning value 1-2-3 will input.
3. The *step value,* the interval between each number, which can be negative or positive.
4. The *stop value,* the ending value 1-2-3 will input.

There are many uses for this command: entering year numbers (1945–1999), month numbers (1–12), dates with equal intervals such as weeks (an interval of 7), and values for amounts that might have intervals of 100, 1000, or -100. You will use this command to enter years in the example that follows.

SAMPLE PROBLEM: SETTING UP DATA FOR ANALYSIS

Problem: You have been asked by the CEO in MTCT to prepare the 1986 income statement data from the spreadsheet INCOME so that he can analyze the effect of inflation rates and the GNP on the company's projected income. You will copy the Sales, Rental Property, and Securities TOTALS data and the row labels from the budget. There is historical data from 1976 to 1985 to input for each income item, GNP, and inflation.

Solution: Copy the column A labels to row 1, column I, and enter the new labels. The values from Total Sales, Rental Property, and Securities for 1986 will be transposed from the spreadsheet. Use the Range Transpose and Range Value command and enter the year numbers 1986–1976, using the Data Fill command.

Notice that in Figure 5.1 the row of labels is in the same order as the column of labels in the original spreadsheet in Figure 5.2. You could type them again in these new cell positions, but using the

Range Transpose command to copy the labels in column A to Row 1 is much easier. Move your cursor to the Home position and enter

/ R T A7.A9

to designate cells A7 to A9 as the column range to transpose FROM. Press ← to complete the command. Then enter

J1

to designate cell J1 as the beginning of the row to transpose TO. Press ← to complete the command.

To improve the clarity of this new section of the spreadsheet, do a little cleaning up. Use the Worksheet Column Set-Width command to set column K to a width of 16 characters and column L to a width of 10 characters, so that you can read the entire label.

Finally, enter the new labels **Period, GNP,** and **Inflation** in cells I1, M1, and N1, respectively. Your spreadsheet should look like Figure 5.3.

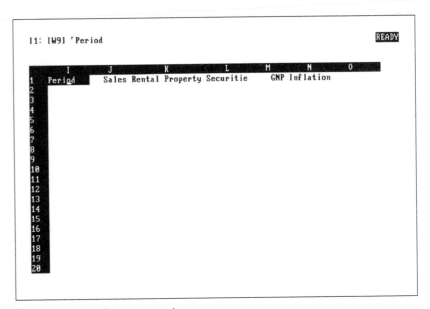

Figure 5.3: Labels transposed

To copy the values for 1986 income from the totals, first convert the formulas to values using the Range Value command. Enter

/ R V F7.F9

to designate cells F7 to F9 as the range to copy values FROM. Press ◄─┘ to complete the command. Then enter

J2

to designate cell J2 as the beginning of the column to copy values TO, and press ◄─┘. Your spreadsheet should look like Figure 5.4.

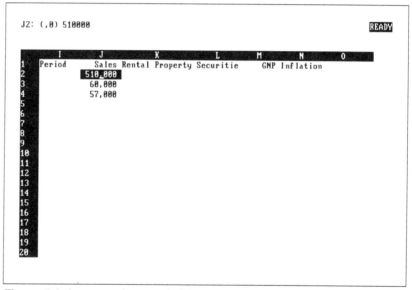

Figure 5.4: Income values copied from income formulas

Finally, transpose the values in the column to a row by entering the sequence

/ R T J2.J4 ◄─┘ J2 ◄─┘

To clean up cells J3 and J4, enter

/ R E J3.J4 ◄─┘

Your spreadsheet should look like Figure 5.5.

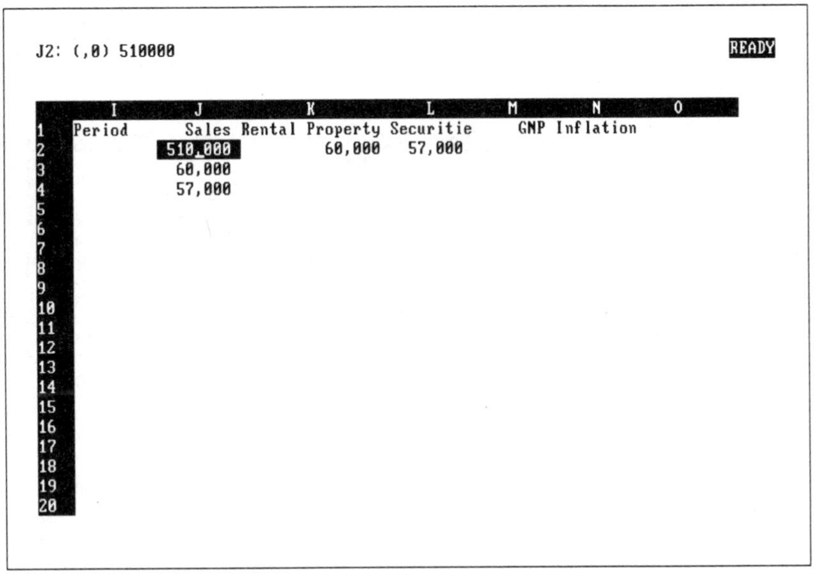

```
J2: (,0) 510000                                                        READY

        I         J         K         L         M         N         O
1  Period        Sales Rental Property Securitie      GNP Inflation
2              510,000          60,000   57,000
3               60,000
4               57,000
5
6
7
8
9
10
11
12
13
14
15
16
17
18
19
20
```

Figure 5.5: Transposition of income values

All that remains to be done in this spreadsheet is to enter the year numbers, 1986–1976, and the sales, rental property, securities, GNP, and inflation data. Notice that the year numbers are in descending order, beginning with 1986 and ending with 1976. Use the Data Fill command to enter the years. To do this, enter

    / D F I2.I12

to designate cells I2 to I12 as the range to receive the data. Press ↩ to complete the command. Then enter

    1986 ↩ – 1 ↩ 1976 ↩

Note from the prompts that you have designated 1986 as the start value, – 1 as the step value, and 1976 as the stop value. The values 1986 through 1976 should appear on your screen in column I. Format the column to General Format using the Range Format General command. Then enter the data for GNP, inflation, and income as shown in Figure 5.6. In only a few minutes, you have finished preparing the spreadsheet as the CEO requested.

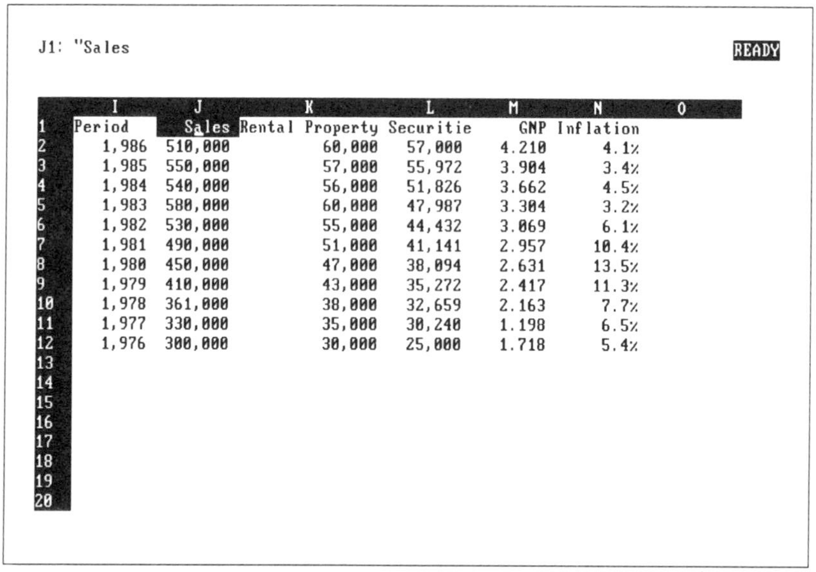

```
J1: "Sales                                                          READY

      I        J       K        L        M       N        O
1  Period     Sales  Rental Property Securitie    GNP Inflation
2     1,986  510,000          60,000   57,000    4.210    4.1%
3     1,985  550,000          57,000   55,972    3.904    3.4%
4     1,984  540,000          56,000   51,826    3.662    4.5%
5     1,983  580,000          60,000   47,987    3.304    3.2%
6     1,982  530,000          55,000   44,432    3.069    6.1%
7     1,981  490,000          51,000   41,141    2.957   10.4%
8     1,980  450,000          47,000   38,094    2.631   13.5%
9     1,979  410,000          43,000   35,272    2.417   11.3%
10    1,978  361,000          38,000   32,659    2.163    7.7%
11    1,977  330,000          35,000   30,240    1.198    6.5%
12    1,976  300,000          30,000   25,000    1.718    5.4%
13
14
15
16
17
18
19
20
```

Figure 5.6: Completed data for 1976–1986

In this section, you have learned to:

- Copy values (the results of formulas) to a new range of cells using the Range Value command
- Copy columns of data to rows of data with the Range Transpose command
- Fill a range with data values using the Data Fill command

Using What-If Analysis

It is common in financial analysis to predict future performance for a company, given factors such as inflation, growth of the company, and increase in demand for a product. These factors may be applied to projections of sales or other types of income, costs, or expenses. For example, suppose you assume that sales for next year will increase by whatever the rate of inflation is for next year. You have studied economists' reports, and their estimates for inflation range from 5% to 6%. You can input the inflation rate as an assumption, or estimate, and enter a formula to instruct 1-2-3 to calculate income, expenses, and net income based on the increase in inflation. This process of testing the effect on one value of changes in another is known as *what-if analysis*.

AUTOMATING WHAT-IF ANALYSIS: THE DATA TABLE COMMAND

Lotus 1-2-3 offers a fast and efficient method of doing what-if analysis—the Data Table command. The Data Table command basically changes a value and writes down the new result of a formula based on that value in an area of the spreadsheet called the *table area*. You determine a list of values that change, called *input values*, and 1-2-3 calculates the formula for each value. This is called the *input formula;* it may refer to any formula in the spreadsheet you want to calculate. For example, you can enter the input formula in a data table as:

Total Net Income*(1 + inflation) = + F29*(1 + B37)

Different inflation rates become the input values. When you use the Data Table command, 1-2-3 recalculates net income for each inflation rate and displays the result for each rate next to the inflation rate in the table area, as shown in Figure 5.7.

USING THE DATA TABLE COMMAND

The Data Table command requires you to specify three types of information. It asks you for the number of inputs, the table area, and the location of the input cells. A data table can have either one or two inputs, or assumptions. Because you are only varying the estimated inflation rate, this is a one-input table. You could add another factor, such as product demand, and it would then become a two-input table.

```
MTCT Corporation                    TODAY'S DATE:        10/23/86
PROJECTED INCOME STATEMENT          TODAY'S TIME:        06:34 PM
FOR THE YEAR 1986

                ~~~~~~~~~  ACTUAL  ~~~~~~~~~~~~    EST     Y-T-D     %
Income:            QTR 1        QTR 2      QTR 3    QTR 4   TOTAL  INCOME
        Sales   110,000      125,000    135,000  140,000  510,000  81.3%
Rental Property  15,000       15,000     15,000   15,000   60,000   9.6%
    Securities   25,000            0     32,000        0   57,000   9.1%
               =========================================================
  Total Income  150,000      140,000    182,000  155,000  627,000 100.0%

Expenses:
    Salaries:
Partner 1        13,750       13,750     13,750   13,750   55,000   8.8%
Partner 2        12,000       12,000     12,000   12,000   48,000   7.7%
Associates       10,500       10,500     10,500   10,500   42,000   6.7%
Administrative    9,000        9,000      9,000    9,000   36,000   5.7%
Clerical          7,000        7,000      7,000    7,000   28,000   4.5%
               --------------------------------------------------------
Total Salaries   52,250       52,250     52,250   52,250  209,000  33.3%
Mngmt Expenses    4,000        5,000      4,500    4,800   18,300   2.9%
         Rent     2,000        2,000      2,000    2,000    8,000   1.3%
     Supplies     2,000        1,800      1,900    2,100    7,800   1.2%
    Telephone     1,800        1,900      2,100    2,300    8,100   1.3%
               --------------------------------------------------------
Total Expenses   62,050       62,950     62,750   63,450  251,200  40.1%
               --------------------------------------------------------
Net Income       87,950       77,050    119,250   91,550  375,800  59.9%
               =========================================================

                            WHAT-IF ANALYSIS

              1987 ESTIMATED          INFLAT NET INCOME

                                       5.00% 394,590
                                       5.25% 395,530
                                       5.50% 396,469
                                       5.75% 397,409
                                       6.00% 398,348
```

Figure 5.7: Data table what-if analysis

SETTING UP A ONE-INPUT TABLE

The table area is a rectangular range that consists of different values for input 1. In this case the values are the inflation rates. The input formula is entered in the next column to the right, one row above where the first result will appear. The *input cell* holds the assumption that will change. It must be a cell in the spreadsheet referenced by the input formula. Figure 5.8 illustrates the cells that make up the one-input table and the location of the input cell containing the initial assumption for inflation.

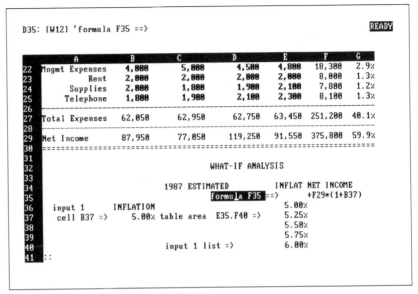

Figure 5.8: One-input data table

Calculating a One-Input Table

To calculate the table, use the Data Table 1-Input command, entering the location of the table and the first input cell to use in the formula. It will take 1-2-3 a few seconds to fill in the values for a data table, depending on how many inputs your table has, the complexity of the formula, and how fast your computer can process.

Setting Up a Two-Input Table

The table area for a two-input table is a rectangular range that consists of a column of the different values for input 1 and a row of the different values for input 2. The input 1 values might be inflation rates and the input 2 values growth factors. The input formula is entered in the cell above the first input cell. The input 1 cell is the input 1 cell referenced by the input formula; the input 2 cell is the input 2 cell referenced by the input formula. In Figure 5.9, cells E35 through G40 make up the two-input table.

```
D31: (G) [W13] 'data table 2                                            READY

        B          C            D           E          F      G       H
21   52,250     52,250       52,250      52,250    209,000  33.3%
22    4,000      5,000        4,500       4,000     18,300   2.9%
23    2,000      2,000        2,000       2,000      8,000   1.3%
24    2,000      1,800        1,900       2,100      7,800   1.2%
25    1,800      1,900        2,100       2,300      8,100   1.3%
26   ------------------------------------------------------------------
27   62,050     62,950       62,750      63,450    251,200  40.1%
28   ------------------------------------------------------------------
29   87,950     77,050      119,250      91,550    375,800  59.9%
30   ==================================================================
31    input 2              data table 2
32   cell B34              WHAT-IF ANALYSIS              input 2 list F35.G35
33    GROWTH
34     2.00%               1987 ESTIMATED NET INCOME     GROWTH
35           formula E35 ==>           +F29*(1+B37+B34)    1.00% 2.00%
36   INFLATION              INFLAT             5.00%
37     5.00% table area   E35.G40 =>          5.25%
38    input 1                                 5.50%
39   cell B37                                 5.75%
40           input 1 list E36.E40 =>          6.00%
```

Figure 5.9: Two-input data table requirements

Calculating a Two-Input Table

To calculate the two-input table, use the Data Table 2-Input command, entering the location of the table, the first input cell, and the second input cell to use in the formula. It will take 1-2-3 more time to fill in the values for a two-input data table than a one-input table, depending again on how many different inputs your table has, the complexity of the formula, and how fast your computer can process.

A sample of using a two-input data table is presented later in the Data Regression section of this chapter.

RECALCULATING THE TABLE WITH THE F8 (TABLE) KEY

When you change the formula or input different values in a table, you need not use the Data Table command again to recalculate. Press the F8 (Table) key instead, and the table will be recalculated using the different formula or input values you have entered. Whenever the spreadsheet file is saved, all the data table settings are saved as well.

SAMPLE PROBLEM: CALCULATING A ONE-INPUT DATA TABLE

Problem: The budget director of MTCT has asked you to project net income for 1987 by multiplying the 1986 estimated year-to-date TOTAL NET INCOME by various estimated inflation rates. The estimates for inflation are 5%, 5.25%, 5.5%, 5.75%, and 6%. Create a table as shown in Figure 5.7 and print the report.

Solution: In order to project net income by the inflation rate, you will enter formulas in cell F35 that will increase the 1986 y-t-d income or expense by each rate. The equation for calculating 1987 values is:

$$1986 \ value \ \times \ (1 \ + \ inflation)$$

where inflation is constant.

Enter this equation as an input formula in cell F35, which refers to the TOTAL Y-T-D INCOME in cell F29 and inflation rate in cell B37.

    +F29*(1+B37)

Using Figure 5.10 as a guide, move your cursor to cell D32 and begin entering the labels and values shown. Remember to enter percents as numbers—.05, or 5%. After you have entered all the data, reformat the cells to the percent format.

To set up the table, enter

    / D T 1 E35.F40

to select a one-input table and designate cells E35 to F40 as the table. Press ⏎ to complete the command. Then enter

    B37

to designate cell B37 as input 1 inflation. Press ⏎ to complete the command.

It will take 1-2-3 a few seconds to fill in the values for net income for each of the inflation rates. Your spreadsheet should look like Figure 5.11.

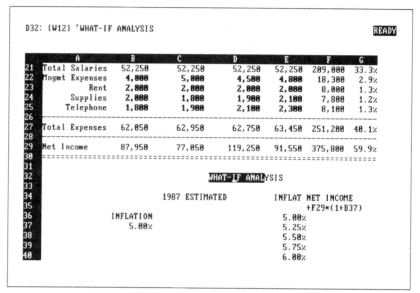

Figure 5.10: What-if analysis labels and values

```
D32: [W12] 'WHAT-IF ANALYSIS                                    READY

         B        C        D        E        F       G       H
21    52,250   52,250   52,250   52,250  209,000  33.3%
22     4,000    5,000    4,500    4,800   18,300   2.9%
23     2,000    2,000    2,000    2,000    8,000   1.3%
24     2,000    1,800    1,900    2,100    7,800   1.2%
25     1,800    1,900    2,100    2,300    8,100   1.3%
26    ----------------------------------------------------
27    62,050   62,950   62,750   63,450  251,200  40.1%
28    ----------------------------------------------------
29    87,950   77,050  119,250   91,550  375,800  59.9%
30    ====================================================
31
32                       WHAT-IF ANALYSIS
33
34              1987 ESTIMATED       INFLAT NET INCOME
35                                        +F29*(1+B37)
36   INFLATION                       5.00% 394,590
37      5.00%                        5.25% 395,530
38                                   5.50% 396,469
39                                   5.75% 397,409
40                                   6.00% 398,348
```

Figure 5.11: Completed what-if analysis using the data table

You might now want to print the results of the completed analysis using the Print command.

Move the cursor to row 41. To print the report, turn on your printer and enter

/ P P A G Q

Your printout should now look like Figure 5.7.

In this section, you have learned to:

- Automate what-if analysis using data tables
- Recalculate a data table using the F8 (Table) key
- Use what-if analysis to change inflation and predict net income

Using Regression Analysis

When you analyze data, you seek not merely to change values but also to establish what the relationships among the different values are. If there is no relationship, then changing one value will have no effect on the other variable. If there is a relationship between the two, you can predict the change in one variable when the other changes. The degree to which one variable changes in accord with the change in another variable is the strength of that relationship. In statistical terms, the relationship is said to be *significant* when the likelihood is small that the relationship you observe is coincidental—a fluke. It is a measure of the confidence you can have that predictions you make based on that relationship will be correct.

Economists and analysts use regression analysis to test the effect of one or more variables on another variable. Values may mutally affect one another—inflation may be affected by rising incomes, and at the same time rising incomes may be affected by inflation. These are said to *vary* together. Or one variable may depend on another, while being independent itself of the value of the other—smoking may cause cancer, but cancer certainly doesn't cause smoking. The variable being affected is known as the *dependent variable,* because the value it has depends on the value of the other factors. The factors, or variables, that affect the value of the dependent variable are called *independent variables,* because any effect the dependent variable might have on them is not being measured. In the above example, smoking is the independent variable and cancer the dependent variable, because the cancer depends on smoking and not the other way around.

In the spreadsheet you just completed, the inflation rate was the independent variable and the net income the dependent variable because you were studying what effect the inflation rate has on net income, not what effect net income might have on the inflation rate.

The custom in regression analysis is to allow X to stand for the independent variable and Y for the dependent variable. Data is compiled for each occurrence of both independent and dependent variables. A regression model determines:

- *R-Squared:* The statistical significance of the relationship between the independent and dependent variables.

- *Constant:* The Y-intercept: the value of the dependent variable regardless of the effects of the independent variable.

- *X-Coefficient(s):* The amount of increase or decrease changes in the independent variable(s) cause in the dependent Y variable.

Estimate of $Y = (X_1 \ coef \times X_1 \ value) + (X_n \ coef \times X_n \ value) + constant$

where n is the number of independent variables.

AUTOMATING REGRESSION ANALYSIS: THE DATA REGRESSION COMMAND

Release 2 of 1-2-3 introduces a new Data Regression command that can perform regression analysis in just a few seconds using one or more independent variables. The regression model can contain up to 16 independent variables. There is no limit for the number of occurrences, except the number of rows your spreadsheet can hold, which will vary depending on how much RAM your computer has installed. The more RAM, the greater the amount of cells available in the spreadsheet. The default of the Data Regression command computes the constant, although you can force it to zero.

USING THE DATA REGRESSION COMMAND

The Data Regression command requires three types of information to be entered by using the options menu below.

X-Range Y-Range Output-Range Intercept Reset Go Quit

The first three options are the three required: the locations of the independent variable(s) X, the location of the dependent variable Y, and where to display the output. You may specify that the intercept be forced to zero; otherwise, the intercept defaults to computing the value. Reset tells 1-2-3 to erase all of the ranges specified. It is used when you want to use new variables or when you make a mistake. The final step is to issue the Go command to instruct 1-2-3 to calculate the regression output.

Estimating a Dependent Variable Using the Constant and Coefficients

The equation for estimating the dependent variable uses the constant, the X1 coefficient, and any other coefficients (X2–Xn) derived from the model's output and the given values for X1–Xn.

When the coefficient is positive, for every one-unit increase in the coefficient, the dependent variable will increase by the value of the coefficient. For example, for every \$1 billion increase in GNP, sales will increase by the coefficient's value. The coefficient is calculated, of course, in terms of the scale of the dependent variable, not of the independent variable. When the coefficient is negative, for every one-unit decrease in the coefficient, the dependent variable will decrease by the value of the coefficient. To construct the formula to estimate a dependent variable with 1-2-3, you would enter:

$$+F20*(+F21*10000)+(+F22*.04)$$

where F20 is the cell with the constant output, F21 is the cell with the X1 coefficient output, 10000 is the estimate for X1, F22 is the cell with the X2 coefficient output, and .04 is the estimate for X2.

Of course, for the estimate of the dependent variable to be useful, the overall model must be significant. Examining and interpreting the R-squared constant is discussed in the next section.

Interpreting R-Squared

R-squared is the constant between 0 and 1 that indicates the overall strength of the relationship between the independent and dependent variables in the model. As a general rule, the higher the R-squared, the greater the degree of relationship between the two variables. When the R-squared value approaches a certain level, depending on the size of the sample studied, the relationship is declared to be significant. Again, significance means that the chance that the relationship you observe in your data is spurious or coincidental is small enough to be disregarded. There's no hard and fast rule about significance. It's a judgment you make, given the rigor of the analysis you did and what the consequences are if you guess wrong.

A high R-squared does not always accurately reflect the strength of the relationship between the dependent and independent variables. It can happen that the sample values entered are not representative of the usual behavior of the variables, even when the results are found to be significant. In general, the greater the number of values tested for each variable, the more chance that the relationship calculated will fairly represent the actual relationship.

Expert opinions vary on what is an acceptable R-squared, but an R-squared result of at least 70% would tend to indicate a significant relationship in the sales model.

In the sample problem below, you will test the relationships between the independent variables GNP and inflation, and the dependent variables sales, rental property, and securities for past years. If you then use that relationship to predict sales in the future, you will have an idea of how much confidence to place in your predictions.

SAMPLE PROBLEM: CALCULATING SALES WITH REGRESSION ANALYSIS

Problem: The Chief Executive Officer needs to predict sales, rental property, and securities for 1987, given different GNPs and inflation rates. GNP and inflation rate are the independent variables. The estimate for GNP is 4.3 billion dollars and for inflation 3.5%. Construct a regression model and the equations to estimate the dependent variables using the given data; interpret the R-squared.

Solution: The data set should be constructed for the CEO from the spreadsheet INCOME in the first section of this chapter. Notice the independent variables in Figure 5.12. Column J contains dependent variable Y1, column K contains Y2, and column L contains Y3. The independent variables X1 and X2 are in column M and N, respectively. There are 11 occurrences or observations of data in this example, one occurrence for each year.

```
J1: "Sales                                                    READY

        I        J         K          L          M       N        O
 1  Period        Sales Rental Property Securities    GNP  Inflation
 2      1986    510,000     60,000    57,000    4.210    4.1%
 3      1985    550,000     57,000    55,972    3.904    3.4%
 4      1984    540,000     56,000    51,826    3.662    4.5%
 5      1983    580,000     60,000    47,987    3.304    3.2%
 6      1982    530,000     55,000    44,432    3.069    6.1%
 7      1981    490,000     51,000    41,141    2.957   10.4%
 8      1980    450,000     47,000    38,094    2.631   13.5%
 9      1979    410,000     43,000    35,272    2.417   11.3%
10      1978    361,000     38,000    32,659    2.163    7.7%
11      1977    330,000     35,000    30,240    1.198    6.5%
12      1976    300,000     30,000    25,000    1.718    5.4%
13
14
15
16
17
18
19
20
15-Nov-85  01:26 AM
```

Figure 5.12: Independent and dependent variables

Now specify the X independent range, the Y dependent range, and where the output range will be displayed. To compute the regression results, enter

/ D R X M2.N12

to designate cells M2 to N12 as the range. Press ⏎ to complete the command. Enter

Y J2.J12

to designate cells J2 to J12 as the range. Press ⟵ to complete the command. Then enter

O J14 ⟵ G

Your spreadsheet should look like Figure 5.13.

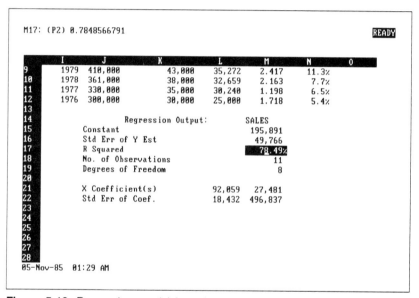

Figure 5.13: Regression model for sales

Estimating Sales Using the Constant and Coefficients

The equation for 1987 sales uses the constant 195,553, the X1 coefficient for GNP of 92,059, and the X2 coefficient for inflation of 27,481 derived from the model. For every $1 billion increase in GNP, sales will increase by $92,059, and for every 1% increase in inflation, sales will increase by $27,481. To construct the 1987 estimate for sales, move your cursor to cell J26 and enter the following:

J26	"GNP =
K26	4.3
L26	"INF =
M26	.035

J27	EST SALES = EST GNP x COEF + EST INFL x COEF + CONSTANT
J28	"SALES =
K28	+(L21*$K$26)+(M21*$M$26) + M15

Your equation for sales should calculate the value $592,708, as shown in Figure 5.14.

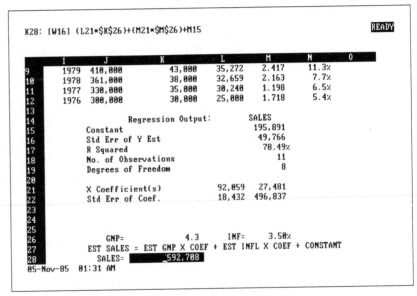

Figure 5.14: Estimate for 1987 sales

Interpreting R-squared

To view R-squared as a percent, reformat the cell M17 by typing

R F P ↵ ↵

Your R-squared result should be 78.49%, which is a significant relationship in the sales model. (The size of the sample used in this example is unrealistically small. With such a small sample, you would actually not have much confidence in your predictions, even with an R-squared of 78.49%. In general, the bigger the sample, the better.)

Try practicing with more Data Regression commands, using securities and rental property as the dependent variables. Figures 5.15 and 5.16 outline the independent and dependent variables and output ranges for each. In Figure 5.15 the dependent variable Y is in column K, while independent variables X1 and X2 are in columns M and N. The output range begins in cell P4. In Figure 5.16 the dependent variable Y is in column L while the independent variables X1 and X2 are in columns M and N. The output range begins in cell V4.

CALCULATING SALES WITH A TWO-INPUT DATA TABLE

The estimate for sales uses a simple formula based on the regression model and the estimated value for GNP and inflation. The estimates for GNP and inflation often vary for many reasons. Suppose you want to vary GNP and inflation and use what-if analysis on sales, rental property, or securities. You can use a two-input data table to perform the what-if analysis using the two inputs GNP and the inflation rate, which make up the "legs" of the table shown in Figure 5.17.

Problem: Test the effect of GNP on sales, asking what if GNP rates equal 4.3, 4.4, 4.5, 4.6, 4.7, and 4.8 billion and inflation rates equal 3.5, 4, and 4.5%, using a two-input table.

Solution: Enter the values for GNP and inflation and lables GNP, SALES ESTIMATE, and INFLATION, using Figure 5.17 as a guide. Reformat the table using the Range Format command. Format the inflation values in row 32 to percents, cell J32 to text, and the GNP values in column J to a fixed format.

The formula in cell K28—the sales estimate—will be used by the data table to test the GNP and inflation values. A two-input data table must contain this formula in the upper-left corner (cell J32) as shown in Figure 5.17. Move your cursor to J32 and type **+K28**. Your table is now ready to calculate sales for each GNP and inflation rate.

Remember that the data table command requires:

1. The table range area location

2. The input cells that should change value

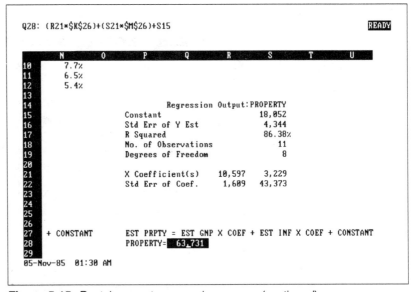

```
K1: [W16] "Rental Property                                        READY

        I        J        K          L          M        N        O
1  Period      Sales  Rental Property Securities    GNP    Inflation
2      1986  510,000          60,000    57,000    4.210      4.1%
3      1985  550,000          57,000    55,972    3.904      3.4%
4      1984  540,000          56,000    51,826    3.662      4.5%
5      1983  580,000          60,000    47,987    3.304      3.2%
6      1982  530,000          55,000    44,432    3.069      6.1%
7      1981  490,000          51,000    41,141    2.957     10.4%
8      1980  450,000          47,000    38,094    2.631     13.5%
9      1979  410,000          43,000    35,272    2.417     11.3%
10     1978  361,000          38,000    32,659    2.163      7.7%
11     1977  330,000          35,000    30,240    1.198      6.5%
12     1976  300,000          30,000    25,000    1.718      5.4%
13
14                Regression Output:      SALES
15         Constant                      195,891
16         Std Err of Y Est               49,766
17         R Squared                      78.49%
18         No. of Observations               11
19         Degrees of Freedom                 8
20
05-Nov-85  01:32 AM
```

Figure 5.15: Rental property regression ranges

```
Q28: (R21*$K$26)+(S21*$M$26)+S15                                  READY

        N        O        P          Q        R        S      T      U
10   7.7%
11   6.5%
12   5.4%
13
14                      Regression Output:PROPERTY
15              Constant                    18,052
16              Std Err of Y Est             4,344
17              R Squared                   86.38%
18              No. of Observations             11
19              Degrees of Freedom               8
20
21              X Coefficient(s)   10,597    3,229
22              Std Err of Coef.    1,609   43,373
23
24
25
26
27  + CONSTANT     EST PRPTY = EST GNP X COEF + EST INF X COEF + CONSTANT
28                 PROPERTY=  63,731
29
05-Nov-85  01:30 AM
```

Figure 5.15: Rental property regression ranges (continued)

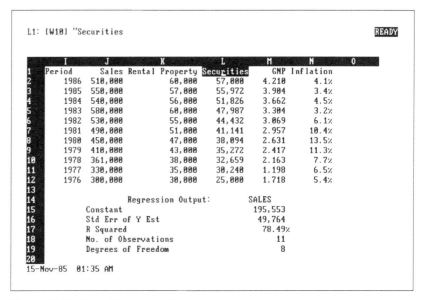

Figure 5.16: Securities regression ranges

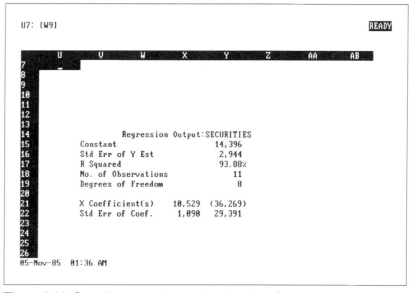

Figure 5.16: Securities regression ranges (continued)

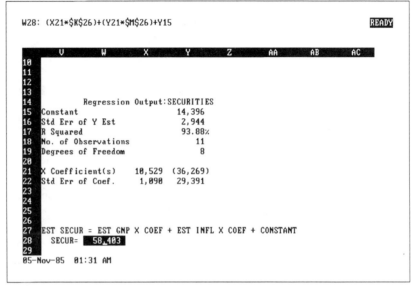

Figure 5.16: Securities regression ranges (continued)

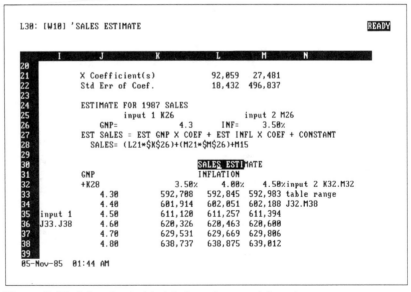

Figure 5.17: Sales data table labels, values, and formula

In the sales estimate, the GNP value in cell K26 and the inflation rate in cell M26 are used as inputs in the formula for sales. The sales estimate table area is located in cells J32 through M38. To calculate the sales estimate for each GNP value and inflation rate, enter

/ D T 2 J32.M38 ⏎ K26 ⏎ M26 ⏎

You have designated cell K26 as input 1 GNP and cell M26 as input 2 INFLATION.

After the data table has been calculated, your spreadsheet should look like Figure 5.17.

If you want to construct data tables that will play what-if with securities and rental property, note that only the table area will change. The table area for rental property is cells P32 through S38 and for securities cells V32 through Y38. When 1-2-3 prompts you to enter input 1 and input 2 for rental property and securities, you need not input them again, because both cells are used in the formulas for rental property and securities. Use Figure 5.18 for the rental property model and Figure 5.19 for the securities model.

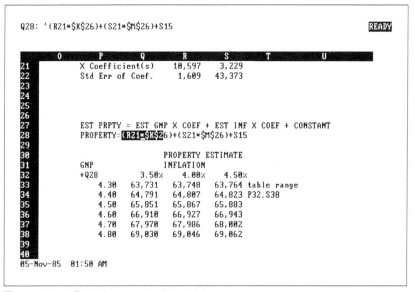

Figure 5.18: Rental property data table

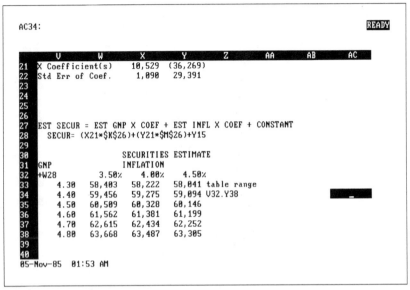

Figure 5.19: Securities data table

In this section you have learned to:

- Perform regression analysis
- Estimate the dependent variable using the regression model
- Interpret R-squared
- Predict future behavior of the dependent variable based on changes in the independent variable
- Use the Data Table command with the Data Regression formula

Using Probability Factors

You can see that forecasts and predictions vary, depending on which values (assumptions) you use. By using probability, you can determine which results are more likely. You can assign a probability factor for each estimate. A probability factor ranges from 0 (impossible outcome) to 1 (certain outcome). You can use your own judgment, along with industry assessments and conventions, to estimate the probability factor for such values as inflation, demand for a product, or the price of a commodity such as oil.

Expected value is the probability of an outcome multiplied by the outcome value. For example, when you toss a coin the probability of "heads" is 0.5 (50% chance). If you will receive $1 for "heads" and $2 for "tails," the expected value is 0.5 × $1, or $.50 for "heads" plus 0.5 × $2, or $1 for "tails." The total expected value for your outcome is:

Expected value outcome 1 + *Expected value outcome* 2 or
($.50 + $1) = $1.50.

In making the final estimate, each value that might occur is weighted by its chances of occurring. Notice in this example that the expected value outcome of $1.50 will never be an actual outcome, just an estimate. The actual outcome will be either $1.00 for heads or $2.00 for tails. Multiplying any estimate for data by probability factors helps make the estimate more accurate. The 1-2-3 command that allows you to make such estimates is the Data Matrix Multiply option, discussed in the following section.

USING THE DATA MATRIX MULTIPLY COMMAND

A *matrix* is a rectangular range of values that contains rows and columns. The sales data table results make up a matrix with six rows and three columns (cells K3–M8), called a 6-by-3 matrix. The probability matrix in Figure 5.20 (cells J13 to O13) is a 1-row-by-6-column matrix, a 1-by-6 matrix.

The Data Matrix Multiply command multiplies one matrix by another matrix. It requires three ranges:

- The first matrix cell range
- The second matrix cell range
- The range to display the output matrix

However, the number of rows on the first matrix must equal the number of columns on the second matrix. If matrix A has 6 rows,

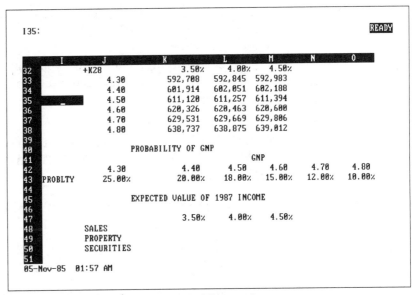

Figure 5.20: Sales matrix and probability matrix

matrix B must have 6 columns for the Data Matrix Multiply command to work properly. That command multiplies the first cell in the first matrix by the first cell in the second matrix. It stores this result temporarily and multiplies the second cells, and so on, until both matrices have been multiplied. The results are then summed and displayed in the area of the spreadsheet you specify.

To compute expected value for sales given 3.5% inflation, multiply each value for sales by the probability factor for the GNP used for the sales estimate. Next, sum these values. The result is the total expected value for sales. The formula for total expected value for sales, assuming 3.5% inflation, is:

GNP	PROBABILITY OF GNP	×	SALES ESTIMATE (3.5% INFLATION)	
4.3	(.25	×	592,665) +	
4.4	(.20	×	601,875) +	
4.5	(.18	×	611,985) +	
4.6	(.15	×	620,296) +	
4.7	(.12	×	629,506) +	
4.8	(.10	×	638,716) =	610,993

You could input formulas for expected value of sales one by one, but 1-2-3's Data Matrix Multiply command does the same thing in a matter of seconds.

In the sample problem below, you will compute the expected value for sales using the probability of the GNP estimates and the estimated value of sales.

SAMPLE PROBLEM: CALCULATING EXPECTED VALUE FOR SALES USING PROBABILITY

Problem: The CEO has learned from a local bank that the probability for GNP ranges from .25, .20, .18, .15, .12, and .10 for 4.3, 4.4, 4.6, 4.7, and 4.8 billion dollars of GNP. Calculate the expected value for sales for each inflation rate by multiplying by the probability estimates for GNP.

Solution: To create the probability matrix, copy the column of GNP values to row 42 using the Range Transpose command. Place the cursor in cell J42 and enter

/ R T J33.J38

to designate cells J33 to J38 as the column range to transpose FROM. Press ⬅ to complete the command. Then enter

J42

to designate cell J42 as the beginning of the row to transpose TO. Press ⬅ to complete the command.

Now enter the estimates for probability factors in row 43 using Figure 5.20 as a guide. Reformat the probability factors in row 43 to Percent format using the Range Format command. Your probability data matrix is now ready to compute the expected value for sales, rental property, or securities.

Multiply the sales matrix by the GNP probability matrix by entering

/ D M M J43.O43 ⬅ K33.M38 ⬅ K48 ⬅

Cells J43 to O43 are matrix 1 (1 × 6), K33 to M38 are matrix 2 (6 × 3), and cell K48 begins the 1 × 3 output matrix. Your spreadsheet should look like Figure 5.21.

```
J47: (P2) [W10]                                               READY

        I        J            K           L           M          N
31            GNP                      INFLATION
32            +K28                  3.50%      4.00%      4.50%
33                    4.30      592,708    592,845    592,983
34                    4.40      601,914    602,051    602,188
35                    4.50      611,120    611,257    611,394 matrix 2 (6x3)
36                    4.60      620,326    620,463    620,600 K33.M38
37                    4.70      629,531    629,669    629,806
38                    4.80      638,737    638,875    639,012
39
40                    PROBABILITY OF GNP        matrix 1 (1x6) J43.043
41                                         GNP
42                    4.30         4.40       4.50       4.60       4.70
43   PROBLTY         25.00%      20.00%     18.00%     15.00%     12.00%
44
45                    EXPECTED VALUE OF 1987 INCOME
46                                                          output
47                                 3.50%      4.00%      4.50%(1x3)
48           SALES            611,028    611,165    611,302 K48
49           PROPERTY
50           SECURITIES
05-Nov-85   01:45 AM
```

Figure 5.21: Expected value for sales

You can repeat the steps above to multiply the property or securities matrix by the probability GNP matrix to create the expected value for property in Figure 5.22 or for securities in Figure 5.23. You could then use these estimates to perform further what-if analyses. You could choose the estimates that assume a moderate inflation rate—say, 4%—and predict 1987 income based on them.

Using the Data Matrix Invert Command

Lotus 1-2-3's Data Matrix command also inverts a matrix mathematically, which can save a lot of time. The matrix must have the same number of columns as rows. The invert operation is used to

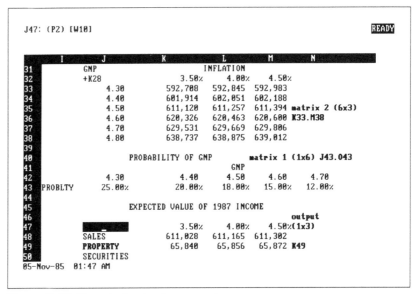

Figure 5.22: Expected value for property

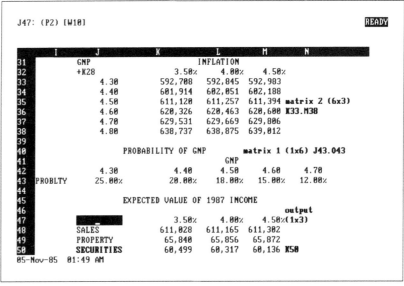

Figure 5.23: Expected value for securities

solve for simultaneous equations in operations research problems, such as finding the shortest distance between several destinations (the traveling salesman problem or the transportation problem); in economic problems, such as maximizing profit; and in manufacturing problems, such as minimizing costs.

To use this command, all you need specify is the input matrix you want to invert and an area of the spreadsheet where you want the resulting inverted matrix to appear.

Problem: A manufacturer of ice cream can produce two types of ice cream, Regular and French. The goal is to maximize profit, assuming Regular sells for $1.00 per gallon and French sells for $2 per gallon. The constraints assume only 2000 gallon of cream and 8 hours of machine time are available. For each gallon, Regular requires ½ quart of cream and .01 hrs per gallon; French requires 1½ quarts of cream and .005 hrs per gallon. Maximize profit.

Solution: Create the matrix for the profit, cream, and machine hours and the maximum resources as shown in Figure 5.24. Invert the basic matrix using the Data Matrix Invert command.

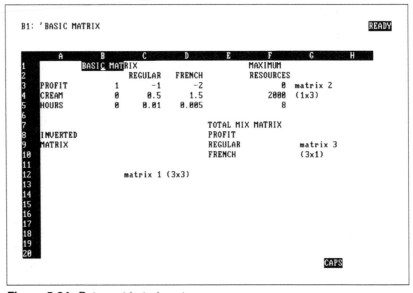

Figure 5.24: Data matrix to invert

Enter

/ D M I B3.D5 ◀─┘ B8 ◀─┘

Your inverted matrix should appear as in Figure 5.25. To find the optimal mix, multiply this matrix by the maximum resource matrix (matrix 2) and direct 1-2-3 to display the result (matrix 3) in cell F8.

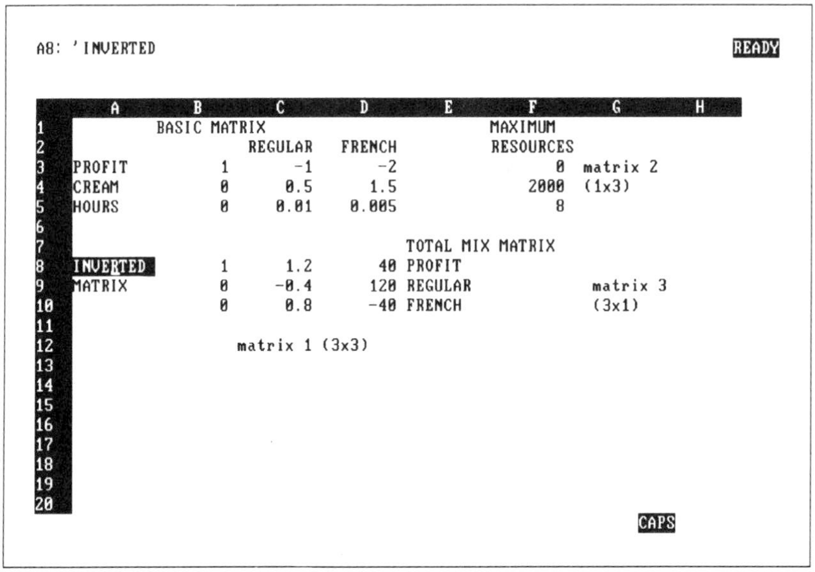

```
A8:  'INVERTED                                                      READY

        A        B        C        D        E        F        G        H
1            BASIC MATRIX                          MAXIMUM
2                     REGULAR   FRENCH             RESOURCES
3    PROFIT       1       -1       -2                     0  matrix 2
4    CREAM        0      0.5      1.5                  2000  (1x3)
5    HOURS        0     0.01    0.005                     8
6
7                                           TOTAL MIX MATRIX
8    INVERTED     1      1.2       40  PROFIT
9    MATRIX       0     -0.4      120  REGULAR            matrix 3
10               0      0.8      -40  FRENCH             (3x1)
11
12                     matrix 1 (3x3)
13
14
15
16
17
18
19
20                                                               CAPS
```

Figure 5.25: Data matrix inverted

Enter

/ D M M B8.D10 ◀─┘ F3.F5 ◀─┘ F8 ◀─┘

The total mix matrix should appear as in Figure 5.26.

In this section, you have learned to:

- Use a two-input data table
- Multiply two matrices
- Invert a matrix

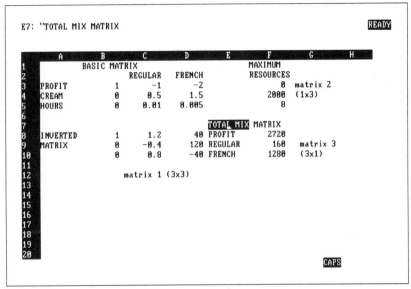

Figure 5.26: Total mix matrix

Summary

In this chapter you have worked with some complicated data analysis and prediction techniques. You have learned to set up data in 1-2-3 for analysis, perform analyses on one and two-input tables, and perform regression and probability analyses. In later chapters, more sophisticated ways of setting up and accessing data for analyses such as these, as well as more general database functions, will be discussed.

The next chapter discusses the graphing features of 1-2-3. Graphing in 1-2-3 is simple and straightforward, and most people experienced with spreadsheets in general and 1-2-3 in particular will find a quick review of the options and processes involved in graphing sufficient for their needs.

In this chapter, you will learn to:

- Create a bar, line, XY, or pie graph
- Add options to graphs
- Catalog graphs for viewing and printing
- Redraw a graph using the F10 (Graph) key
- Print graphs on paper using the PrintGraph program

A good executive or manager is the person who can make quick decisions based on the information at hand. Yet it can be difficult to extract subtle trends or notice gradual changes in performance from rows and columns of financial and other numeric information. Results obtained from a spreadsheet are often skimmed over quickly. In the process, you and others may miss fundamental conclusions about performance. An illustrative picture—a graph—showing the results as they change helps many people to recognize patterns and trends they would otherwise overlook.

Graphing data in 1-2-3 is quick, easy, and flexible. Figure 6.1 shows the various types of graphs available.

Different types of graphs are better used with certain types of data. A line graph plots points and connects them with a line. A bar graph constructs a vertical bar up to the data point with a shaded pattern. Stacked bar graphs construct a vertical bar for one data point and insert or "stack" another bar inside the first bar for the second data point. (Stacked bar graphs are commonly used to show revenue as the first data point, expenses as the second bar, and profit as the third bar, for example. Thus, expenses are stacked on top of profit, and revenues are stacked on top of expenses.)

An X-Y graph is used to plot the intersection of an X data point with a corresponding Y data point, such as height and weight or a dependent variable versus an independent variable.

A pie graph shows data points as "slices" of a circular pie or as percentages of the data points' total. These graphs usually show such factors as how large (or small) a slice of profit is of sales, or any other application in which the parts add up to 100% of the whole.

In this chapter, you will learn how to create, modify, and print 1-2-3 graphs. You must have a graphics adapter for your computer

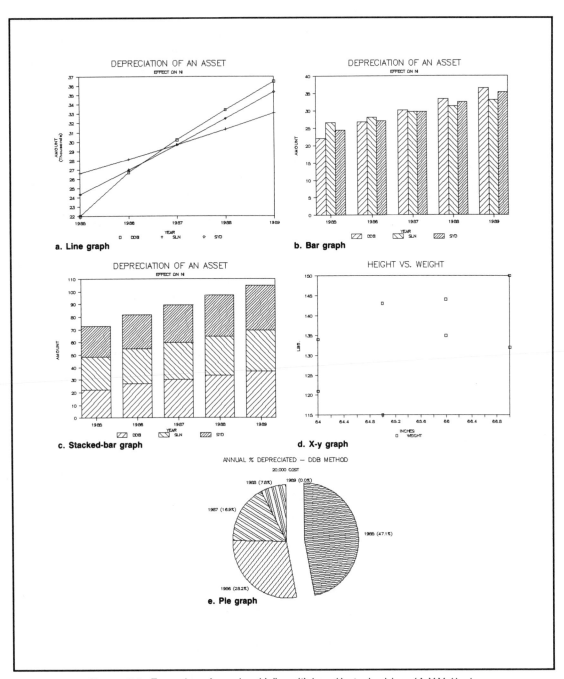

Figure 6.1: Examples of graphs: (*a*) line, (*b*) bar, (*c*) stacked bar, (*d*) X-Y, (*e*) pie

to display the graph on your computer screen, but you need not have a graphics adapter to create the graph. You can save the invisible graph and print it out by using the PrintGraph program. Most dot-matrix printers on the market can print graphs. The types of graphics adapters and graphics printers 1-2-3 can use are listed in Appendix A.

Creating a Bar, Line, or X-Y Graph

To create a graph, you basically call up the Graph Menu, specify the locations of the numeric data you want to graph, and select from the options available for graphs. The Graph Menu, which is selected from the Main Menu, has the following submenu:

Type X A B C D E F Reset View Save Options Name Quit

The options allow you to select:

- The type of graph
- The X-axis values from the spreadsheet
- The set of data values—A,B,C,D,E, or F—to plot from the spreadsheet

They also allow you to:

- Save and name the graphs you create
- Add enhancements to graphs
- Quit the Graph Menu

There are three basic steps for creating any type of graph: (1) select the type, (2) select an X-axis, and (3) select the data values. The sections that follow discuss each of the three steps.

CHOOSING THE TYPE OF GRAPH

The first step is to choose the type of graph you want to create, selecting from line, bar, X-Y, stacked bar, or pie (Figure 6.1). To choose the graph type, just select Type from the Graph Menu and then select the appropriate type of graph.

The next basic requirement for creating a graph is to draw the X axis and plot the data points. The next section explains how to specify and identify these numbers.

X AND Y AXES

Graphs have two axes—the Y axis and the X axis. The Y axis is the vertical axis, and the X axis is the horizontal axis. The X axis is the backbone of a graph. Without it, the graph has no reference from which to begin plotting points. Labels from the spreadsheet are used to describe the associated data points for the X axis.

For example, say you want to plot quarterly sales for your company. The labels that describe the quarters are on the X axis: they are the reference points for the sales data. In other graphs, periods of time may be the labels of the X axis.

You will be given step-by-step instructions for creating a line graph showing depreciation effects on net income for the years 1985–1989, as shown in Figure 6.2, using the file DEPREC you created in Chapter 4. You will then print the graph on paper, using the PrintGraph program.

If you have already created the depreciation spreadsheet from Chapter 4, retrieve the file DEPREC now. If you didn't create it before, take a few minutes to do so now. When you have the file DEPREC up on the screen (as shown in Figure 6.3) you are ready to start your graph.

1. To start, create the X axis for the periods 1985–1989 for the depreciation line graph. Enter

X B7.F7 ←┘

You will have a complete graph as soon as you specify the data points (or data values, to use 1-2-3's language). The next section concerns how you specify the data values to be used in the graph.

SPECIFYING DATA VALUES TO PLOT

Data values are the data points you want to plot. You can plot six different sets of data values, called the A, B, C, D, E, and F

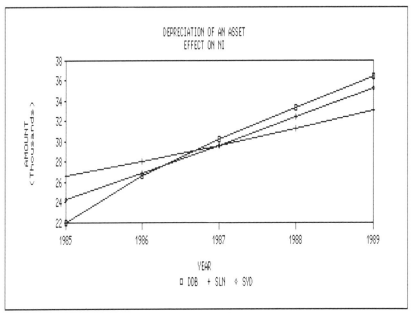

Figure 6.2: Depreciation analysis line graph

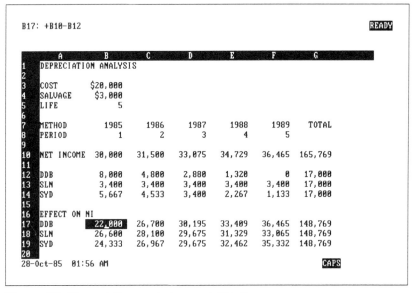

Figure 6.3: Depreciation analysis spreadsheet

axis. In this graph, you want to plot the effect on net income for each of three depreciation methods, using the A, B, and C data ranges. Data ranges identify each area of the spreadsheet that contains the data values to be graphed.

2. To designate the A, B, and C axes for the depreciation line graph, enter

A B17.F17 ↵ B B18.F18 ↵ C B19.F19 ↵

Once you have specified the X axis and at least one data value, you can view the graph, assuming you have a graphics adapter. If not, you'll have to wait until the graph is printed to get a look at it.

VIEWING THE GRAPH

3. If you have a graphics adapter, select VIEW from the menu to see your basic line graph. Press any key to stop viewing the graph.

If you don't have an adapter, you will save the graph onto disk and print it on paper, as described later in this chapter. Figure 6.4 shows the basic line graph you just created.

In this section, you have learned to:

- Create a line graph
- Specify the X axis and data values
- View the graph

What Options Can Do for Graphs

The graph you just created isn't particularly easy to read. It is impossible to tell which line represents data points for A, which for B, and which for C. There's no way to know what the graph is about, because there are no headings or descriptions. It is also difficult to tell

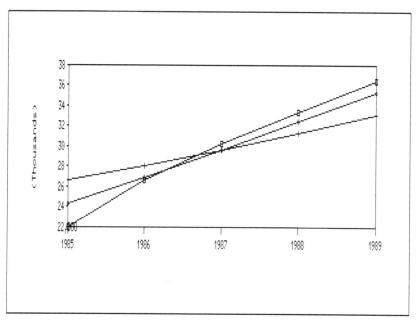

Figure 6.4: Basic line graph

the exact value for each data point plotted. If you have a color monitor, you can see that all the lines are the same color.

Fortunately, there is more to 1-2-3's graphics capabilities than meet the eye in this simple first example. You can add options to your graph that make it easier to understand and more interesting to view. Pie charts, which we will look at later, can be shaded with different patterns and exploded. Below is the Graphs Options submenu, from which this fine tuning can be accomplished:

Legend Format Titles Grid Scale Color B&W Data-Labels Quit

Each of the options is discussed in the following sections.

USING TITLES AND LEGENDS

Your graph can be made easier to read by adding options from the Graph Menu. A *legend* describes each data type and matches the symbol used on the graph to the description of the data type. *Titles* label the graph with headings and also label the X axis and the Y axis.

The Legend menu option specifies a description for each data type as you want it to appear on the graph. Another way to enter a description for a data type is to reference a cell label already on the spreadsheet that describes the data type. To do this, precede the location of the description with a \. Keep in mind that if you erase or change the referenced cell, the legend will also change. You can think of it as a floating legend—a legend that changes as the value of the cell changes. You will use a floating legend in the depreciation graph example.

The depreciation graph displays the effect of three depreciation methods on net income. When you add legends, each method's value will be identified on the graph. A title explaining the graph is also useful.

1. To add legends and titles to the graph as shown in Figure 6.5, use the following sequence of commands. Watch the prompts on your screen as you enter

   O L A \A17 ↵

2. You have now designated A17 as the legend for A. To designate cell A18 as the legend for B, enter

   L B \A18 ↵

3. Likewise, to select a cell for the C legend, enter

   L C \A19 ↵

4. Now, to create titles for the first row, enter

   T F DEPRECIATION OF AN ASSET ↵

5. For the second row, enter

   T S EFFECT ON NI ↵

6. Then to enter the X axis title, enter

   T X YEAR

7. Then to enter the Y axis title, enter

   T Y AMOUNT ↵

8. Enter

   Q V

to quit the options menu and view the graph.

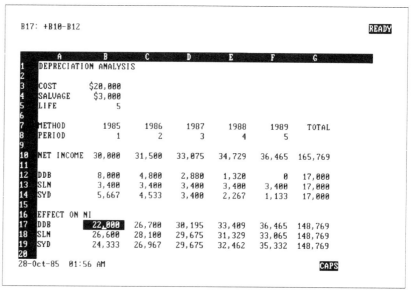

B17: +B10-B12   READY

	A	B	C	D	E	F	G
1	DEPRECIATION ANALYSIS						
2							
3	COST	$20,000					
4	SALVAGE	$3,000					
5	LIFE	5					
6							
7	METHOD	1985	1986	1987	1988	1989	TOTAL
8	PERIOD	1	2	3	4	5	
9							
10	NET INCOME	30,000	31,500	33,075	34,729	36,465	165,769
11							
12	DDB	8,000	4,800	2,880	1,320	0	17,000
13	SLN	3,400	3,400	3,400	3,400	3,400	17,000
14	SYD	5,667	4,533	3,400	2,267	1,133	17,000
15							
16	EFFECT ON NI						
17	DDB	22,000	26,700	30,195	33,409	36,465	148,769
18	SLN	26,600	28,100	29,675	31,329	33,065	148,769
19	SYD	24,333	26,967	29,675	32,462	35,332	148,769
20							

28-Oct-85   01:56 AM   CAPS

Figure 6.5: Line graph with legends and titles

Note that all data values cross over at one of the values, but you can't clearly see which one using the Y axis as a guide. You can actually make the graph tell you what the crossover point is if you use a data label.

MAKING A GRAPH TALK WITH DATA LABELS

Data labels allow you to enter labels, comments, or actual data values above, below, right, center, or to the left of any data point.

The graph in Figure 6.6 illustrates a comment and a data value entered as data labels.

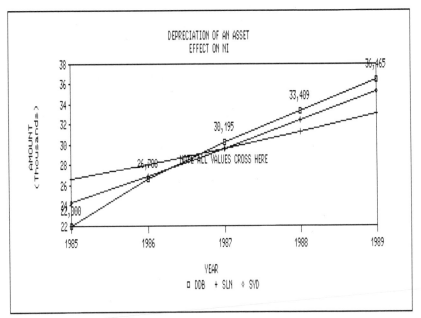

Figure 6.6: Line graph with data labels

To associate a data label with any of the A, B, C, D, E, or F data points, use the Graph Options Data-Labels command. Then select any of the data ranges to attach data labels to. The program asks for the location on the spreadsheet that contains the label. Most people reference the actual data values, but you can enter text in cells and reference those cells to describe a data point. After you enter the range, 1-2-3 will ask you where to display the data labels—center, left, above, right, or below, relative to the data point.

Some comments might be: "breakeven point" for operating costs, "highest quarter" for a salesperson's performance, or "see note on page 2" to reference a text report. Keep the comments short, however, because 1-2-3 tends to condense them during display.

You can remove the lines from a line graph to allow for longer data labels by using the Graph Options Format command discussed in the next section.

FORMATTING LINE GRAPHS WITH SYMBOLS

Lotus 1-2-3 allows you to adjust the format of a line graph's symbols—the small square, cross, and diamond. You can also temporarily remove lines from the graph. The Graph Options Format submenu offers these options:

Lines Symbols Both Neither

Normally, a line graph displays both lines and symbols for a data range. If you only want data range points to show, you can adjust the format of a graph to display only the points by using the Graph Options Format Symbols command. You may want to use a color pen to connect the points yourself when you print the graph out on paper. If you have included data labels near the data points, it is easier to read them without lines. Figure 6.7 shows a line graph with lines removed.

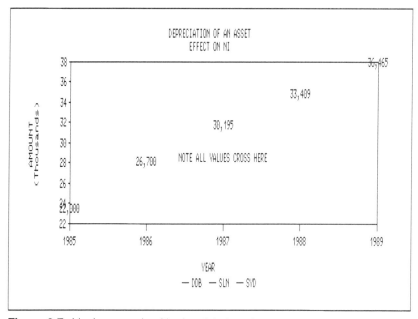

Figure 6.7: Lineless graph with data labels only

Sometimes symbols overlap and make it difficult to read the graph. You can remove symbols from a graph by choosing the Lines option of the command.

Finally, 1-2-3 can be told to remove both symbols and lines from a line graph when you only want data labels to show. To do this, choose the Neither option. To add symbols and lines back to a line graph, choose the Both option.

DRAWING GRID LINES

When data points are drawn on a graph, it can be difficult to see the X or Y scale's corresponding value. Your eye tries to align the data point in the middle of the graph with the scale value, but if the point is between two scales, it is difficult to estimate the data value. Using the Graph Options Grid command, you can add grid lines to a graph. The Grid option submenu includes:

Horizontal Vertical Both Clear

Select the Horizontal option to draw grid lines that extend the Y axis and the Vertical option to draw grid lines that extend the X axis. The Both option includes horizontal and vertical grids, as shown in Figure 6.8.

Remove grids by selecting the Clear option from the Grid submenu. Grids are especially helpful in checking data values in X-Y graphs. You cannot use grids with a pie graph.

USING SCALES

The *scale* is the range of values that appears on the X or Y axis used to plot the data range values. Lotus 1-2-3 uses the X range you specify as the upper and lower limits and automatically creates upper and lower limits, based on your data range values, for the Y axis. Units are also displayed in the same magnitude as the original data. This is known as Automatic scaling; it makes the graphing process very simple. The Graph Options Scale submenu offers these options:

Y Scale   X Scale   Skip

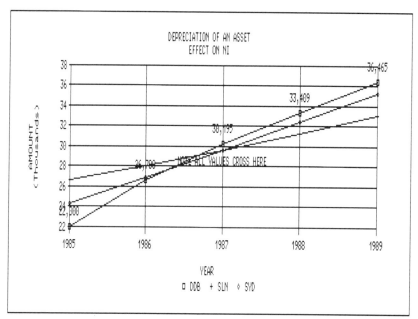

Figure 6.8: Line graph with grid lines

To alter a Y or X scale, first choose the Y or X option. Both of these options have the same submenu:

Automatic Manual Lower Upper Format Indicator Quit

Automatic is the default scale. It may be chosen to cancel the manual, format, or indicator options for the X or Y scale. Note that this submenu is for either the Y or X scale and would have to be used twice, once for the Y and once for the X scale, if manual scaling were desired for both.

The Manual option allows you to specify an upper or lower limit for the axis, change the type of format (Currency, Comma, Date, or any other type) for the axis, or hide the magnitude indicator for that scale. You must select Manual before leaving the submenu to ensure that the upper or lower limit, format, or indicator changes.

Separate graphs are often overlayed to show similar types of information with very different values. It is common for analysts to revise a trend line for economic growth or inflation from quarter to quarter.

The upper and lower limits may vary for each revision, yet it is handy to see revisions with consistent upper limits. Figure 6.9 shows that the upper limit for the Y scale on the line graph that previously displayed 37 is now set to $40 and the lower limit is set to $20, formatted using Currency format. Some mathematical graphs require that the origin, the lower Y and X scale, be set to 0.

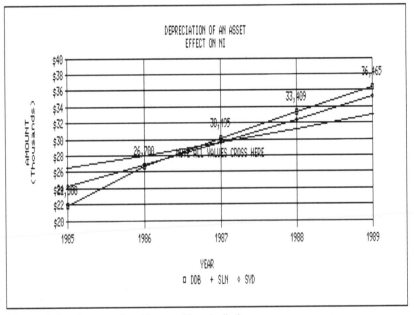

Figure 6.9: Line graph with new Y-scale limits

The next option on the axis submenu is Format. Format types are the same as the spreadsheet format types. 1-2-3 will format the scale as it appears on the spreadsheet. You may want the graph to display one format type but display the spreadsheet values using another. The Format option offers you formats for either scale.

After Format comes the Indicator option. It allows you to turn off the automatic scale label feature. This option solves, at least partially, a common problem with the indicator. Very often in spreadsheets, data in millions is entered abbreviated to thousands for the sake of economy on the spreadsheet. When you graph the results, the indicator for the graph automatically says THOUSANDS for the Y scale.

You find yourself whiting out THOUSANDS and retyping MIL-LIONS on every graph to label the scale accurately. Release 2 of 1-2-3 allows you to hide the indicator by using the Indicator No option. Unfortunately, 1-2-3 does not allow you to retype a new indicator. However, you could use the Graph Options Titles Second command to have a scale indicator label appear on the graph.

The Skip option hides descriptive data values in the X-axis range for a specified interval. This is useful when the X-axis scale appears crowded. You can skip labeling every nth X scale where n is the interval between 1 and 8192. For example, say your X scale is 1985–2000, with data plotted for each year. You could label the X axis for every fifth year by specifying a skip of 5. 1-2-3 hides the scale for four years between each fifth year plotted.

You can practice assigning upper and lower limits, using different formats, and hiding indicators with a line, bar, or X-Y graph. Pie graphs don't use manual scales, as you'll see in the section on pie graphs later in this chapter.

There is now one more option to explore—the possibilities of using colors in your graphs.

USING COLOR IN GRAPHS

If you have a color monitor, you won't want to miss 1-2-3's Graph Options Color command to make your graph bloom. RGB (red, blue, and green) monitors display 1-2-3 graphs using white, red, and blue colors. The IBM Enhanced monitor offers even more colors.

You will want to use the color option when shading and exploding pie graphs to make them really stand out. If you want to print a graph in color, you need to use one of the color printers or plotters listed in Appendix A of this book. If you are using a color monitor but a black-and-white printer, select the B&W option for black and white before you use the Graph Save option. Otherwise, when you print a pie or a bar graph the bars or slices will be solid black and difficult to read. More details are in the sections on saving and printing graphs later in this chapter.

In this section, you have learned to:

- Add legends and titles to graphs
- Make graphs communicate with data labels

- Format line graphs with symbols
- Draw grid lines
- Alter scales
- Add color to graphs

Cataloging Graphs

Lotus 1-2-3 draws several distinctions about using graph files that can be somewhat confusing. The rules are summarized here:

- To save a graph for viewing, you have to name it first. You can have more than one graph associated with a single spreadsheet, and each graph must have a unique name. Naming the graph with the Graph Name command saves it for later viewing but does not save it for later printing.
- To print a graph, you must first save it by using the Graph Save command. Once you save a graph for printing, you cannot view its saved version by using PrintGraph before sending it to the printer.

These rules are discussed in detail in the following sections.

NAMING A GRAPH

To save more than one version of a graph with different options, or to save a graph of another area of the spreadsheet for viewing with a file, you must first name the graph. The name can be any 15-character meaningful abbreviation for what the graph represents. Naming a graph is done with the Graph Name command.

You must also save the entire spreadsheet file to save the graph name. Think of the graph name as an option that is saved in the same way as (and at the same time as) the values in the spreadsheet cells.

1. To name the current depreciation graph LINE, enter

/ G N C LINE ↵

2. Next, change this graph to a bar graph by selecting the Type option and Bar. Name the bar graph BAR, using the same Graph Name command as before. Don't forget to Quit the Graph menu when you have finished naming the bar graph. You can call up a named graph by using the Graph Name Use command.

3. Save your file DEPREC and the named versions of the graphs LINE and BAR again now.

You can create new graphs that use different options easily by using the Graph Reset command, as explained in the next section.

CHANGING GRAPH SETTINGS

Once you have created a graph with many options and data values, it can be confusing to try to create a new graph from it. To erase or reset the settings of the original graph, use the Graph Reset command. This command does not destroy your named graphs; it just allows you to redefine the settings necessary for a new graph more quickly.

You can also use this command to reset one or more data ranges for the A,B,C,D,E, and F axis or the X axis. All other options would remain as they were before reseting any single data range.

4. To prepare for creating a pie graph later in this chapter, reset the graph you have already created. Enter

   / G R G

Now that you have reset the settings, you can easily create another graph from scratch without having to cancel each option for the previous graph.

REVIEWING GRAPHS

After you have assigned names to each of your graphs, you can use the Graph Name Use command to view a graph that has been created. When you bring the graph onto the screen, you can change the type to see the same data graphed in different ways.

You can then name each type as you view it.

5. To call up the original graph LINE, enter

      / G N U LINE ⏎ Q

You can enter the name LINE by moving your cursor to it with the arrow key. You could also call up BAR, the version of the depreciation graph saved as a bar graph, using the same command sequence.

In the next section, you will see how to save a graph for printing.

SAVING A GRAPH FOR PRINTING ON PAPER

Lotus 1-2-3 graphs that you want to print on paper are saved in special files with a .PIC extension name. To tell 1-2-3 to save the graph in a .PIC file, use the Graph Save command. This is similar to saving your regular files, except 1-2-3 saves only the graph image.

First, call up the graph you want to save and make it current by using the Graph Name Use command and entering the name of the graph. Once a graph is current, 1-2-3 knows that it is the graph to save when you use Graph Save. You must assign a name that is eight characters or fewer to the saved graph. Be sure to give the file a meaningful name, because you can't view a graph saved in this way before you print it.

6. To save the graph LINE, make sure it is current by calling it up with Graph Name Use. Then enter

      / G S LINE ⏎ Q

7. Use the Graph Name Use command for the LINE and BAR graphs and save each of them. Now you are ready to print the graphs using the Lotus PrintGraph program.

LISTING SAVED GRAPHS

You can view all of the names of the saved graph files on your disk that can be printed by using the command File List Graph. The screen displays the file names of any graphs that are saved. You can change any number in your spreadsheet after saving a permanent version of the graph, and then redraw the graph to see the changes.

In this section, you have learned to:

- Name a graph for viewing
- Reset graph settings
- View various graphs on the screen
- Save a graph for printing
- List saved graphs

Redrawing a Graph with the F10 (Graph) Key

If you change a value in a spreadsheet on which a graph is based, the graph will also change. You can sit back and watch 1-2-3 automatically redraw the graph by simply pressing the F10 (Graph) function key. This key redraws the most recently looked-at graph in the file.

If your spreadsheet has more than one graph, call up the graph you want to view by using the Graph Name Use command. Once the graph has been made current by being called on, you can use the F10 key to redraw it, updating it with any changes that have been made to the spreadsheet data.

For example, in the depreciation spreadsheet, change the asset cost to $25,000 by typing **25000** in cell B4 and pressing ◄─┘. Then press the F10 key to redraw it.

Creating a Pie Chart

A pie graph (or pie chart) is often used to determine what percent each of a series of values is to a total value. For example, say you want to view the annual percentage depreciation for the DDB (double-declining balance) method of depreciation for the years 1985–1989. You could create a formula that would divide each year's depreciation by the total. But using 1-2-3's pie graph, you can have the program divide for you and display the results in a pie graph, as shown in Figure 6.10.

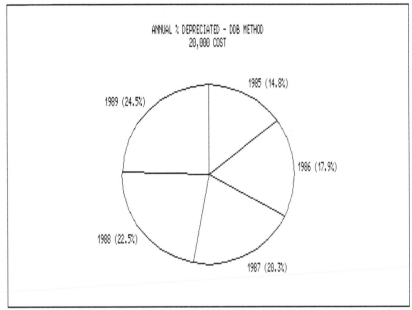

Figure 6.10: Pie graph

To create a pie graph, you need only specify the A-axis data points that, when added together, produce the total you want each item divided by. It is a common error to try to specify each value to be divided by the total in a separate A axis, B axis, and so on. If you specify only one value for the A axis, that value is the total, and the pie graph cannot be drawn. You must have at least two values to create a pie chart, as each "slice" of the pie becomes a value proportional to the total. Using the information computed for DDB depreciation in Figure 6.2, you can follow these steps to construct a pie chart.

1. Enter

/ G T P A B12.F12 ⏎

You can explode the slices of the pie or shade them as shown in Figure 6.11.

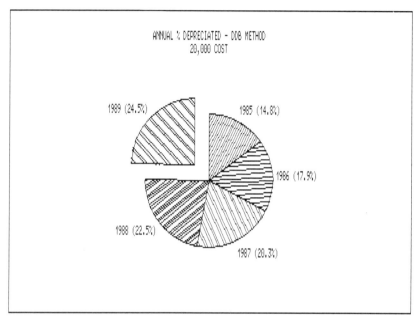

ANNUAL % DEPRECIATED - DDB METHOD
20,000 COST

1989 (24.5%)   1985 (14.8%)

1986 (17.9%)

1988 (22.5%)

1987 (20.3%)

Figure 6.11: Exploded pie graph

EXPLODING AND SHADING PIE GRAPHS

To explode or shade a pie chart, you must specify a B range on the spreadsheet to use for the shading and explode codes. To explode a slice, enter a number greater than 100 in the position of the range relative to the data in the A range. To shade a slice, enter a number between 1 and 7 to vary the shading pattern. See the Lotus *Reference Manual* for more on shading.

2. For example, to shade the pie graph in the spreadsheet DEPREC, specify empty cells B16 to F16 as the B range. Enter the values **101, 2, 3,** and **4** in the spreadsheet to explode the first slice and shade all slices. Press the F10 (Graph) key to redraw the exploded pie graph.

Hint: You can hide the shading and explode codes so that they don't appear on the spreadsheet by using the Range Format Hidden command.

You should now be able to create graphs and have saved a few for printing. The next section discusses how to use the Lotus Print-Graph program.

In the last two sections, you have learned to:

- Redraw the current graph
- Build a pie graph

Printing Graphs on Paper Using PrintGraph

You cannot use the Print command in the Main Menu to print a graph. Instead, you use the special Lotus program called Print-Graph. To use PrintGraph, however, you must first quit 1-2-3.

There are two ways to enter the PrintGraph program. (Steps 1, 2, and 3 below are used for a floppy-based system, or when Print-Graph is not on your hard disk. If you have PrintGraph installed on a hard disk, use step 1 only.)

1. You can enter from DOS by placing the PrintGraph disk in drive A and typing **pgraph.** Or if your screen shows the Lotus Access Menu, you can select the PrintGraph option from the menu.

2. Next, Lotus will instruct you to insert your PrintGraph disk in drive A. Place the disk in drive A and close the door.

3. Next press ← to tell Lotus your disk is in place. Then wait a few seconds for the PrintGraph menu to appear (Figure 6.12).

You are now ready to tell PrintGraph which type of printer or plotter you will use. The next section explains this step.

FIRST STEPS

1. If you are using the program for the first time, check to make sure the printer type displayed is the same as your printer or

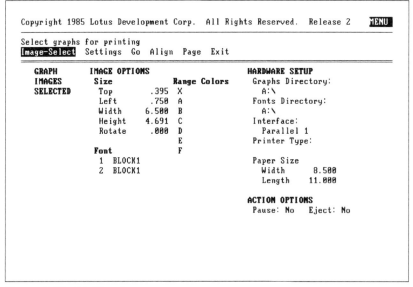

Figure 6.12: PrintGraph menu

plotter model. To select your printer/plotter model for the first time, enter

S H P

Move the cursor to the name of your printer with ↑ or ↓. Press the space bar until a # sign appears to the left of your printer's name. Then press ↵ to confirm the selection of the model.

2. To save this setting, enter

Q S Q

Note: If your printer is not listed, see Appendix A. You may also need to change the directory specifications for the PrintGraph program or your graph data files if you are using a hard disk system or a two-drive system. This is also discussed in Appendix A.

Now you have permanently set up the PrintGraph program to use the printer model specified. You need not repeat this step unless you change printer models.

PrintGraph is now ready to use. You can learn more about its features in the next section.

OPTIONS FOR PRINTING GRAPHS

Once you have created and saved a graph, there are still a few options you can add by using PrintGraph. The options available are:

- Colors: If you have a color printer or plotter, you can specify a color for each data range and the grid (if you have added a grid). If you are using a color plotter, Lotus will tell you on the screen when to switch color pens.
- Fonts: The style of the character used to print text.
- Size: The size of the printed graph.
- Density: The darkness of the type—how many times the printer will overprint the graph.
- Mode: You can tell Lotus to form-feed to the top of a new page after printing the graph.
- Directories: This option tells Lotus where to look for the PrintGraph program (Fonts) and the saved graphs (Pictures).

You can change any of these options by selecting the option from the options submenu. Don't forget that the F1 (Help) key still works with PrintGraph, and you can ask 1-2-3 for help at any time. Figure 6.13 shows the Help screen for Fonts.

Printing Graphs Darker or Using Density

Density refers to the darkness of the graph on paper. Lotus 1-2-3 will print in single density as a default—that is, there will be one pass of the printer for each part of the graph. To increase the quality of the printed graph, you can specify double, triple, or quad density. Bear in mind that generating these densities will take more time (quad will take about 10 minutes) and you should only use them when you are sure the final graph is correct.

Changing Fonts

The *font* is the type of characters used to print the titles and legends. Main titles are printed in large letters, and other titles and

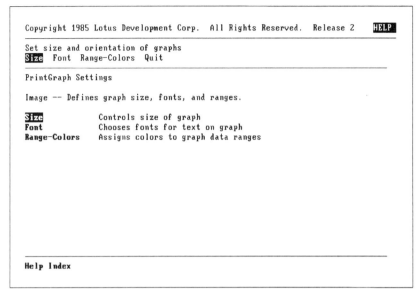

Figure 6.13: PrintGraph Help screen

legends are printed in smaller letters. Lotus defaults to BLOCK style font, which is the easiest to read. You can select ROMAN, ITALICS, or SCRIPT styles, which are illustrated in Figure 6.14.

To change a font from BLOCK, just select the Options Font sequence and specify the new font style. Note that SCRIPT is very difficult to read.

Changing the Graph's Size

Lotus 1-2-3 prints graphs on the top half of a 8½ × 11-inch page. Thus the default size is half, for half page. You can enlarge the graph to be printed full size, or use the entire page of paper. A half-size graph is printed top to bottom, and a full-size graph is printed right-side to left-side, or rotated.

You can also specify a different size—between full and half—by changing the width or height of the graph to the desired finished measurements of the graph. Note the maximum width is 6.8 inches and the maximum length is 9.4 inches. You can rotate the direction 1-2-3 will print the graph 90 degrees and change the left or top

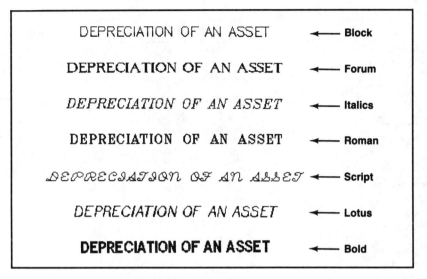

Figure 6.14: Examples of fonts

margins. Practice changing size settings to see which size your graphs look best in.

Hint: If you reduce the size of the graph, you can then use a word processor to print a text description on the same page or use 1-2-3 to print a spreadsheet on the same page. Just leave the same paper with the graph in the printer, making sure the paper is advanced to the end of the graph.

After you have specified a few options, try printing graphs using the Select command in the next section.

SELECTING GRAPHS FOR PRINTING

First, specify the name of the graph you want to print by selecting the Image Select option from the menu. A list of all graphs or the PICTURES directory will appear on the screen. A typical list of graph files is shown in Figure 6.15

The directions for selecting files are on the right side of the screen. To select a graph to print, press ↓ to highlight the name of the graph and then press the space bar to mark it. You may mark

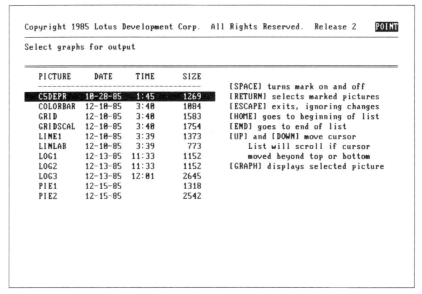

Figure 6.15: Graph listing

several graphs, and 1-2-3 will print them one after another. If you do this, you may want to select the Page-Eject option from the menu, so that each graph will appear on a new page.

Printing a graph can be a slow process, depending on your printer model. Be prepared to wait a few minutes with most printers. Letter-quality printers cannot print graphs. See Appendix A for a list of printers you may use to print graphs.

After printing a graph, you can exit PrintGraph and return to 1-2-3.

EXITING THE PRINTGRAPH PROGRAM

To exit the PrintGraph program, just select Exit from the menu. You won't be able to exit until your graph has finished printing. Your options are saved if you have chosen the Save option to write them permanently onto your disk.

In this section, you have learned to:

- Set up PrintGraph for the first time

- Change the font, density, or size of a graph
- Select graphs for printing
- Load and exit the PrintGraph program

Summary

In this chapter you have explored 1-2-3's graphing features. As you have seen, transforming rows and columns of relatively meaningless numbers into immediately intelligible displays is a matter of a few keystrokes. The graphs are easy to do, elegant to view, and a most effective means of presenting information.

The next chapter covers some important 1-2-3 housekeeping utilities: formatting options, cell and password protection, file handling (including transferring of files back and forth to other software packages), and managing disk space. The chapter also presents print procedures, options, and commands.

Chapter 7

Formatting, Printing, and File Handling

In this chapter, you will learn to:

- Use formats to improve appearance
- Take security measures with spreadsheet files
- Use print options
- Customize printed reports
- Print a spreadsheet to a word processing file
- Store, retrieve, list, and erase 1-2-3 files
- Combine 1-2-3 files
- Consolidate duplicate files
- Measure worksheet memory
- Translate files using the Lotus Access Translate utility

Usually the only person who sees your spreadsheet on the screen is you. What everyone else sees are the printouts you produce. In fact, there are ways to protect your spreadsheet, to make sure you control who sees it and who doesn't, by adding passwords to the file. You can allow someone else to see the spreadsheet but protect its contents against accidental change or erasure.

Your printouts can appear in different formats from your spreadsheets. You can exclude sensitive and confidential information from printouts by hiding it. You can change type styles, page lengths, and add headers and footers in 1-2-3. You can even move 1-2-3 files to other programs such as WordStar and MultiMate and add textual notes. You can combine different spreadsheets in one report; for example, you can combine monthly budgets into quarterly and yearly budgets. You can transfer data between 1-2-3, Symphony, dBaseII and III, VisiCalc, and Jazz.

These printing, spreadsheet protection, and file handling options available in 1-2-3 are discussed in the sections that follow, starting with the format options used to prepare a spreadsheet for printing.

Using Formats to Improve Spreadsheet Appearance

The way a spreadsheet looks is almost as important as the information it contains. If the layout is unclear or confusing, the important results of the spreadsheet might be overlooked or ignored. For example, $120,000 is much clearer than 120000. Dollar signs in front of values and fixing values displayed to the right of decimals help make the spreadsheet legible.

Changing the presentation of data so that it is easier to read is called *formatting* in 1-2-3. Table 7.1 lists the format options available.

Menu Item	Description	Example
Fixed	Number of decimals	**1024.50** (Fixed 2)
Scientific	Scientific notation	**102.45E +01**
Currency	$ sign before entry	**$1,024.50** (Currency 2)
, (comma)	Separating commas between thousands	**1,024.50** (,2)
General	Zeros right of decimal not shown; displays as entered.	**1024.5**
+/-	Horizontal bar graph + = 1, − = −1. Fills cell with symbol.	**+ + + +** (Represents 4)
Percent	Trailing % with decimals	**12.4%** (Percent 1)
Date	1 DD-MMM-YY	**01-Oct-86**
	2 DD-MMM	**01-Oct**
	3 MMM-YY	**Oct-86**
	4 MM/DD/YY	**10/1/86**
	5 MM/DD	**10/01**
Time	1 HH:MM:SS AM/PM	**02:30:14 PM**
	2 HH:MM AM/PM	**02:30 PM**
	3 HH:MM:SS 24 Hr Long Intl	**14:30:14**
	4 HH:MM 24 Hr Short Intl	**14:30**
Text	Formulas instead of values appear as entered; any other entries such as labels or numbers appear as entered.	**+b15/2** **1024.5**

Table 7.1: 1-2-3 Format Options

Menu Item	Description	Example
Hidden	The cell's contents temporarily do not appear on the screen but are still stored in the cell.	
Reset	Resets the default numeric format for the cell.	

Table 7.1: 1-2-3 Format Options (continued)

A word of caution about using fixed decimal places for Fixed, Currency, or Comma formats. Suppose the value in a cell is:

Value Displayed Before Format	*Value Stored*
123.467	123.467

When a fixed format using two decimal places is selected, the value displayed is:

Value Displayed After Format	*Value Stored*
123.47	123.467

Note that when you format a number, the value displayed on the screen is no longer the same as the value stored. If you use the cell in a formula or function, it is the value stored—123.467—that is used, not the value as the format displays it—123.47. In a printout of the spreadsheet, the totals will not appear to equal the sum of the numbers displayed.

To have the value displayed be used in a formula or function, the value stored must be changed to match. In this case, the value 123.467 can be changed to 123.47 with the @ROUND function, permanently rounding off the stored value to equal the formatted value. @ROUND is discussed further in Chapter 4.

Also note that the date and time formats can only be applied to dates and times entered as functions, not on textual dates. To format textual dates, you must convert them to functions using @DATEVALUE and @TIMEVALUE. For more details on date functions, see Chapter 4.

You can format an entire spreadsheet at once by using the Worksheet Global Format command, or format it range by range by using the Range Format command. The two methods are discussed in the following sections.

USING GLOBAL FORMATS

Use the Worksheet Global Format command to set a format option for the entire spreadsheet when most of the spreadsheet will use that format. (You can go back later and change the format of specific columns with the Range Format command discussed in the next section.)

Lotus 1-2-3 automatically displays numbers without punctuation and without decimal places. Usually you will want some punctuation, and often you will want decimal places to display. When you use the Global Format command, all new numbers entered into a spreadsheet will automatically be formatted with the new format that you specify.

Some of the Global Format options are more commonly used than others; their usefulness varies according to their application. A financial analyst, for example, will probably never format an entire spreadsheet in scientific notation, but an engineer will do so often.

If most of your values are financial and greater than 1000, you will probably want to select either the Comma option, which inserts commas in all numeric values greater than 999, or the Currency option, which displays dollar signs ($) in front of values in addition to adding a comma in the thousands place.

FORMATTING A RANGE

You often need to specify a different format for a particular cell or for a group of cells. A *range format* specifies a small area within the spreadsheet that will display a particular format. You can use the Range Format command sequence and select any of the format types, but the most common uses for range formats is to display percents in particular columns.

You can format a range of cells before you enter any values in it. Once a cell format has been specified, the format becomes an attribute of the cell. When the cell is copied, the format is also copied.

A COMMON FORMAT ERROR

A common error that comes up in spreadsheets is that the format selected generates larger numbers than the width of the column can allow. When the number becomes larger than can be displayed in the selected format, 1-2-3 fills the cell(s) with asterisks. These asterisks are a warning that the format display selected is longer than the width of the column. To solve the problem, increase the column width by using the Worksheet Column Set command.

COPYING FORMATS

When you copy a cell with an assigned format type to another cell or cells, the new cells take on the same format as the original cell. There doesn't have to be a value in a cell to copy the format to another cell, so numbers generated later can unexpectedly take on inappropriate formats.

You may often find yourself copying cells and then forgetting the new cell format. When you enter a new value in the new cell, it displays the value using the previously copied format. Simply reformat the cell using the Range Format command when this happens.

Sometimes you may want to prevent the appearance of parts of the spreadsheet altogether, for security reasons. You can accomplish this with the Hidden option, which is discussed in the next section.

In this section you have learned to:

- Improve spreadsheet appearance by formatting cells
- Copy cell formats

Using Special Formats for Worksheet Security

In the world of financial reporting, there is often data that should only be available to top management or other selected personnel. A few new security measures are now available in 1-2-3 to prevent unauthorized access to spreadsheet information. Internal measures hide selected data on the screen and printed reports, and external measures prevent access to the entire spreadsheet.

The MTCT budget built in Chapter 3 is used in this section to illustrate the internal measures available. If you didn't create that spreadsheet, don't bother for this example; just follow along as if you had.

INTERNAL SECURITY MEASURES

Lotus has added to the internal measures available in Release 1A (protecting cells) new features that allow hiding columns and cells. The measures are referred to as *internal* because you apply them once you are already in the spreadsheet. Hiding data is used chiefly to prevent sensitive or unnecessary data from being displayed in printed reports. Protecting cells is used primarily to keep unsophisticated users from accidentally overwriting or erasing important data.

HIDING CELLS

You will often want to produce printouts in which some confidential data is not displayed. Another occasion for hiding cells is when they contain intermediate formulas or macros that, while necessary to the spreadsheet's computation, are completely unrelated to the data being analyzed or the results produced.

Hint: Once these kinds of cells are hidden, you might forget where you put them in the spreadsheet, or that they exist at all. Make a note of where these hidden ranges are by giving them names made up of the locations of the cells and the purpose of the range, such as A1MACRO-ENTER.

The easiest way to avoid printing a range, of course, is to select only the ranges of data you want to print. In a budget, for example, confidential information such as income, bonuses, and certain expenses may be located only in certain columns, which you can exclude from printing when you specify the range. When the sensitive information is arranged by rows, however, not by columns, or when only certain cells should be excluded in an otherwise necessary column, then some means of hiding those cells becomes necessary. You can hide this information temporarily for printing using the Range Format Hidden command. Once you have hidden a cell, you can still get a look at it by placing the cursor in that cell. There is no way to hide a cell so that it cannot be "unhidden" by someone else, short of erasing it entirely.

Problem: Hide the MTCT salaries for partners, associates, and other personnel.

Solution: Use the Range Format Hidden command to hide cells B15 through G19. The MTCT spreadsheet should look like Figure 7.1, with the cells concerning the breakdowns in salaries hidden.

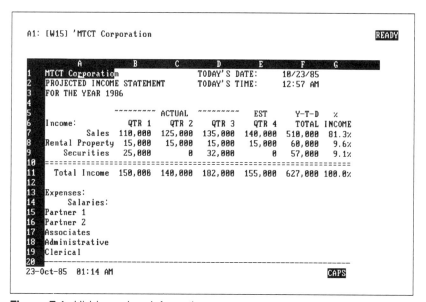

Figure 7.1: Hidden salary information

Total Salaries still computes in row 21, while the individual salaries by partner, associate, and other personnel are gone. You could now print a report that excludes salary information and then unhide (display) the hidden cells for your own use.

Unhiding Hidden Cells

To unhide hidden cells, simply reformat the hidden cells using the Range Format command and the original type of format specified. You can most quickly reset the cell to the global default by choosing the Reset option.

Hiding Columns

Being able to hide columns is particularly useful when you print reports that contain intermediate formulas or confidential information in a column. The Worksheet Column Hide command removes the column quickly from the screen, while the columns that still display retain their proper column number. That is, if you hide column A, the first column in the spreadsheet will be labeled B and will contain column B's information.

To hide columns, place the cursor in the first column to be hidden. Then use the Worksheet Column Hide command and move the cursor with ← or →, highlighting any additional columns you want hidden. Press ↵ when all the columns to be hidden have been selected.

Problem: In the MCTC spreadsheet, hide the estimate for the fourth quarter, the Y-T-D totals, and % Income columns, E, F, and G, respectively.

Solution: Move your cursor to column E, the first column to hide. Enter

   / W C H . → → →

Your budget spreadsheet should now look like Figure 7.2.

Unhiding Hidden Columns

Columns currently hidden, but displayed with the Worksheet Column Display command, are indicated by asterisks * in the column title border at the top of the screen, as in Figure 7.3.

You can unhide columns by using the Worksheet Column Display command and pointing the cursor to the columns you want displayed. To select more than one column, point to the first, type a period, move the cursor to the last column to be displayed, and press ↵.

You may want to save both versions of a spreadsheet, one with and one without hidden columns, by giving one version a different file name. Again, it is unfortunate that anyone with access to the spreadsheet can "unhide" a column, but at least you can prevent accidental damage by using the Protect command discussed in the next section.

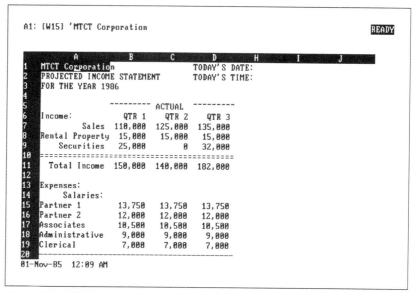

Figure 7.2: Hidden columns E through G

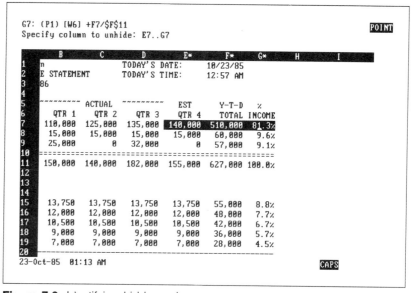

Figure 7.3: Identifying hidden columns

Protecting Cells

When inexperienced users have access to your spreadsheets, you can protect cells, especially those that contain complex formulas, against accidental overwriting.

As a simple precaution, you should protect all formulas, labels, and other values that are not likely to change once the spreadsheet setup has been completed. Cells that are unprotected appear on the screen in a brighter intensity for easy identification.

It is easier to protect the entire spreadsheet and then go back and unprotect the cells that are likely to change. Use the Range Protect command, which is similar to the Range Format command except that you specify a range to protect rather than to format. The protection does not go into effect until you also turn on global protection, described after the next procedure, for unprotecting cells.

Unprotecting Cells

To unprotect a range of cells that have data values so that you can enter new values while protection is turned on, use the Range Unprotect command and specify the range to be unprotected. Leave formulas, labels, and functions protected most of the time. If you later find that one of these needs to be changed, go back and unprotect it then.

When the income, salary, and expense data have been unprotected, the MTCT spreadsheet looks like Figure 7.4.

Turning on Global Protection

Lotus 1-2-3 requires that you enable protection (that is, turn it on) by using the command Worksheet Global Protection Enable, which locks your spreadsheet against accidental data entry errors.

Once protection has been turned on, you will not be able to enter into or erase any protected cell. The program will beep and display the status ERROR in the upper-right corner.

To make changes to protected cells, either use the Worksheet Global Protection Disable command or unprotect the cell. The Disable procedure is the same as the Enable procedure, except it turns off protection.

A more stringent security measure, password protection, is described in the next section.

```
A1: [W15] 'MTCT Corporation                                    READY

        A           B        C        D        E        F        G
1  MTCT Corporation                    TODAY'S DATE:    18/23/85
2  PROJECTED INCOME STATEMENT           TODAY'S TIME:    12:57 AM
3  FOR THE YEAR 1986
4
5                     ~~~~~~~~ ACTUAL ~~~~~~~~  EST     Y-T-D   %
6  Income:            QTR 1    QTR 2    QTR 3   QTR 4   TOTAL  INCOME
7          Sales     118,888  125,888  135,888 148,888 518,888 81.3%
8  Rental Property   15,888   15,888   15,888  15,888  68,888   9.6%
9       Securities   25,888        8   32,888       8  57,888   9.1%
10 ========================================================================
11    Total Income  150,888  148,888  182,888 155,888 627,888 188.8%
12
13 Expenses:
14     Salaries:
15 Partner 1         13,758   13,758   13,758  13,758  55,888   8.8%
16 Partner 2         12,888   12,888   12,888  12,888  48,888   7.7%
17 Associates        18,588   18,588   18,588  18,588  42,888   6.7%
18 Administrative     9,888    9,888    9,888   9,888  36,888   5.7%
19 Clerical           7,888    7,888    7,888   7,888  28,888   4.5%
20 ------------------------------------------------------------------------
   23-Oct-85  81:28 AM                                          CAPS
```

Figure 7.4: Unprotected cells with protected cells

EXTERNAL SECURITY MEASURES

You can externally protect a file, keeping out all unathorized users, by assigning a password as described in this section. The password cannot be removed except by someone who already has the password.

Additional security measures include locking your floppy disks in a container or cabinet, locking your hard disk with a key on the power switch, and clearing the screen by using the Worksheet Erase Yes command whenever you leave your desk for more than a few moments. This next section will show you how to password-protect files.

Password-Protecting Files

You can assign a password only to an entire spreadsheet file. A password is a code word you must type in when you want to use a file. Once assigned, you can't retrieve the file without typing the password. Lotus 1-2-3 is case sensitive about passwords: it distinguishes etween upper- and lowercase letters. If the password is PANDORA, 1-2-3 will not accept the password pandora.

To assign a password to an existing file, first cancel the original file name by pressing the Escape key when the name appears. Then reenter the name, followed by a space and the letter P. If the file name is INCOME, for example, cancel it and reenter INCOME P.

To assign the password KEY to an existing file INCOME, use the File Save command with the P option. Enter

/ F S

and press Esc to cancel the file name. Then enter

INCOME P

to select INCOME as the name of the file with a password. Press ◄┘ to complete the command. Enter

KEY

and press ◄┘ to assign the password KEY. Then retype

KEY

and press ◄┘ to verify the password KEY. Pressing

R

replaces the file with the new password. You can see the password prompt in Figure 7.5.

Retrieving Password-Protected Files

To retrieve a password-protected file, use the File Retrieve command. When you select the name of the password-protected file, 1-2-3 will prompt you to type in the password you gave the file. Make sure you type the password in exactly as it was first entered, using the same upper- or lowercase combinations. Your screen will look like Figure 7.6, displaying the password retrieval prompt.

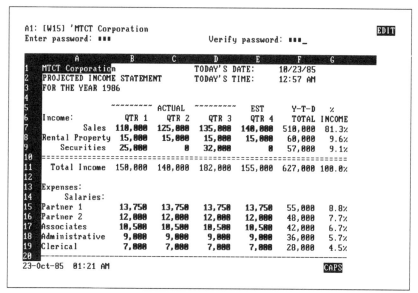

```
A1: [W15] 'MTCT Corporation                                          EDIT
Enter password: ■■■          Verify password: ■■■_

          A         B         C         D         E         F       G
1  MTCT Corporation                TODAY'S DATE:        10/23/85
2  PROJECTED INCOME STATEMENT      TODAY'S TIME:        12:57 AM
3  FOR THE YEAR 1986
4
5                  ~~~~~~~~~ ACTUAL ~~~~~~~~~    EST     Y-T-D    %
6  Income:          QTR 1     QTR 2    QTR 3    QTR 4    TOTAL  INCOME
7         Sales   110,000   125,000  135,000  140,000  510,000  81.3%
8  Rental Property  15,000    15,000   15,000   15,000   60,000   9.6%
9       Securities  25,000         0   32,000        0   57,000   9.1%
10 ================================================================
11   Total Income  150,000   140,000  182,000  155,000  627,000 100.0%
12
13 Expenses:
14      Salaries:
15 Partner 1         13,750    13,750   13,750   13,750   55,000   8.8%
16 Partner 2         12,000    12,000   12,000   12,000   48,000   7.7%
17 Associates        10,500    10,500   10,500   10,500   42,000   6.7%
18 Administrative     9,000     9,000    9,000    9,000   36,000   5.7%
19 Clerical           7,000     7,000    7,000    7,000   28,000   4.5%
20
23-Oct-85  01:21 AM                                              CAPS
```

Figure 7.5: Password prompt

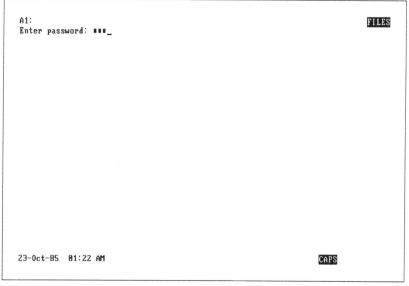

```
A1:                                                                FILES
Enter password: ■■■_










23-Oct-85  01:22 AM                                              CAPS
```

Figure 7.6: Password retrieval prompt

Removing a Password

To remove a password, save the file again with the File Save command. When the file name appears, press the Backspace key and type the file name, this time without the P: INCOME, not INCOME P.

To remove the password from the file INCOME, for example, enter

    / F S

Press the Backspace key to cancel the password option. Press ⏎ to select INCOME as the name of the file without a password. Pressing

    R

replaces the old version with the updated version of the file.

In this section, you have learned to:

- Hide columns
- Hide cells
- Protect your spreadsheet
- Enable protection
- Assign passwords
- Retrieve a password-protected spreadsheet
- Remove passwords

Customizing Printed Reports

Lotus 1-2-3's Print command allows you to print copies of your spreadsheet either to a *printer* or to a *file*. If you print to a file, you can use a word processor to edit and enhance a report further. We will look in more detail later in this chapter at the various things you can do by printing to a file.

This section discusses 1-2-3's print options,which you can use to adjust margins, insert headers and footers, change print type size, and display special formats. You can also enter special characters that control page breaks and character size.

The options available within 1-2-3 for printing are:

Range Line Page Options Clear Align Go Quit

- The Range option specifies which section of the spreadsheet to print.
- The Line option causes your printer to advance the page by one line.
- Page causes the printer to advance to the top of the next page.
- Clear sets all defaults to default settings.
- Align and Go are the final commands you use to print a report.

SETTING UP PRINT RANGES

The Print Printer Range and Print File Range options allow you to select the range to be printed, to a printer and to a file, respectively. In this section we will discuss printing with a printer; printing to a file is covered in the section "Printing to a File" later in this chapter.

To print to a printer, first highlight the range to print. Move the cursor to the first cell, type a period to anchor the range, and then either move the cursor to the last cell to be printed or type in the first and last range cell locations, separated by a period (for example, A1.H28). To print the entire spreadsheet, press the Home key, type a period to anchor, then press the End key and the Home key again.

SENDING A REPORT TO A PRINTER

To tell 1-2-3 to begin printing, first make sure your printer in turned on and is on-line. Then select Align, which sets the number of lines printed to 0, and Go, which actually prints the range. If you don't select Align first, 1-2-3 starts counting the number of lines from the last spreadsheet you printed. If you print a 30-line report, the line count will then be 31. If you then print a second report of 50 lines without first selecting Align, the printer will print the first 30 lines (which equals the number of lines 1-2-3 thinks are on one page). The printer then advances to another page to print the remaining 20 lines. Selecting Align in between each printout would prevent this by returning the line count to 0.

Hint: If you want the printout to have a page number other than 1, you can use this feature: first choose Align, which sets the page count to 0; then press the Page option the number of times less one that equals the page number you want the printout to have. Do not select Align again; select Go, and the printout will print with the page number you want.

USING PRINT OPTIONS

There are several options in 1-2-3 available for adjusting margins, headers, and footers. The menu options available are:

Header Footer Margins Borders Setup Pg-Length Other Quit

The sections that follow will describe each option in detail.

Adding Headers and Footers

A *header* is a line that appears at the top of each page of a printed spreadsheet. A *footer* is a line that appears at the bottom of each page of a printed spreadsheet.

You could insert a header in the printout that displays, for example, the current date on the right side of the top line and a footer that prints the name of the file and the author. The command to select a header (or footer) is Print Printer Options Header (or Footer).

Once you have selected Header or Footer, there are special characters you can use to align the text. To center the text of a header or footer, enter the special character ǀ before the text. To right justify the text of a header or footer, precede the text by ǁ. If you do not precede the text by either ǀ or ǁ, the text will be left justified.

The special symbol @ in a header or footer will be replaced by the current date when the file is printed, and the symbol # numbers pages automatically.

Code	*Result*
¦@	Centered date
¦¦@	Right-justified date
¦#	Centered page number
¦¦#	Right-justified page number

To specify a right-justified date heading in a spreadsheet print-out, enter

/ P P O H

Then type

¦¦@

to specify a right-justified date code; press ⟵. Enter

Q

to quit the Options menu.

A printed report with a date heading looks like the report in Figure 7.7.

You can use the Option Footer command to create a centered footer with a page number. In the example above, substitute F (Footer) for H (Header) and ¦Page for ¦¦@.

Adjusting Margins

You can use the Print Printer Options Margin command to change the left, right, top, and bottom page margin specifications. The program automatically sets the left margin to 4 and the right margin to 76. If your printer can print more than 80 characters of text, you can set the right margin to a maximum of 240 characters. To alter a right margin to its maximum, enter

/ P P O M

```
                                                    14-Feb-86

MTCT Corporation                  TODAY'S DATE:    10/23/86
PROJECTED INCOME STATEMENT        TODAY'S TIME:    06:17 PM
FOR THE YEAR 1986

                  ~~~~~~~~ ACTUAL  ~~~~~~~~   EST    Y-T-D    %
Income:           QTR 1    QTR 2    QTR 3   QTR 4   TOTAL INCOME
        Sales    110,000  125,000  135,000 140,000 510,000  81.3%
Rental Property   15,000   15,000   15,000  15,000  60,000   9.6%
     Securities   25,000        0   32,000       0  57,000   9.1%
                ========================================================
   Total Income  150,000  140,000  182,000 155,000 627,000 100.0%

Expenses:
   Salaries:
Partner 1         13,750   13,750   13,750  13,750  55,000   8.8%
Partner 2         12,000   12,000   12,000  12,000  48,000   7.7%
Associates        10,500   10,500   10,500  10,500  42,000   6.7%
Administrative     9,000    9,000    9,000   9,000  36,000   5.7%
Clerical           7,000    7,000    7,000   7,000  28,000   4.5%
                ------------------------------------------------------
Total Salaries    52,250   52,250   52,250  52,250 209,000  33.3%
Mngmt Expenses     4,000    5,000    4,500   4,800  18,300   2.9%
         Rent      2,000    2,000    2,000   2,000   8,000   1.3%
     Supplies      2,000    1,800    1,900   2,100   7,800   1.2%
    Telephone      1,800    1,900    2,100   2,300   8,100   1.3%
                ------------------------------------------------------
Total Expenses    62,050   62,950   62,750  63,450 251,200  40.1%
                ------------------------------------------------------
Net Income        87,950   77,050  119,250  91,550 375,800  59.9%
                ========================================================
```

Figure 7.7: Printed report with date heading

Press

> **R**

to select **Right** and enter

> **240**

to set the right margin to 240 characters. Then press ◄─┘ and enter

> **Q**

to quit the Options menu.

To print the full 240 characters of a large spreadsheet, you will also need to condense the type size of the printed characters from the default type size of 10 pitch to 12 pitch. (*Pitch* refers to the number of characters per inch). You will learn how to change type size later in this chapter.

Printing Long and Wide Reports with Borders

The Print Printer Options Borders command allows you to print column labels, row labels, or both on a multipage report, such as a 12-month budget. If you use a column of 9 characters for each month, you can't print 9 × 12 characters on one page (80 characters is the limit). The program will print the first 80 characters, skip to a new page, and then print the remaining characters. Normally, the second page would not contain the first column and row labels that describe sales, costs, expenses, or profit.

The Borders Columns option causes the row labels to be copied to each successive page that is still printing a portion of the first page of the wide spreadsheet. You specify the range to be copied as the column that contains the row labels, which is usually column A.

To print an extra-long spreadsheet so that the row of field labels prints at the top of each page, use the Print Printer Options Borders Row command. Again, specify the range, this time using row instead of column labels, such as A1.K1 for column labels that begin in column A of row 1.

Watch for duplication of borders when you use either Borders option. Double-check the print range specified in the Range option to make sure it does not include the Border range as well. Otherwise, you will print double borders on the first page.

To cancel the Borders option, use the Print Printer Clear Borders command.

Condensing Type—Using Setup Strings

Setup strings are codes used to print characters in a different style, size, or density. These codes are mainly used to print extra-wide spreadsheets that normally would take several pages with a printer that prints a maximum 80-character line. You can increase the number of characters printed per line by condensing the type size. You specify this as a *setup string* under Options in the Print menu.

Setup strings are the control codes your printer expects to receive for changes in default settings. Your printer reference manual has a chart of the codes that represent various settings. Look for the codes necessary to produce condensed (15 characters per inch) or elite (12 characters per inch) type.

Depending on which printer you have, you can choose other styles such as italics, roman, or script. Once you enter the codes, 1-2-3 translates them into setup strings. (For a chart of the translation 1-2-3 performs, see pages 306–7 of the 1-2-3 *Reference Manual*).

For condensed type, an Epson printer expects the sequence control-O. Looking at the chart on page 306, you find that the LICS code (Lotus code) for control-O is 15. The setup string must begin with a \0, so the complete control sequence you enter is \015 to specify condensed type for a spreadsheet using an Epson printer.

A printed condensed type size report looks like Figure 7.8. You can now also vary the type size within a page, using 1-2-3's new embedded codes, explained later in this chapter.

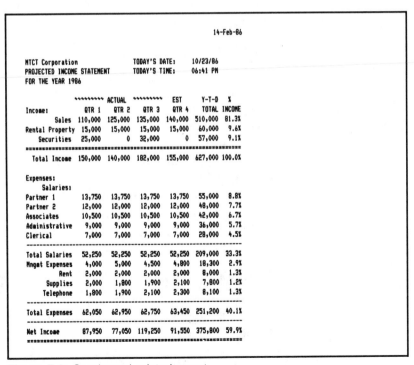

Figure 7.8: Condensed printed report

Beware: Save your file before you select the setup string option. If your printer requires a series of default setup strings, they will be listed when you select the setup string option. (1-2-3 inserted the codes for the printer when you selected it during the Install procedure.) If your printer was not on the list of printers and was custom installed, be careful not to risk losing the setup string sequence. Make sure it's written down somewhere—in the front of your printer manual, for example.

The setup string for condensed type should be added to the end of whatever strings were already there. If you inadvertently erase some of these codes, the printer won't work until you exit 1-2-3 and reenter them. (You may also need to turn your printer off and on to reset it.)

Setup strings entered from the Print menu will only be in effect for the current spreadsheet. To permanently select a different default setup string (such as condensed type), use the Worksheet Global Default Printer command, discussed later in this chapter in the section "Using Global Printer Settings."

Changing Page Length

The default for page length is 66 lines per page. You can change it to a number between 20 and 100 with the Print Printer Options Page-Length command. This is useful when you use longer paper such as legal-size paper or $8^1/_2$ × 13-inch paper, which contains 88 lines.

You also can use setup strings to change the page length for a spreadsheet permanently, as we will discuss in the section "Using Global Printer Settings."

For more complicated page handling, you may want to purchase the new Report Writer package, discussed in Appendix B, especially for printing special forms such as checks, invoices, or time cards from database records.

Printing Cell Formulas: The "Other" Option

You can check your spreadsheet formulas by causing the formulas themselves to print (rather than the usual result of the formula) using the Print Printer Options Other Cell-Formulas command. The formulas, values, and labels are printed in the same order as they appear on the screen. For example, the formula

+4 +5 +6 will normally appear on the screen and on printouts as 15, the result of the calculation. When you select the Other option, +4 +5 +6 prints instead of 15. It's a good idea to use this option to print out your spreadsheets as backup documentation of formulas, which could prove invaluable should you lose the file and have to reenter it from scratch. A printout of cell formulas for the MTCT budget appears in Figure 7.9.

```
                              14-Feb-86


A1: [W15] 'MTCT Corporation
D1: 'TODAY'S DATE:
F1: (D4) @DATE(86,10,23)
A2: [W15] 'PROJECTED INCOME STATEMENT
D2: 'TODAY'S TIME:
F2: (D7) @NOW
A3: [W15] 'FOR THE YEAR 1986
B5: (G) \~
C5: ^ACTUAL
D5: (G) \~
E5: [W9] ^EST
F5: "Y-T-D
G5: [W6] ^%
A6: [W15] 'Income:
B6: (G) "QTR 1
C6: "QTR 2
D6: "QTR 3
E6: [W9] "QTR 4
F6: "TOTAL
G6: [W6] 'INCOME
A7: [W15] "Sales
B7: (,0) U 110000
C7: (,0) U 125000
D7: (,0) U 135000
E7: (,0) U [W9] 140000
F7: (,0) @SUM(B7..E7)
G7: (P1) [W6] +F7/$F$11
A8: [W15] "Rental Property
B8: (,0) U 15000
C8: (,0) U 15000
D8: (,0) U 15000
E8: (,0) U [W9] 15000
F8: (,0) @SUM(B8..E8)
G8: (P1) [W6] +F8/$F$11
A9: [W15] "Securities
B9: (,0) U 25000
C9: (,0) U 0
```

Figure 7.9: Cell formula listing

When you have printed the formulas, remember to cancel the command with the Print Printer Options Other As-Displayed command.

SAVING PRINT SETTINGS

When you save your file after specifying headers, footers, margins, and setup strings, these settings are saved also and will automatically be included whenever you print your spreadsheet again. You can specify different ranges to print sections of a spreadsheet and keep the file saved with a specific section to be printed as the default.

USING PAGE BREAK CODES

Many spreadsheets you print will take up more than one page. You can force page breaks in particular places on the spreadsheet by using a page break code. Simply move your cursor to the cell that you want to be the first line of the new page. Use the Worksheet Page command to mark this as the new page. You can insert page breaks anywhere in your spreadsheet.

The MTCT spreadsheet created in Chapter 3 originally had the budget and memo on the same page. After inserting a page break before the memo, two colons appear in the cell, representing the page break, as shown in Figure 7.10. Note that 1-2-3 has also inserted a row in the spreadsheet for the page break line.

HIDING ZEROS

In many formal reports the value zero is not displayed. Lotus 1-2-3 calls this *zero suppression*. You can hide these zeros by using the Worksheet Global Zero option. You need not specify a range; 1-2-3 suppresses all zero values with this command. Should any zero value subsequently change to a nonzero value, 1-2-3 will display the new value.

A spreadsheet with hidden zeroes looks like Figure 7.11, with the zeros appearing blank in cells C9 and E9.

CHANGING TYPE SYZE WITHIN A REPORT— USING EMBEDDED CODES

You may often want to enlarge or vary the type style of titles, subtitles, and other special parts of reports for emphasis and easier

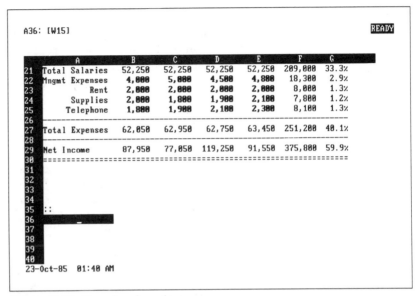

Figure 7.10: Page break code

A1: [W15] 'MTCT Corporation   READY

	A	B	C	D	E	F	G
1	MTCT Corporation			TODAY'S DATE:		10/23/85	
2	PROJECTED INCOME STATEMENT			TODAY'S TIME:		01:40 AM	
3	FOR THE YEAR 1986						
4							
5		~~~~~~~~	ACTUAL	~~~~~~~~	EST	Y-T-D	%
6	Income:	QTR 1	QTR 2	QTR 3	QTR 4	TOTAL	INCOME
7	Sales	110,000	125,000	135,000	140,000	510,000	81.3%
8	Rental Property	15,000	15,000	15,000	15,000	60,000	9.6%
9	Securities	25,000		32,000		57,000	9.1%
10	===						
11	Total Income	150,000	140,000	182,000	155,000	627,000	100.0%
12							
13	Expenses:						
14	Salaries:						
15	Partner 1	13,750	13,750	13,750	13,750	55,000	8.8%
16	Partner 2	12,000	12,000	12,000	12,000	48,000	7.7%
17	Associates	10,500	10,500	10,500	10,500	42,000	6.7%
18	Administrative	9,000	9,000	9,000	9,000	36,000	5.7%
19	Clerical	7,000	7,000	7,000	7,000	28,000	4.5%
20							

23-Oct-85 01:41 AM

Figure 7.11: Suppressed zeros

reading. Double-wide characters, italics, boldface type, and other print enhancements are available on most dot-matrix printers through the use of control codes. In Figure 7.12, notice that the MTCT memo was printed with TO and FROM in double-wide characters, and the rest of the report was printed with regular type.

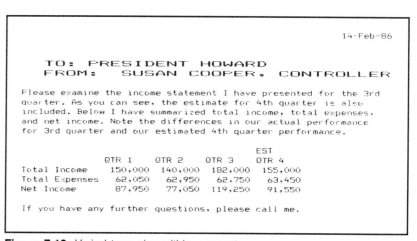

Figure 7.12: Varied type size within a report

To print the entire spreadsheet in a special font or type style, enter the control code as a setup string, which we described earlier.

To change only a portion of the spreadsheet, you can embed the control codes directly into the spreadsheet. First, look up the control code for the font or type style you want in your printer manual. Look for the codes necessary to print double-wide or expanded type, for example:

Printer	*Control Code*	*Function*
Gemini	ESC W 1	Double-wide pitch
Epson FX	ESC W 1	Double-wide pitch
Okidata 82	ESC W 1	Double-wide pitch
Gemini	ESC W 0	Cancels double-wide pitch
Epson FX	ESC W 0	Cancels double-wide pitch
Okidata 82	ESC W 0	Cancels double-wide pitch

To translate these codes to 1-2-3, use the chart on pages 306 through 307 of the 1-2-3 *Reference Manual*. Match each control code character the printer expects to the LICS (the code you will type into 1-2-3 that represents the printer code). The Star Gemini sequence is:

Control Code	*LICS code*
ESC	27
W	87
1	01
0	00

A \0 precedes each code. To input the entire code in the spreadsheet, move your cursor to the line above the text you want printed double wide. (You may also want to prevent the control codes themselves from appearing on the printout by preceding them with the characters ǁ.)

To enter a code to start double-wide printing, type

ǁ\027\087\001

in a blank cell on a blank row. (You may need to insert a row if one is not available.) This will start double-wide printing. To cancel the double-wide printing, enter

ǁ\027\087\000

in a blank cell in a blank row below the text. The MTCT spreadsheet with embedded codes looks like Figure 7.13.

USING GLOBAL PRINTER SETTINGS

As mentioned previously with regard to setup strings, you can specify any print option either locally (for the current spreadsheet only) by using the Print Printer command or globally for all the work you do with 1-2-3 by using the Worksheet Global Default Printer command. The options that can be set are shown in the status display in Figure 7.14.

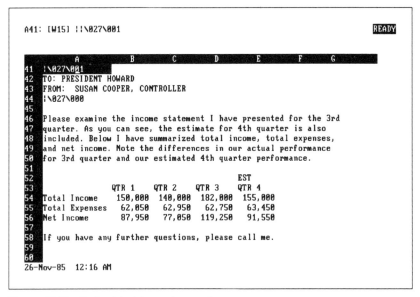

Figure 7.13: Embedded type size codes

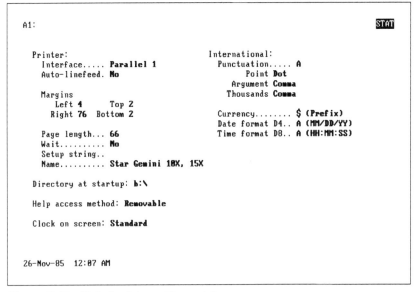

Figure 7.14: Global printer settings status

To permanently change worksheet settings such as margins, setup string, or page length, simply select the menu option and change the default settings to the new settings you want. To permanently install the new settings on the 1-2-3 disk, first remove the write-protect tab from the disk and choose Update from the Default menu. All printing options for any spreadsheet created will reflect these new settings.

Other status settings can also be changed here, such as startup directory, Help access method, clock display, and nationality of currency and date formats.

SELECTING AN ALTERNATE TEXT PRINTER

You may have more than one text printer available to you. Once you have installed the printers (see Appendix A), you can select the printer you want to use with the Worksheet Global Default Printer Name command.

After you select Name, 1-2-3 displays a menu of options beginning with 1 and ending with N, where N is the number of printers you selected for text printing in the install option. You simply select the printer you use most frequently from the menu and then quit the Printer menu. This selects a particular printer model only for the spreadsheet you are currently working in. When you save the file, the printer default you selected is also saved.

You can install one text printer model as the default for all spreadsheets on the 1-2-3 disk. First, remove the write-protect tab from the disk and then choose Update from the Default menu. Your 1-2-3 disk will now automatically look for that printer type when you print spreadsheets, unless you specifically choose a different printer for a particular spreadsheet with the Worksheet Global Default Printer Name command.

Printing to a File

You can print either directly to your printer, by using the Print Printer option, or you can print to a special .PRN file on your disk by using the Print File option. Unlike your original spreadsheet files, .PRN files can be viewed, edited, and otherwise manipulated by most word processing and communications programs.

CREATING A FILE TO STORE A REPORT

To create a .PRN file, use the Print File command. The program will ask you to specify a file name. The file name must be 8 characters or fewer and may not begin with a number. Do not enter the .PRN extension; 1-2-3 assigns it automatically.

After you name the file, specify the range to print by using the Range option in the Print menu. When you print a range to a file (usually for further editing with a word processing program), 1-2-3 will list the files you have already created with this command and ask you to name a file into which the range should be printed. You can either move the cursor to one of the files offered or type in a new file name. If you choose a file that already exists, 1-2-3 will not add this printout to that file; it will instead erase the old file contents and replace them with the current printout. The program then asks you to select Cancel, which returns you to the Print menu, or Replace, which carries out the Print command. (To combine different printouts, print them in separate files and combine them with DOS or in the word processing program you will be using.)

USING PRINT OPTIONS WHEN PRINTING TO A FILE

Most of the time, you won't want 1-2-3 to add margins, because your word processor will automatically print the file using a page offset (a default fixed number of characters from the left side of the page). In fact, if you do specify a left margin, the document will appear in the word processing program with spaces in front of each line, which you will then have to remove. Top and bottom margins will add unnecessary blank lines to the document. If you have previously specified left, top, and bottom margins other than 0 for printing to a printer, respecify them with the Options Margins command as follows:

Left = 0   Right = 80   Top = 0   Bottom = 0

You will probably also want to suppress page breaks, headers, and footers by using the Options Other Unformatted command.

After you have suppressed the formatting options, select Quit from the Options menu.

After you complete printing the spreadsheet to a file, make sure you use the Options Other Formatted command to tell 1-2-3 to resume printing margins and page breaks.

THE FINAL STEP: PRINTING TO THE FILE

All that's left to do is to choose Align and Go from the Print Menu. After you select Go, make sure you leave the menu by selecting the Quit option rather than pressing the Esc key. Selecting the Quit option closes the .PRN file you have created.

TRANSLATING A 1-2-3 FILE
TO WORDSTAR AND MULTIMATE

To edit the new document using WordStar, type **D** at the WordStar opening menu. Then type the full name (including the .PRN extension). You can readily add any print enhancements or text to the spreadsheet.

To edit the document using MultiMate, you must first convert the file to the special MultiMate format using the utility program FILECONV. Select to convert the ASCII file you created to MultiMate. It is then ready to edit using MultiMate.

In this section, you have learned to:

- Print a spreadsheet with a printer
- Add useful headers and footers
- Adjust margins
- Print long and wide reports with borders
- Reduce type size for a report by using setup strings
- Change page length
- Print cell formulas
- Save print settings

- Use page break codes
- Hide unwanted zeros
- Change type size within a report
- Use global printer settings
- Select a different text printer
- Print to a file
- Edit 1-2-3 reports with word processing programs

File Handling

The 1-2-3 program has considerable resources for exchanging and combining data in separate spreadsheet files. This is useful for consolidating spreadsheets that are structured in a similar way, such as bringing together four quarterly balance sheet statements into a year-end summary. The commands for such file operations are accessed through the File menu.

The commands in the File menu are shown below. Those commands used for transferring information to and from existing spreadsheets are marked with an asterisk (*):

Command	*Purpose*
Retrieve	Load an existing spreadsheet file into memory.
Save	Save the current spreadsheet to a disk file.
Combine*	Incorporate information from another spreadsheet into the current spreadsheet.
Xtract*	Save a portion of the current spreadsheet to disk as a separate spreadsheet file.
Erase	Erase a spreadsheet file from the current disk directory.
List	Display a listing of spreadsheet files in the current directory.
Import*	Incorporate information from a file into the current spreadsheet.
Directory	Display and/or change the current directory.

SAVING AND RETRIEVING FILES

In 1-2-3, you can retrieve files in one of two ways, depending on whether the file is password protected. If the file is not password protected, simply select Retrieve, type in the file name, and press ◄┘. If the file is password protected, enter the file name plus the password and press ◄┘.

When you select Retrieve, a list of the first four spreadsheet files on your default drive is presented. You can use the arrow keys to move to one of these; then press ◄┘ to retrieve the highlighted file. If the file you want isn't among the first four, you can either use ↓ to view the next four or press the F3 key, which presents a list of all the files on the disk. Then use the Home, End and arrow keys to move around the list. Home moves the cursor to the first file, and End moves the cursor to the last file. Files are listed in alphabetical order.

To save a file, select Save and type the name of the file. You can save the current work you have done into a different file simply by saving it with a different name. Remember, to password-protect a file, name it FILENAME P and then enter the password.

LISITNG OR ERASING A FILE

The options List and Erase each present the same submenu:

Worksheet   Print   Graph   Other

When you select the kind of file you want, a list of all the files of that type is presented. To erase a file, move the cursor until the file is highlighted; then press ◄┘. You might use the F3 key with the Erase option to list all the files on the screen at the same time.

SPECIFYING THE CURRENT FILE DIRECTORY

To change the directory into which your files will be saved, use the Directory command. The current directory is displayed. Use the backspace or ← to move to the beginning of the entry. When you are entering a new directory, specify the drive name as well, as in:

    C:\budget86

This is a temporary specification, and if you want to tell 1-2-3 to permanently look at a different directory, use the Worksheet Global Default Directory command, discussed in Appendix A.

MEASURING WORKSHEET MEMORY

The Worksheet Status command reports the amount of RAM available for the spreadsheet you are currently working on as the percent of RAM remaining. If the RAM left is 50%, your spreadsheet can be twice as large as it is right now before you run out of space. If the RAM left is 75%, your spreadsheet can be four times as large as it is right now before you run out of RAM.

Remember, RAM is not the same as the disk space on your floppy or hard disk. You will usually run out of RAM before you run out of disk space, but it is possible to run out of disk space first. Lotus 1-2-3 displays a MEM indicator in the lower-right corner of your screen when you finally run out of memory. At that point you will be unable to enter additional information or save your work, so it is a good idea to check the amount of RAM remaining from time to time when you are working with very large or very many spreadsheets.

COMBINING FILES

The File Combine command allows you to bring information stored in another spreadsheet into the current spreadsheet. It retains the work currently in progress while incorporating additional information from another spreadsheet file.

During File Combine operations, the position of the cell pointer determines where in the current spreadsheet any new information from other spreadsheet files will appear. The position of the cell pointer marks the upper-left cell of the incoming spreadsheet (or range of cells). The range of cells being brought in from another spreadsheet will overlay cells in the current spreadsheet. The results of this overlaying of cells will vary, depending on the cell contents in the current spreadsheet and the secondary options chosen (Copy, Add, or Subtract).

When you use the File Combine command, be careful to add information to an area of the current spreadsheet where incoming values and labels will not interfere with existing cell entries in unexpected ways. It is usually best to use a blank area in the current spreadsheet for File Combine Copy operations. In addition, be sure to save your current spreadsheet before using the File Combine command, in case any cells get unexpectedly overlaid.

Such settings as named ranges, print settings, and database-related ranges contained in the other spreadsheets are not brought into the current spreadsheet during File Combine operations.

You can select three options that control how this additional information is brought into the current spreadsheet. The secondary menu that appears after selecting the Combine command contains the following commands:

Command	*Purpose*
Copy	Replaces cell entries in the current worksheet with a copy of labels and values from another spreadsheet.
Add	Adds values from within another spreadsheet (including the current values of formulas) to cell values contained in the current spreadsheet.
Subtract	Subtracts values from within another worksheet (including the current values of formulas) to cell values contained in the current spreadsheet.

A final selection within the File Combine command menu offers the options of incorporating the entire spreadsheet specified or a portion of the spreadsheet specified:

Option	*Purpose*
Entire-File	Incorporate all cell values and labels from a specified spreadsheet.

Option	*Purpose*
Named/ Specified- Range	Incorporate only those cell values and labels contained within a designated range within the specified spreadsheet.

Copying Duplicate Information from 1-2-3 Files

To copy one 1-2-3 file into another, use the File Combine Copy Entire-File command. Suppose you have a 1-2-3 database containing names of employees and financial information in one file and you wish to build another database that contains all of this information plus productivity measurements in a second file. Rather than retype the employee names in the second file, you can use this command to copy all of the first file to another area in the second file.

To copy values from a file that contains formulas, use the File Combine Add command, which will duplicate the results of the formulas rather than the formulas themselves. (See "Copying Parts of Files" later in this chapter.)

Consolidating Duplicate Files

The File Combine Add and File Combine Subtract commands are powerful tools for consolidating information from a group of similar spreadsheets. The structure of the individual spreadsheets must be identical; otherwise the results will be unpredictable and often meaningless.

For example, these commands can be useful in combining two or more division budgets to calculate a total budget for a company. Suppose there are three divisions, A, B, and C. Each division keeps its budget in a separate spreadsheet file. The corporate office keeps the master budget format with zero values and uses each division's budget to calculate the total budget. The master budget, which contains zeroes for values, contains formulas identical to the division spreadsheet.

To use the command, retrieve the master budget file. Then locate the cursor in the Home position. To add a division's budget, use the File Combine Add Entire-File command and specify the name of the file for division A. Repeat the sequence for divisions B and C.

Combining Parts of Files

The option for bringing only certain cell ranges into the current spreadsheet lets you obtain specific information from within other spreadsheets. For example, you can combine (copy) small ranges within other spreadsheets into your current spreadsheet, eliminating the need to have copies of several spreadsheets in memory at the same time. This reduces memory requirements and allows the current spreadsheet to be maintained in a compact, manageable format.

For example, suppose you have a cash balance spreadsheet for each month. The spreadsheet computes the ending balance for the current month, and the next month uses the ending balance for its beginning balance. If the balance contains several values, you can copy them automatically instead of retyping them.

The new 1-2-3 allows you to copy data from a file by using either the data's cell locations or its range name. To do this, you assign a range name to the ending balance or record the cell location of the cell(s) you want to copy, using the Range Name Create command. Make sure to resave the file after creating the range name. Then retrieve the next month's spreadsheet and use the File Combine Add Named/Specific-Range command to copy the values to the beginning balance for the month.

EXTRACTING PARTS OF A FILE

The File Xtract command saves a specified section of the current spreadsheet to a separate spreadsheet file. This command is used primarily to separate parts of a spreadsheet that has become larger than can be comfortably managed. Once sections of a spreadsheet have been extracted, you can recombine them by using the File Combine commands.

For example, in the company with three divisions A, B, and C, suppose each division is responsible for a different area of sales. The master spreadsheet contains all categories of sales, separated by division. The division managers do not see the sales for the other divisions. The overall sales director extracts the portion of the sales report having to do with each division and delivers that portion to each division manager. The division managers make corrections and return the files to the sales manager, who recombines them into the master report.

The options available for the File Xtract command are:

Option	Result
Formulas	Save a copy of the specified cell range to a new spreadsheet file, including formulas and cell references.
Values	Save a copy of the specified cell range to a new spreadsheet file, converting all formulas to their current values.

After you select either Formulas or Values, 1-2-3 asks you to name the file into which the extracted material should be placed. It also asks for the range of cells to be extracted:

Message	You enter:
Enter xtract file name:	The file name for the new spreadsheet.
Enter xtract range:	A cell range (e.g., A1..C10)

If you choose Formulas, a copy of the selected spreadsheet section that is functionally equivalent to the original is saved. All formula and cell-reference relationships are maintained, and print settings, database ranges, and range name positions are saved in the extracted spreadsheet. Extracting formulas is useful for isolating sections of a spreadsheet for further calculations and for delivering portions of spreadsheets that other people will be responsible for filling with data (as in the three-division example earlier.)

Choosing Values saves a copy of the selected spreadsheet section in which only the results of formulas are included, not the formulas themselves. The extracted spreadsheet will appear exactly like the original but will not be functionally equivalent because formulas and most cell-reference relationships will be lost. Extracting values is useful for preserving current values on a spreadsheet that undergoes periodic revision, for later historical analysis.

Problems may result if a spreadsheet range selected for a File Xtract Formulas operation contains cell formulas that reference other cells lying outside the extract range. If a cell contains a formula that references another cell outside the extract range, the formula may produce unpredictable results in the newly extracted spreadsheet. As a general rule, it is best to use File Xtract Formulas operations on areas of a spreadsheet that are self-contained; that is, that do not depend on other cells located elsewhere in the spreadsheet for calculations. If the layout of a spreadsheet is such that cell references are widely distributed, then File Xtract Values operations may be more appropriate.

IMPORTING WORD PROCESSED OR TEXT FILES

The File Import command is used to incorporate a print file created with the Print File command (or any other plain ASCII file) into the current spreadsheet. Print files produced by 1-2-3 consist of ASCII text characters and have the extension .PRN that identifies them in a directory listing. ASCII text is a relatively standardized file format for microcomputers, and many word processing, database, and communications programs produce such files. You must use the DOS RENAME Command to include the .PRN extension before using the File Import command. This command is useful as a means of importing information from other sources into 1-2-3 spreadsheets.

Note: A WordStar file created with the D (document) option cannot be imported directly into 1-2-3. To import it, print the WordStar file to another file with a .PRN extension. This strips the control codes and carriage returns from the file. Files created and edited exclusively with the N (non-document) option can be imported directly into Lotus 1-2-3.

The File Import command has two options. Selecting Text imports information from a print file as a "long label" of text, extending from the current cell pointer position. Selecting Numbers imports numeric values from a print file into columns to the right of the cell pointer.

After choosing Text or Numbers, the program will prompt you for the file name of the print file to be imported. You need not type the .PRN.

Depending upon your choice of Text or Numbers and the contents of the specified print file, the characters and text in the print file will be imported into the current spreadsheet at the cell pointer position.

With 1-2-3 Release 2, you can use the Data Parse command to convert an ASCII text file of mixed text and value "long labels" imported into the current spreadsheet (with a File Import Text operation) to a format that can use 1-2-3's standard commands and functions. This procedure is discussed in Chapter 10, "Data Sharing Techniques."

USING THE ACCESS SYSTEM
FILE TRANSFER UTILITY

The 1-2-3 Utility disk contains a program that controls the conversion of files created by other programs into files that 1-2-3 can interpret. This Translate utility can be accessed through the Lotus Access System's Translate option.

Before using the Translate utility, make sure your system is set up to retrieve files from the correct disk drive, either B for a two-drive system or C for a hard disk. You need not convert 1-2-3 release 1A files using Translate, even though it is listed as an option. For further considerations in translating to and from dBase II or III, see Chapter 10, "Data Sharing Techniques."

The Translate utility is menu driven, which makes it easy to operate. After you select the Translate option from the Lotus Access menu, the following menu is displayed:

What do you want to translate FROM?

1-2-3, release 1A
1-2-3, release 2
dBase II
dBase III
DIF
Jazz
SYMPHONY, release 1.0
SYMPHONY, release 1.1
VISICALC

After you select the program to translate from, 1-2-3 asks you to select the program you will translate to:

What do you want to translate TO?

1-2-3, release 1A
dBase II
dBase III
DIF
SYMPHONY, release 1.0
SYMPHONY, release 1.1

Not all of the programs listed can be translated to one another using the Translate utility. The translations that work are listed in Table 7.2.

From	*To*
1-2-3, Release 1A	1-2-3, Release 2
	dBase II
	dBase III
	DIF
	Symphony, Version 1.0
	Symphony, Version 1.1
1-2-3, Release 2	1-2-3, Release 1A
	dBase II
	dBase III
	DIF
	Symphony, Version 1.0
	Symphony, Version 1.1
dBase II and III	1-2-3, Release 1A
	1-2-3, Release 2
	Symphony, Version 1.0
	Symphony, Version 1.1

Table 7.2: Translations Possible with 1-2-3, Release 2

From	To
DIF	1-2-3, Release 1A
	1-2-3, Release 2
	Symphony, Version 1.0
	Symphony, Version 1.1
Jazz	1-2-3, Release 1A
	1-2-3, Release 2
	Symphony, Version 1.0
	Symphony, Version 1.1
VisiCalc	1-2-3, Release 1A
	1-2-3, Release 2
	Symphony, Version 1.0
	Symphony, Version 1.1
Symphony, Version 1.0	1-2-3, Release 1A
	1-2-3, Release 2
	Symphony, Version 1.0
	dBase II
	dBase III
Symphony, Version 1.1	1-2-3, Release 1A
	1-2-3, Release 2
	Symphony, Version 1.1
	dBase II
	dBase III

Table 7.2: Translations Possible with 1-2-3, Release 2 (continued)

In this section, you have learned to:

- Save and retrieve files
- List or erase files
- Specify a current file directory
- Measure 1-2-3 worksheet memory space
- Combine and consolidate 1-2-3 files

- Extract parts of a 1-2-3 file
- Import word processed or ASCII text files
- Use the Lotus Access file transfer program

Summary

In this chapter, you have explored some fundamental 1-2-3 housekeeping functions: handling, protecting, and printing files; altering how text, numbers, and dates appear on the screen and in print; and managing disk space. The techniques and practices outlined in this chapter are designed to give you the tools you need to have your 1-2-3 work at your fingertips in the format you need, quickly and efficiently.

The next chapter introduces the notion of databases in general and setting up databases in 1-2-3 in particular. The chapters that follow it then discuss how to sort, select, copy, and edit database information.

Part III

The Database

Chapter 8

Building a Database

In this chapter, you will learn to:

* Create a database
* Compute fields
* Improve the appearance of a database
* Print the database

As a manager, you should have easy access to the information that is relevant to the efficient operation of your organization. For instance, you should be able to keep track of salaries by department, find out the number of employees in a department, and calculate how long employees remain in your company. This record-keeping process is usually done on paper and stored away in file cabinets, and you may often find yourself spending more time looking for the information than using it. But with 1-2-3 you can use database management to organize company information so that it is easy to update, collate, and find.

A database holds information organized so that it can be managed. In 1-2-3, database information is held in tables. All the information associated with a given value is located on the same row as that value, much like an ordinary data table is arranged. What makes such a table a database in 1-2-3 is the way the program can manipulate the information once the database is set up. Each group of information—each row—is called a *record,* and each column is called a *field.* A *field name* describes the kind of information to be found in that column for each record.

For example, if your database contains the names, addresses, and telephone numbers of your clients, you would have a separate record for each client. Within each record, the information is divided into fields, one for the last name, one for the first name, one for the phone number, and so on. Release 2 allows you to have up to 256 fields and up to 8192 records, depending on how much RAM memory your computer has. The database is headed by field titles, which serve as an index for items you are keeping track of.

What are databases used for? To name only a few applications:

* Lists of information
* Accounting—payables and receivables

- Asset and liability records
- Time billing records
- Investment portfolio amounts and details
- Calendars of events
- Research data
- Medical case histories
- Real estate listings
- Scholastic records
- Contract details
- Client orders and addresses
- Mailing lists
- Donor lists
- Campaign information
- Demographic information
- Survey results

. . . the list is endless. Once you have information in a database, the ways you can organize and manage it are almost unlimited.

In this chapter, you will contruct a database containing personnel information. It will track employee first and last name, job function, department, ethnic code, sex, management level, annual salary, monthly salary, and hire date. This database will be used to demonstrate step-by-step how to create field names, enter data records, enter formulas for records, format data records, and print a database. Because this is the first chapter on databases, the steps are outlined in detail. Subsequent database chapters will assume you have the basic familiarity with databases that this chapter provides. If you are already familiar with 1-2-3's database capabilities, you may wish to turn to Chapter 9, "Using a Database," for material on sorting and querying a database as well as using statistical analysis and database functions, or turn to Chapter 10, "Data Sharing Techniques," for discussions of how to link 1-2-3 databases and transfer data in them to and from other database products.

Creating a Database

Creating a database is very similar to creating a spreadsheet. You first enter labels that are used for field names in the first row of the database. Data records are then entered, one per row, filling in each field for each record. A database can store label entries (called *text fields*), number entries (called *value fields*), formulas, and functions.

Database design, like spreadsheet design, requires some careful thought. Make sure that you design the database for your future needs as well as your immediate ones. Sketch the design on paper before you sit down at the computer. You can change the database after it is created and add new fields by inserting columns and new records by inserting rows, but designing your database well in the first place will save a good deal of time later.

Using a poorly designed database can be very time consuming, and using a well-designed one can be an enormous time saver. Your first step is to decide which information to include in the database, which you should plan carefully with paper and pencil, as discussed above. The second is deciding the order of the fields.

ORDERING FIELDS

When designing a 1-2-3 database, you must decide the order in which the data will be entered and viewed. When you enter data into a field, the cursor moves to the right so that you can enter the next item of data. If your database is designed so that data is entered in logical sequences, it is easy to enter records. For example, if a database is to contain names, addresses, and sales amounts, set up your fields so that you enter the first name, last name, address, and sale amount, in that order. If the data to be entered is being taken from a printed form or report, design the database so that the information is entered in the same order as it appears on the report. Sometimes you will discover that the form is not well designed, and then you may want to change the form rather than change the database.

Again, should you later discover that you have to change the field order or add a field, you will find that 1-2-3 allows you to insert a field or column, move fields, change the width of fields, or specify new formulas for fields. In many other database programs, these are formidable, if not impossible, chores.

Once you have specified the order of the fields, you are ready to create the database.

WIDENING FIELDS AND COLUMNS

1. First, adjust the columns to the widths shown below so that you can see the entire column as you build the example database. Move the cursor to the column to be adjusted and then use the Worksheet Column Set command.

A	B	C	D	E	F	G	H	I	J
11	13	11	9	6	4	6	9	8	10

ASSIGNING AND ENTERING FIELD NAMES

Each field name must be unique. Although field names can be entered in either upper- or lowercase, using only uppercase letters will help to distinguish field names from data records. Just as in any ordinary table heading, you will want to use more than one row for the longer field names, so that none of the columns are overly wide.

2. Using Figure 8.1 as a guide, enter the field names for the employee database.

WHAT KINDS OF DATA CAN BE USED IN RECORDS?

Most of the data in this particular database is either label (text) or numeric, but functions and formulas are allowed as well. Labels can contain up to 240 characters. Formulas, functions, and numeric fields have the same limits and parameters as in a regular spreadsheet.

3. Using Figure 8.2 as a guide, enter the label and numeric data fields for each of the 15 records.

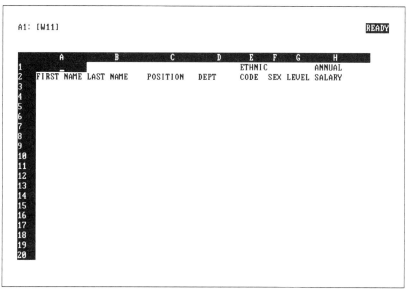

Figure 8.1: Field names for employee database

After entering all the records, the two computed fields, MONTHLY SALARY and HIRE DATE, will require a formula and a function, described in the next section.

In this section, you have learned to:

- Select the order for database fields
- Assign and enter field names
- Identify the kinds of data that can be used in a database

Computing Fields

You may put formulas and functions in fields and compute them like spreadsheet cells. The formulas may rely on other data records (cell locations) or use @ functions. Any of the regular spreadsheet formula signs, such as +, −, /, and *, can be used to create a formula. You could, for example, specify an @SUM that will add values across the cells in a given record in a database that tracked

```
A1: [W11]                                                              READY

         A           B           C          D       E    F    G        H
1                                                        ETHNIC         ANNUAL
2   FIRST NAME  LAST NAME    POSITION    DEPT      CODE  SEX LEVEL  SALARY
3   Glenn       Tucker       Musician    Pub Rel     1  M      2    25000
4   David       Jenkins      Sen Prog    DP          1  M      2    35000
5   Peter       Avila        Jun Prog    DP          2  M      3    27000
6   Elaine      Rubenstein   Trainer     Personnel   2  F      3    27000
7   Judy        Gabriel      Telec Spec  Tech        1  F      2    35000
8   Alice       Hennetig     Counselor   Personnel   1  F      2    32000
9   Janice      Schooler     Train Spec  Finance     1  F      2    38000
10  Leon        Callinan     Counselor   Health      4  F      3    29000
11  Mark        Bruno        Writer      R D         2  M      3    28000
12  Matthew     Bronson      Mngmt       Tech        3  M      1   100000
13  Paul        Kaplan       Mngmt       Sales       1  M      1    80000
14  Bill        Mees         Mngmt       Finance     1  M      1    90000
15  Lisa        Salvetti     VP          Mrktg       2  F      2    30000
16  Cindy       Revel        VP          Finance     3  F      2    30000
17  Ed          Levine       Pres        Sales       4  M      1    75000
18
19
20
```

Figure 8.2: Label and numeric fields

quarterly sales for each year. Instead of entering the value in the Total field, you could compute the sum of the four quarters. The total will change whenever any of the data in the computation changes, just as in an ordinary spreadsheet. All of the @ functions work just as they do in 1-2-3 spreadsheets.

In your personnel database, you will create a computed field for monthly salary based on annual salary equal to annual salary divided by 12.

ENTERING A FORMULA FOR A FIELD

You enter the formula for a field as you do in a spreadsheet, referencing the cells in the database involved in the computation. Then you can copy the formula to any other cells in the database.

1. Enter the formula for the first employee's monthly salary in cell I3. Enter

   +H3/12

In the next section you will enter the HIRE DATE for the same employee, using the @DATE function.

ENTERING A FUNCTION FOR A FIELD

The 1-2-3 @NOW, @DATE, and @TIME functions refer to your computer's internal clock, rather than to any field in the database. Once entered, these functions can be copied just as formulas can be, using relative and absolute references.

2. In this database, enter @DATE for the first employee's hire date in cell J3 as

@DATE(82,7,15)

Your database should now look like Figure 8.3.

Figure 8.3: Database with a formula and function

The hire date is stored using a function rather than as plain text so that you can later use arithmetic and logical operations on it to select employee records.

You are now ready to copy the formula and function you entered for one employee to the rest of the employee records.

COPYING A FORMULA FOR A FIELD

It is easier and faster to copy a formula or a function into the remaining database records than to enter each one separately. When you later insert new database records, remember that it will be faster to copy any formulas or functions from an existing record's cell in this case also.

   3. To copy the monthly salary formula, copy cell I3 to cells I4 through I17, using the Copy command.

When the copying is finished, your database should look like Figure 8.4.

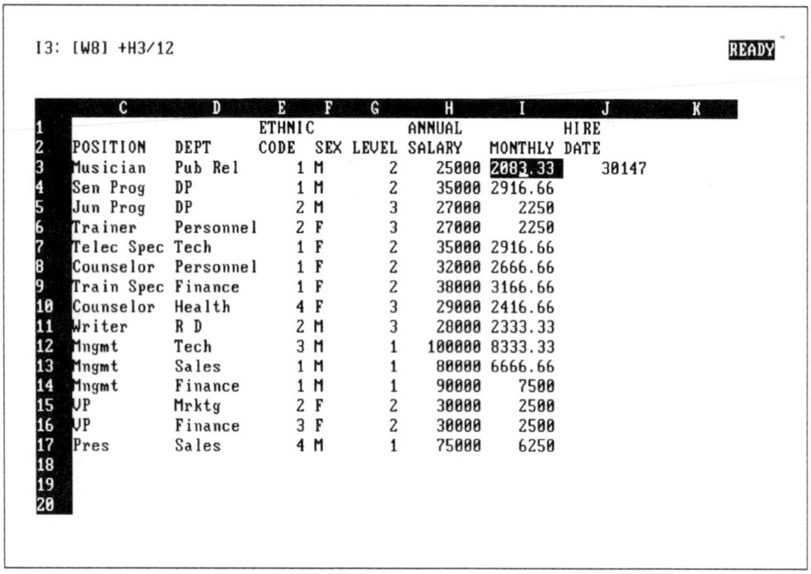

```
I3: [W8] +H3/12                                              READY

         C         D       E   F   G      H        I       J       K
1                        ETHNIC          ANNUAL         HIRE
2   POSITION    DEPT      CODE SEX LEVEL SALARY  MONTHLY DATE
3   Musician    Pub Rel    1  M    2     25000  2083.33   30147
4   Sen Prog    DP         1  M    2     35000  2916.66
5   Jun Prog    DP         2  M    3     27000   2250
6   Trainer     Personnel  2  F    3     27000   2250
7   Telec Spec  Tech       1  F    2     35000  2916.66
8   Counselor   Personnel  1  F    2     32000  2666.66
9   Train Spec  Finance    1  F    2     38000  3166.66
10  Counselor   Health     4  F    3     29000  2416.66
11  Writer      R D        2  M    3     28000  2333.33
12  Mngmt       Tech       3  M    1    100000  8333.33
13  Mngmt       Sales      1  M    1     80000  6666.66
14  Mngmt       Finance    1  M    1     90000   7500
15  VP          Mrktg      2  F    2     30000   2500
16  VP          Finance    3  F    2     30000   2500
17  Pres        Sales      4  M    1     75000   6250
18
19
20
```

Figure 8.4: Database with formula copied

COPYING A FUNCTION FOR A FIELD

To save time, you can copy most functions, just as you can copy formulas. Where your functions reference relative cells, 1-2-3 will automatically adjust the cell locations specified in the function. If, for example, you sum all the cells in row I in one function and then copy the function to row J, the copied function will sum J's cells, not I's. If you want the cell locations specified in the function to remain constant when the function is copied, insert a dollar sign ($) before the column and row references in the original function, as in @SUM($I$1..$I$10).

Usually when you use the @DATE function, the dates to be entered will be different from record to record and must therefore be entered separately. You can still copy the @DATE function, however, and then edit the year, month, and day using the F2 (Edit) key.

4. Using the Copy command, copy the function in cell J3 to cells J4 through J17. Then edit each cell using the information in Figure 8.5.

In this section, you have learned to:

- Enter a formula for a field
- Enter a function for a field
- Copy a formula for a field
- Copy a function for a field

Improving Database Appearance

You can make your databases more legible by using various 1-2-3 format options. The format options available in a spreadsheet are available for databases as well.

Numeric and computed fields should be formatted so that their value and meaning are apparent. To format each column or group of columns in a different format, use the Range Format command. If the entire database will have the same format (which usually occurs only when it consists entirely of numbers), use the Worksheet Global Format command. When you use the Global Format command, new records will automatically take on the format of the whole database.

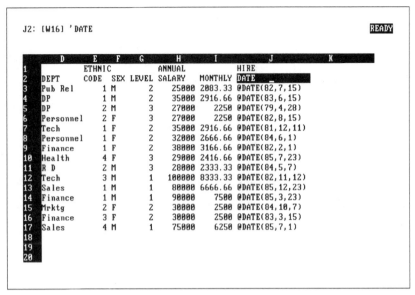

Figure 8.5: @Date functions copied and edited

In the example, the ANNUAL SALARY column needs a Currency format, the MONTHLY SALARY column a Comma format, and the HIRE DATE column a Date format.

1. Format the database now using the Range Format command, specifying the appropriate format type for each column. Your database will then look like Figure 8.6.

2. Save your database in a file called DBASE so that you can use it in later exercises.

In this section, you have learned to:

- Format database records

Printing a Database

You use the same Print command to print a database as you use to print a spreadsheet, specifying the range from the first cell to be

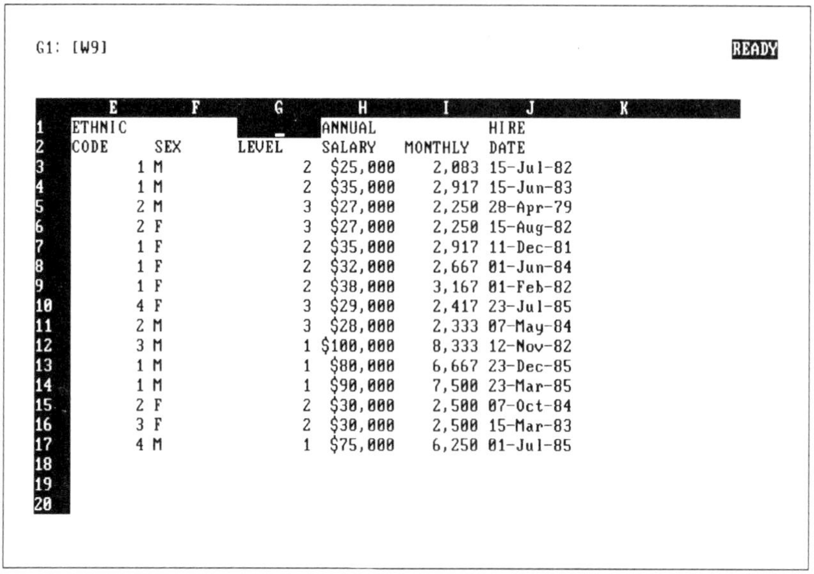

```
G1: [W9]                                                          READY

              E        F        G       H        I        J        K
  1  ETHNIC                        ┌───┐ANNUAL            HIRE
  2  CODE          SEX     LEVEL     SALARY   MONTHLY   DATE
  3           1 M                2  $25,000   2,083 15-Jul-82
  4           1 M                2  $35,000   2,917 15-Jun-83
  5           2 M                3  $27,000   2,250 28-Apr-79
  6           2 F                3  $27,000   2,250 15-Aug-82
  7           1 F                2  $35,000   2,917 11-Dec-81
  8           1 F                2  $32,000   2,667 01-Jun-84
  9           1 F                2  $38,000   3,167 01-Feb-82
 10           4 F                3  $29,000   2,417 23-Jul-85
 11           2 M                3  $28,000   2,333 07-May-84
 12           3 M                1 $100,000   8,333 12-Nov-82
 13           1 M                1  $80,000   6,667 23-Dec-85
 14           1 M                1  $90,000   7,500 23-Mar-85
 15           2 F                2  $30,000   2,500 07-Oct-84
 16           3 F                2  $30,000   2,500 15-Mar-83
 17           4 M                1  $75,000   6,250 01-Jul-85
 18
 19
 20
```

Figure 8.6: Formatted database

printed through the last cell. To print the DBASE example, use the
Print Printer Range command to specify cells A1 through J30. Figure 8.7 shows the personnel database printout.

```
                                      ETHNIC         ANNUAL           HIRE
FIRST NAME LAST NAME    POSITION    DEPT     CODE  SEX LEVEL SALARY   MONTHLY DATE
Glenn      Tucker       Musician    Pub Rel    1   M      2  $25,000   2,083 15-Jul-82
David      Jenkins      Sen Prog    DP         1   M      2  $35,000   2,917 15-Jun-83
Peter      Avila        Jun Prog    DP         2   M      3  $27,000   2,250 28-Apr-79
Elaine     Rubenstein   Trainer     Personnel  2   F      3  $27,000   2,250 15-Aug-82
Judy       Gabriel      Telec Spec  Tech       1   F      2  $35,000   2,917 11-Dec-81
Alice      Hennetig     Counselor   Personnel  1   F      2  $32,000   2,667 01-Jun-84
Janice     Schooler     Train Spec  Finance    1   F      2  $38,000   3,167 01-Feb-82
Leon       Callinan     Counselor   Health     4   F      3  $29,000   2,417 23-Jul-85
Mark       Bruno        Writer      R D        2   M      3  $28,000   2,333 07-May-84
Matthew    Bronson      Mngmt       Tech       3   M      1 $100,000   8,333 12-Nov-82
Paul       Kaplan       Mngmt       Sales      1   M      1  $80,000   6,667 23-Dec-85
Bill       Mees         Mngmt       Finance    1   M      1  $90,000   7,500 23-Mar-85
Lisa       Salvetti     VP          Mrktg      2   F      2  $30,000   2,500 07-Oct-84
Cindy      Revel        VP          Finance    3   F      2  $30,000   2,500 15-Mar-83
Ed         Levine       Pres        Sales      4   M      1  $75,000   6,250 01-Jul-85
```

Figure 8.7: Employee database printout

Because with Release 2 you can create as many as 256 fields in the database, you will often not be able to print all the columns at the same time.

When you want to print only selected database columns, use the new Worksheet Column Hide command to hide some of the columns temporarily.

For example, to get a printout of an entire spreadsheet that is too wide to print at once, print the spreadsheet in sections. Say that the database contains 20 fields that are each 10 spaces wide, for a total width of 20 × 10, or 200 spaces. Most standard printers print only 80 spaces wide.

To print this database, first hide all but the first eight fields. Save and print the database. Then go back and hide all but the second set of eight fields, save the database, and print it again. Continue until all the fields have been printed. Tape the printouts together in order. You now have a complete printout of the database. (For cosmetic reasons, you might want to reduce the printouts and copy them onto a single sheet, using a standard copying machine.) You could also use the embedded control codes described earlier to condense the type size, which would eliminate the need for cutting and pasting.

In this section, you have learned to:

- Print the entire database
- Print selected database fields

Summary

This chapter has presented the basics of designing and using a database. You have seen how to create a simple database, use computed fields, work with formatting commands, and print out a database.

The next chapter discusses how you can name ranges in the database so that you can print different sections, move to different sections, or insert new sections by typing in the range name instead of entering cell locations. It also presents the different methods available for selecting, reporting, editing, and deleting information in the database. Statistical analysis and what-if analysis are covered in Chapter 9, while Chapter 10, "Data Sharing Techniques," presents advanced techniques for sharing data among databases.

Chapter 9

Using a Database

In this chapter, you will learn to:

- Organize a database with range names
- Sort a database
- Query a database
- Classify data using frequency bin ranges
- Perform statistical analysis on a database
- Build data tables that compute database statistics

The last chapter introduced the fundamentals of setting up a database in 1-2-3. While this setup is important, it is all preliminary. A database really begins to be useful only after you have it set up and are ready to put it to work.

There are two primary ways of accessing and selecting information in your database: *sorting* and *querying*.

First, you can sort records based on the values in a particular field. You could, for example, arrange sales entries in order of decreasing amount, so that the highest sale amount is at the top of the database, and the lowest is at the bottom. You could then tell which clients owed the most money and take the appropriate action, sending invoices or follow-up letters. Because you can sort records in 1-2-3, you don't have to enter the records in a particular order. In this example, you would most likely enter the records in chronological order as the sales occur. When you need the monthly sales report, you would sort the database as described here.

Another use of sorting is to alphabetize entries. You might, for example, want to produce an alphabetical list of sales clients from the database just sorted in sales amount order. Or you might sort the products you sell as a cross reference for inventory purposes. Sorting automatically arranges the entire database in any order you specify. In 1-2-3, you can sort by two fields as well as by one. For example, you might choose first to sort chronologically, by the date products are sold, and within that, sort alphabetically by product name so that each day's products sold are listed in alphabetical order.

The second method of manipulating data is *querying*—selecting records in a particular range, based on a value or series of values you specify.

Querying allows you to ask the database questions. Lotus 1-2-3 then searches the records and gathers the information that answers those questions. You might, for example, ask 1-2-3 to look at the database and show all records for employees who work in Finance. Once 1-2-3 selects these records, it either presents them to you one at a time for editing or deletion or outputs copies of them to another area of the spreadsheet, which can then be printed.

Another use of query is to search through a database and display all unique values for a field, ignoring repeats. You might, for example, ask for a list of all unique clients for a mailing, so that a customer who made two purchases would only receive one letter.

Lotus 1-2-3 database fields can also be easily classified into *bins*, which are separate ranges based on values in a particular field. You might, for example, want to discover how many employees earn between $0 and $20,000, $20,000 and $30,000, and $30,000 and $40,000. You could then create a distribution range, displaying the number of employees in each range.

More advanced 1-2-3 database applications covered in this chapter include computing totals for salaries by department, calculating costs and expenses by category, and determining and averaging sales by region. You can derive such tables of information from the data fields by combining database @ functions with the Data Table command, which will be discussed in the latter part of the chapter.

Organizing a Database

So far you have learned to design and build a simple database. As you begin to use the database, however, you will need to begin separating it into distinct regions by specifying range names in order to sort, query, print, and perform various other operations. The sections that follow describe how to name ranges, how to keep track of range names, and how to take advantage of the range name feature to simplify entering new records.

USING RANGE NAMES
TO CATALOG SECTIONS

So that you do not have to memorize the cell locations of the various ranges in which you are interested, you can specify range names. These are particularly useful for cataloging the cell locations of various sections in your databases and large spreadsheets. To create a range name, you use the Range Name Create command. Each name must be 15 characters or fewer and must not have spaces in it. After you have assigned a name, you specify the cell locations of the section you are naming. You can modify the cell locations in a range name using the same command you used to create it, but you cannot modify the name itself. If you misspell a range name, delete it and start over, using Range Name Delete command.

A range name can represent a single cell as well as a series of cells. Using range names in this way can be useful in building formulas. Once you have created a range name, you can quickly move to the area it represents. You can also print any area of the database or spreadsheet by range name.

To move to a named range, press the F5 (Goto) key once and the F3 (Name) key twice. The list of range names will appear on the screen. Select the name of the range to which you want to move.

To print a named range, select Range from the Print menu. Press the F3 (Name) key twice to produce a list of range names and select the range name that represents the section you want to print.

KEEPING TRACK OF RANGE NAMES

The more you use range names, the more you will create, and you may lose track of the names you have used. Release 2 of 1-2-3 allows you to print a list of the range names on your spreadsheet by using the Range Name Table command. Figure 9.1 shows a table of range names.

Make sure your cursor is on a clear area of the spreadsheet before trying this command, because the range name table will overwrite any values or text in the cells in which it is displayed.

When 1-2-3 asks you to specify a range, press the F3 (Name) key to call up the list of range names and then select the appropriate one. You will use range names extensively in this chapter. Range names are also discussed in regard to macros in Chapter 11.

The first use of the range name feature that we will examine is when it is used to insert new records in a database.

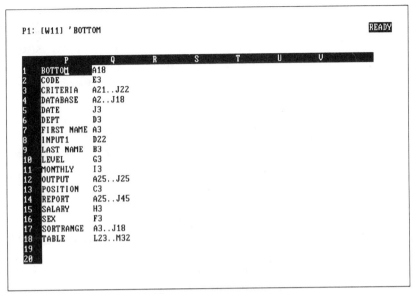

```
P1: [W11] 'BOTTOM                                              READY

             P         Q         R         S         T         U         V
 1   BOTTOM      A18
 2   CODE        E3
 3   CRITERIA    A21..J22
 4   DATABASE    A2..J18
 5   DATE        J3
 6   DEPT        D3
 7   FIRST NAME  A3
 8   INPUT1      D22
 9   LAST NAME   B3
10   LEVEL       G3
11   MONTHLY     I3
12   OUTPUT      A25..J25
13   POSITION    C3
14   REPORT      A25..J45
15   SALARY      H3
16   SEX         F3
17   SORTRANGE   A3..J18
18   TABLE       L23..M32
19
20
```

Figure 9.1: Range name table

INSERTING RECORDS

When you insert a row in a spreadsheet, every row below it moves down and all the formulas are adjusted. For this reason, it is best to insert new records just before the last record in the database. Each time you insert a new record, the cell location of the last record in the database will change, so that you cannot use the cell location of the last record as a marker for the end of your database in formulas or for moving to the end of the database to enter new records. If you name the cell location of the first field in the last record with a range name, this end cell will "float," moving down automatically and becoming a permanent name for the end of the database.

Give the cell a name such as BOTTOM or END to mark it as the end of the database, so that you will be able to go directly to it to enter new records and can reference the end of the database permanently in formulas.

To enter new rows in a database, you do not simply move down to the next blank row with the arrow key, as you normally would in a spreadsheet. In a database you must insert a new record between the last database record and the row above it. If you insert a new row below the row in which the END cell is located, END will lose its place as the last record. Also note that if you sort the database into a different order, the last record will change, and you will have to adjust the range names for both the new and previous last records.

Use the Range Name Create command to create the range name BOTTOM for the last record of the personnel database. Note that Figure 9.2 shows the location of the range name at cell A17.

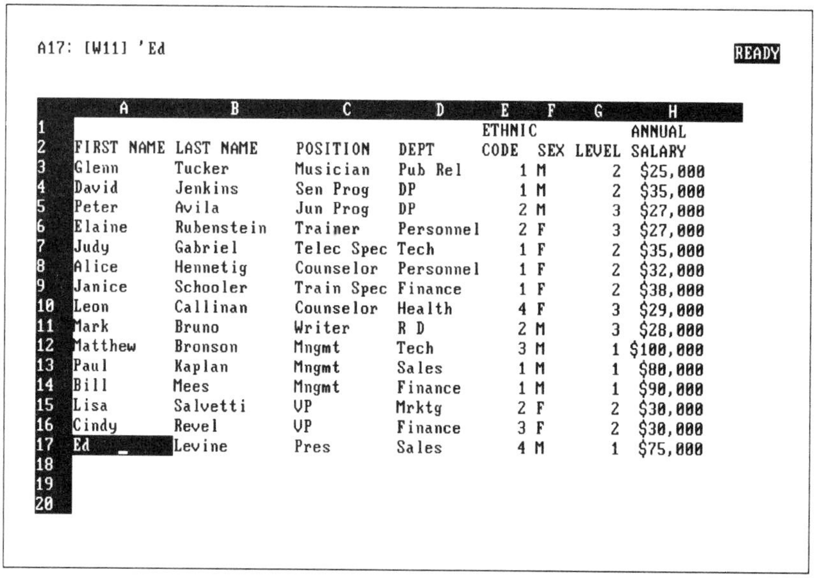

Figure 9.2: Range name BOTTOM

Now press the F5 (Goto) key and then the F3 (Name) key to bring up the table of range names. Select the range name BOTTOM. The cursor moves immediately to the row of the last record of the database. Insert a new row here using the Worksheet Insert Row command. Figure 9.3 shows that the range name BOTTOM is located in cell A18 after the blank row has been inserted. The range name BOTTOM has moved down and continues to mark the last record of the database.

As you can see, naming the last record simplifies movement within the database as well as database housekeeping. Other

```
A18: [W11] 'Ed                                                        READY

        A           B           C           D       E   F   G      H
1                                                  ETHNIC        ANNUAL
2   FIRST NAME  LAST NAME   POSITION    DEPT       CODE SEX LEVEL SALARY
3   Glenn       Tucker      Musician    Pub Rel      1 M      2  $25,000
4   David       Jenkins     Sen Prog    DP           1 M      2  $35,000
5   Peter       Avila       Jun Prog    DP           2 M      3  $27,000
6   Elaine      Rubenstein  Trainer     Personnel    2 F      3  $27,000
7   Judy        Gabriel     Telec Spec  Tech         1 F      2  $35,000
8   Alice       Hennetig    Counselor   Personnel    1 F      2  $32,000
9   Janice      Schooler    Train Spec  Finance      1 F      2  $38,000
10  Leon        Callinan    Counselor   Health       4 F      3  $29,000
11  Mark        Bruno       Writer      R D          2 M      3  $28,000
12  Matthew     Bronson     Mngmt       Tech         3 M      1 $100,000
13  Paul        Kaplan      Mngmt       Sales        1 M      1  $80,000
14  Bill        Mees        Mngmt       Finance      1 M      1  $90,000
15  Lisa        Salvetti    VP          Mrktg        2 F      2  $30,000
16  Cindy       Revel       VP          Finance      3 F      2  $30,000
17
18  Ed    _     Levine      Pres        Sales        4 M      1  $75,000
19
20
```

Figure 9.3: Range name BOTTOM after inserted row

methods of automating record insertion by using macros are introduced in Chapter 11.

Hint: You can mark a formula such as MONTHLY SALARY with a range name such as FORMULA1 and then copy from the range name to a newly inserted row's cell.

After you insert new records, the next step is usually to rearrange the database into a particular order, so that new records are organized within the database as a whole. The next section discusses sorting the database.

In this section, you have learned to:

- Catalog sections with range names
- Keep track of range names
- Insert records in a database

Sorting a Database

Whenever you want to see your database records in a different order, you can sort them on any of the fields they contain by using the Data Sort command. Sorts can be made on both alphabetical and numerical data, in either ascending or descending order.

You will usually want to sort a database several times, based on values in a different field each time, for different applications. Sometimes you will want to sort by two fields rather than one. The next sections discuss these processes, ending with a sample problem demonstrating an alphabetical sort.

AUTOMATING SORTING: THE DATA SORT COMMAND

The Data Sort command automates the sorting process. Unlike many other database programs, 1-2-3 takes only a few seconds to sort most databases. Sometimes it sorts a database so fast that you don't even notice the new order.

The items to be sorted need not be very many for the Data Sort command to be useful; in fact, they could be just a single column of numbers or labels.

When you use the Data Sort command, you specify three items. The first is the range you want sorted. For a sort of the entire database, this range is the first field of the first record through the last field of the last record. Do not include rows that are not data, such as field names, blank rows, and the like, or they will be included in the sort, which can lead to strange results. Note that any column not included in the range specification will not be sorted.

After specifying the range, select a field to be used to sort the database. For instance, you might want to sort by client name. Client name is then the *key field* you want the sort to use.

When you sort, you can specify two keys, a *primary* and a *secondary key*. When you specify a secondary key, the database is first sorted strictly by the order of the primary key. Then, within each group of like primary values, 1-2-3 goes back and sorts by the secondary key. For example, if a database contains client purchase records, you could sort first by client name and then, within each client name, by amount of purchase. The primary key is client name and the secondary key is amount of purchase.

The last step specifies the sort order. Select ascending for alphabetical sorts from A to Z and numerical sorts from lowest to highest.

Select descending for alphabetical sorts from Z to A and numerical sorts from highest to lowest.

In summary, to sort a database: specify the range, the key or keys to sort by, and the order—either ascending or descending.

The next sections discuss the specific options of the Data Sort menu.

USING THE DATA SORT COMMAND

It is much more efficient to use range names rather than cell locations to identify the range that will be sorted. Once you have named a range, 1-2-3 will look at the area bounded by the range name. As the database grows, 1-2-3 automatically makes the sort range larger, as long as new records are inserted within the boundaries specified for the range name.

The range name for the sort range should be called something like SORTRANGE, but can be any name fewer than 15 characters that reminds you that this range name contains only data records to be sorted. In Figure 9.4, SORTRANGE consists of cells A3..J17.

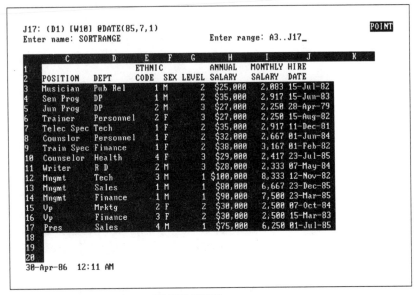

Figure 9.4: Database with SORTRANGE range name

Always save your file before using a Sort command, just in case. Then you can recall the file without having to reenter any data or "unsort" the database if the sort doesn't turn out the way you expect.

The steps involved in performing any sort are outlined below, followed by the sample problem.

First, invoke the Data Sort command and select Data-Range. Press the F3 (Name) key and move the cursor to the name SORTRANGE, or whatever name you have given the range to be sorted. When the name is highlighted, press ◄─┘ to complete the process.

Next, select the primary key by highlighting any data value in the column of the field you want to sort by and pressing ◄─┘. (It doesn't matter here which value you select in the column. You are selecting the entire column, not a particular value in the column.)

Now specify the order of the sort, either ascending or descending. Type **A** or **D** and press ◄─┘.

Repeat this same process—select a value and specify the sort order—to select a secondary key.

The final step is to select Go from the menu, which begins the sort.

When you save the file, the most recent sort settings are also saved. To resort a database with the same settings, specify a new key or keys and select Go. The database range is permanently referenced by the range name SORTRANGE; even if you insert a new record, you can resort the entire database, including the new record, by selecting Go.

SAMPLE PROBLEM: SORTING ALPHABETICALLY AND INSERTING A NEW RECORD

Problem: Alphabetize the personnel database by last name. Use the Sort command to perform an ascending sort. Then insert a record for a new employee between Kaplan and Levine, using the information below and today's date as the hire date.

FIRST NAME	LAST NAME	POSITION	DEPT	ETHNIC	SEX	LEVEL	SALARY
Cathy	Larson	Auditor	Finance	1	F	2	32000

Solution: First create the range name SORTRANGE. To create the range name, enter

/ R N C

Enter

SORTRANGE

to designate SORTRANGE as the range name and enter

A3. J17

to designate A3 to J17 as the database records. Press ⏎ to complete the command.

Then specify the Data-range, Primary-Key and Ascending order using the Data Sort command. Enter

/ D S D F3

Move the cursor to SORTRANGE and press ⏎. Enter

P

and move the cursor to cell B4 to designate LAST NAME as the primary key. Then press

⏎ A ⏎ G

Your spreadsheet should look like Figure 9.5.

Next, insert a row between Kaplan and Levine, where the new record can be entered. Place the cursor in the cell with Levine's name, B11, and enter

/ W I R ⏎

Finally, enter the new record in row 11, reformat the ANNUAL SALARY and HIRE DATE cells, and copy the formula for

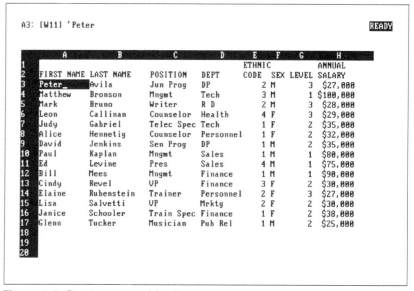

A3: [W11] 'Peter

Figure 9.5: Database sorted by last name

MONTHLY SALARY using the Copy command. Your spreadsheet should look like Figure 9.6.

Hint: You can insert a new record anywhere in the database and resort the database by typing / **D S G.**

In this section, you have learned to:

- Automate sorting with the Data Sort command
- Use the Data Sort command
- Sort alphabetically
- Insert a new record

Querying a Database

You will often want to select only certain information from a database, based on the value or values found in different fields of each record. For example, you might want a list of clients who purchased

```
A1: [W11]                                                      READY

          A          B            C          D      E    F    G      H
                                                    ETHNIC         ANNUAL
 1                                                  CODE  SEX LEVEL SALARY
 2   FIRST NAME LAST NAME     POSITION   DEPT
 3   Peter      Avila         Jun Prog   DP         2  M      3  $27,000
 4   Matthew    Bronson       Mngmt      Tech       3  M      1  $100,000
 5   Mark       Bruno         Writer     R D        2  M      3  $28,000
 6   Leon       Callinan      Counselor  Health     4  F      3  $29,000
 7   Judy       Gabriel       Telec Spec Tech       1  F      2  $35,000
 8   Alice      Hennetig      Counselor  Personnel  1  F      2  $32,000
 9   David      Jenkins       Sen Prog   DP         1  M      2  $35,000
10   Paul       Kaplan        Mngmt      Sales      1  M      1  $80,000
11   Cathy      Larson        Auditor    Finance    1  F      2  $32,000
12   Ed         Levine        Pres       Sales      4  M      1  $75,000
13   Bill       Mees          Mngmt      Finance    1  M      1  $90,000
14   Cindy      Revel         VP         Finance    3  F      2  $30,000
15   Elaine     Rubenstein    Trainer    Personnel  2  F      3  $27,000
16   Lisa       Salvetti      VP         Mrktg      2  F      2  $30,000
17   Janice     Schooler      Train Spec Finance    1  F      2  $38,000
18   Glenn      Tucker        Musician   Pub Rel    1  M      2  $25,000
19
20
```

Figure 9.6: New record inserted into database

more than $500 worth of merchandise last month. Or you might want the list of all purchases made in the first half of the month. For database inquiries of these kinds, use the Data Query command.

The Query command allows you to specify both the conditions under which to select a particular record and which information in the record to report about. If, for example, you have a large database (keeping track of names, phone numbers, addresses, purchases, amounts due and paid, and so forth), you will want to restrict queries to just the information needed. Query could return only the name and telephone number, for example, or only the amounts due and paid. Once the records have been selected, they are either brought to the cursor one by one for editing or deletion, or they are copied to a separate blank section of the spreadsheet (from which they can be edited and printed without affecting the values of the original database).

The sections that follow discuss using the Data Query command, specifying the criteria by which records should be selected, and specifying the area on the spreadsheet where a query report should be displayed.

AUTOMATING QUERY:
THE DATA QUERY COMMAND

Like the Data Sort command, the Data Query command starts
out by asking where the data range from which to select records is
located. The only difference is that the data range must also include
the row of labels (the field names) for the database. This tells
Query where the database starts and where to start searching for
information.

To use the Data Query command, you must create two special
areas on the spreadsheet—a criteria section and an output section.
In the criteria section, you specify the basis on which to evaluate
each record for inclusion in the selection. Each criterion is called a
condition. The condition specifies what to look for, such as "all
names that begin with A" or "all values less than 1000."

Lotus 1-2-3 creates a report of the selected records, copying them
to a region of the spreadsheet specified as the output section. The
output section is where the results of the query are displayed.

In the next section, you will see how to set up the Query command for each type of query.

USING THE DATA QUERY COMMAND

Figure 9.7 shows the three sections—database (A2..J18), criteria
(A21..J22), and output (A25..J25)—for the employee database.
(This first look at queries will assume that you want to output the
result to an empty area of the spreadsheet for printing, and so an
output section is included in all steps. When the query is for editing
or deletion, the output section need not be created.)

To begin a query, you create a range name (such as DATA-
BASE) for the range that begins with the first cell in the field name
row and ends at the last field of the last record. Then identify an
empty area of the spreadsheet (either below the database or to the
right of the last field of the database) where the criteria for
the query will be identified. Next, identify the criteria: copy the field
names that will be used to specify search conditions from the original
database to the criteria section. Because you will often use all of
the fields to search for information, you might want to copy the
entire field name row.

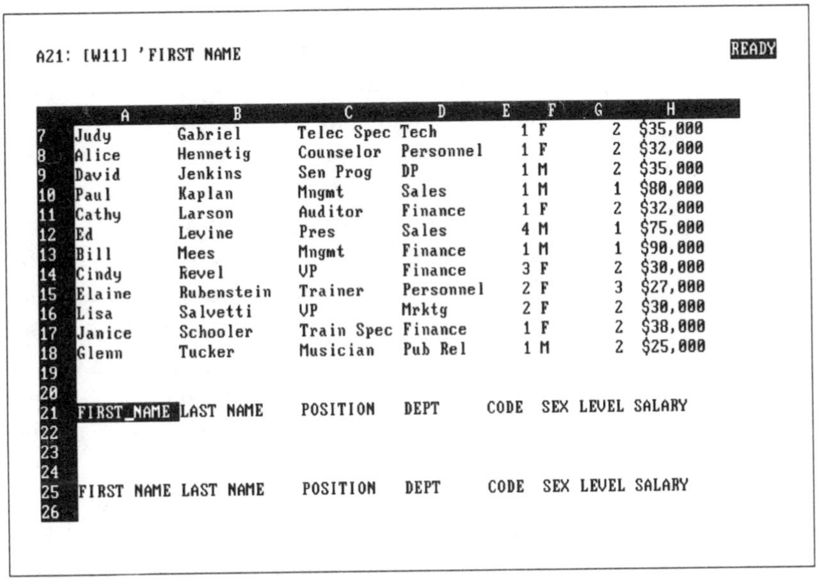

A21: [W11] 'FIRST NAME — READY

	A	B	C	D	E	F	G	H
7	Judy	Gabriel	Telec Spec	Tech	1	F	2	$35,000
8	Alice	Hennetig	Counselor	Personnel	1	F	2	$32,000
9	David	Jenkins	Sen Prog	DP	1	M	2	$35,000
10	Paul	Kaplan	Mngmt	Sales	1	M	1	$80,000
11	Cathy	Larson	Auditor	Finance	1	F	2	$32,000
12	Ed	Levine	Pres	Sales	4	M	1	$75,000
13	Bill	Mees	Mngmt	Finance	1	M	1	$90,000
14	Cindy	Revel	VP	Finance	3	F	2	$30,000
15	Elaine	Rubenstein	Trainer	Personnel	2	F	3	$27,000
16	Lisa	Salvetti	VP	Mrktg	2	F	2	$30,000
17	Janice	Schooler	Train Spec	Finance	1	F	2	$38,000
18	Glenn	Tucker	Musician	Pub Rel	1	M	2	$25,000
19								
20								
21	FIRST NAME	LAST NAME	POSITION	DEPT	CODE	SEX	LEVEL	SALARY
22								
23								
24								
25	FIRST NAME	LAST NAME	POSITION	DEPT	CODE	SEX	LEVEL	SALARY
26								

Figure 9.7: Database query ranges

Next, create the output section by copying the field names that will be displayed as a result of the search from the original database to another empty section of the spreadsheet, either below or to the right of the database. (Make sure the original database, the output section, and the criteria section don't overlap.) Here too the usual method is to copy the entire field name row to the output section, retrieving all of the information contained in the database for the records that are selected. Sometimes you will be sure that you want only a few fields for a particular query, such as name and phone number and not address. In that case, select only the desired fields.

Then create a range name for the criteria section called CRITERIA. It should include the row of copied field names and the blank row below it. This blank row will be used to enter the conditions used to select records.

You can define the final range, named OUTPUT, in two ways. First, you can specify an unlimited output section, wherein 1-2-3 will copy as many records as it finds that meet the conditions. To do this, just specify the range as the row of copied field names in the section you have designated for output. But beware: this alternative instructs 1-2-3 to retrieve as many records as meet the criteria. If there are cells below the output section that contain data you care about, they will be overwritten if the output of the query is large enough to reach them.

The second way is to limit the output section by naming the range that contains the row of field names and a fixed number of rows below it to which output can be copied. For example, you would specify 30 rows when you know the 31st row contains the beginning of another database or other data you want to preserve.

Unless the output section is designated as the bottom of the entire spreadsheet, with no data below it at all, it is better to use the limiting method. But when 1-2-3 queries the database and retrieves more records than will fit in the limited output range, you will receive the message "Range is full". To display all of the retrieved records, you will have to insert more rows in the output section. (Because the output section has a range name, it will automatically adjust to include any newly inserted rows.)

After all of the ranges have been named, select each of them, one at a time, by pressing the F3 (Name) key and selecting the proper range name for each range. When you save the spreadsheet file, the most recent settings are saved as well. And again, because the ranges are named, you need not redefine them after inserting or deleting records. The named ranges will expand or contract as the database size does.

The next sections explore the various conditions you can specify to search for records in the database.

Establishing Query Conditions

In the last section, the criteria section was described as consisting of the row of field names copied from the original database and the blank line below, where the actual conditions that the fields being evaluated must meet to be included in the query are specified.

You establish conditions merely by typing the criterion under the appropriate field name in the criteria section. For example, the criteria section below instructs 1-2-3 to select the record of every employee in the Finance department.

FIRST NAME	LAST NAME	POSITION	DEPT	CODE	SEX	LEVEL	SALARY
			Finance				

You cancel a condition by erasing the contents of the cell or cells containing the condition, using the Range Erase command. (Do not use the space bar/⏎ sequence here, because an apostrophe would be entered in each cell and become a condition that 1-2-3 would search for.)

The condition can specify that a field must match or partially match another label or value in the database or that it match or partially match a comparison of other values.

The following sections explore each of these alternatives.

Matching. When the condition is that a particular field value equal another value exactly, the condition is called a match.

For example, a query might ask for all employee records that match the criteria "work in Finance" by typing **Finance** under the label DEPT in the criteria section. Spell any label used to match records exactly as it appears in the database.

Another example of a value match is to ask for all records of employees who earn $25,000 by typing **25000** under the label SALARY in the criteria section.

These are simple matching conditions; they search for records that match exactly what you type. You can also require multiple matches, for example, all employees who work in Finance and earn $25,000 and are ethnic code 1, as shown below.

FIRST NAME	LAST NAME	POSITION	DEPT	CODE	SEX	LEVEL	SALARY
			Finance	1			25000

Partially matching. Partially matching compares part of a label or value with another label or value, using the special characters *, ? and ˜ to represent the parts of the values that 1-2-3 can ignore. For example, to retrieve all records for employees whose last names begin with A, type **A*** below LAST NAME in the criteria section. The A indicates starting with A, and the * is a *wildcard* symbol indicating *anything that follows*.

The wildcard symbol ? is used to stand for a single character to be ignored in the evaluation. Use a ? to mark each place before the real criteria portion of the value is reached. For example, in the code section you might not care about the first two digits of a three-digit code, as long as the last digit is 5. You would specify the criterion ??5, as shown below.

CODE

??5

The wildcard symbols can also be combined with other conditions. The example below causes the retrieval of all records in which the department begins with P and the salary equals exactly $25,000:

FIRST NAME LAST NAME POSITION DEPT CODE SEX LEVEL SALARY
                                      P*   25000

The ? character is useful when you aren't sure about the spelling of a certain condition, or when the spelling varies from record to record. For example, if you wanted to select all employees from Finance and you weren't sure whether the "F" is capitalized, you would enter the condition below.

DEPT

?inance

1-2-3 would select all records that contain either "Finance" or "finance" in the DEPT field.

The ˜ character, placed at the beginning of a label condition, indicates that all the values *except* those that follow it are to be selected. It is the equivalent of "not equal to."

For example, the following condition would result in the selection of all employee records *except* those who work in Personnel:

DEPT

˜Personnel

Comparing values. The most powerful form of conditional selection is comparing values. In the example database, most employees earn between $25,000 and $38,000. If you want to know how many employees earn more than $30,000, you can have 1-2-3 compare each record against the number 30000 and select the matching records.

Comparisons are formulas and, like any other spreadsheet formula, start with the + sign. The formula then names the cell in the first record of the database in the column of the field being compared as the place to start the query. For example, to obtain a list of all employees who earn more than $30,000, start by creating the formula that will evaluate the first record:

SALARY

+H3>30000

The value displayed as a result of this comparison is 0, since the first record in the example database is for Avila, who earns $27,000, which is less than $30,000 and thus does not meet the comparison criterion. The program is testing to see if the record is true, meaning that it matches the criterion, or false, meaning that it does not. Avila earns $27,000, which is less than $30,000, so the test is false. False results display as 0, and true results display as 1.

Most of the time, you will want to reformat this entire row so that formulas will display as text by using the Range Format Text command. Whenever a new formula is entered, the formula is displayed instead of the 1 or 0.

Hint: To remember what is in cell H3, you can create a range name that is identical to the field name. The same formula would read:

SALARY

+SALARY>30000

To create range names for each field quickly, use the Range Name Labels Down command in each column. The program will name the range (and therefore every cell in the range) as the name of the field in that column.

Now when you enter +**fieldname** in any formula in the criteria section, every cell with that name will be included in the evaluation.

You can enter multiple conditions that compare values such as SALARY > 30000 and SALARY < 35000, as shown below.

SALARY
+ SALARY>30000#AND#SALARY<35000

These conditions select from the database the list of employees who earn between $30,000 and $35,000. You can also use the other multiple conditional operators in 1-2-3—OR and NOT—in the criteria formulas. For more discussion of these operators, see the section "Logical @ Functions" in Chapter 4.

Multiple conditions. Even more complex multiple conditions can be created. Suppose you want a list of employees who work in Finance, DP, and Tech. You can extend the criteria section to include two more condition rows, as shown here.

DEPT

Finance

DP

Tech

Because you initially defined the criteria range as the row of field names and the single blank line below it, you need to tell 1-2-3 there are two more rows of conditions by extending the range name CRITERIA. To modify a range name, call it up by using the Range Name Create command and use the arrow keys to stretch or shrink the range. In this case, press ↓ twice and then press ←┘ to complete the command. The new criteria section now includes the three condition rows.

Hint: With Release 2, you can enter the same multiple condition entered on three rows above as a formula in the first row:

+ DEPT = "Finance"#OR#DEPT = "DP"#OR#DEPT = "Tech"

When the criteria section has been extended to include multiple rows and you then want to use a single row condition, remember to redefine the range name CRITERIA, contracting the range to the field name row and the line below it, or the Query command will continue to look for multiple conditons.

The 1-2-3 *Reference Manual* contains good material about matching, partially matching, and comparing criteria. For further experience, try the sample problem at the end of this section.

Once the the criteria have been established, the final step is to decide whether to copy selected records to the output section and print a report, edit the records, or delete the records by selecting either Extract, Find, or Delete from the menu, as discussed in the following sections.

Copying Selected Database Records with Query Extract

The Extract command copies the selected records to the output section. Before selecting Extract, make sure that the database, criteria, and output sections are set up and the conditions are specified. Then start the query process with the Data Query Extract Quit command.

Remember that if more records are selected than will fit in the output section, you will have to increase the output section's size.

When the query completes successfully and the selected records are displayed in the output section, you can obtain a printout of the output section by specifying it with the Print Printer Range command. You might create a range name for the output section called OUTPUT_RPT. The _ (underline) uses a blank space to separate OUTPUT from RPT in the range name.

The next section discusses using the Query Find command to edit records.

Editing Database Records with Query Find

In the old 1-2-3, you had to search through the database "manually" to edit records. For example, if you used the Data Query Find command to locate employees hired one year ago, 1-2-3 would deliver the proper records but would only allow you to review them, not edit them. You would still have to locate and edit the records manually in the original database after the query completed. Now 1-2-3's Data Query Find command will highlight the selected records one by one and allow you to change the value of any or all of their fields. A "found" record looks like Figure 9.8.

```
A3: [W11] 'Peter                                                    FIND

        A          B            C          D      E   F    G      H
1
2    FIRST NAME LAST NAME    POSITION    DEPT    ETHNIC        ANNUAL
                                                 CODE  SEX LEVEL SALARY
3    Peter      Avila        Jun Prog    DP        2   M    3    $27,000
4    Matthew    Bronson      Mngmt       Tech      3   M    1    $100,000
5    Mark       Bruno        Writer      R D       2   M    3    $28,000
6    Leon       Callinan     Counselor   Health    4   F    3    $29,000
7    Judy       Gabriel      Telec Spec  Tech      1   F    2    $35,000
8    Alice      Hennetig     Counselor   Personnel 1   F    2    $32,000
9    David      Jenkins      Sen Prog    DP        1   M    2    $35,000
10   Paul       Kaplan       Mngmt       Sales     1   M    1    $80,000
11   Cathy      Larson       Auditor     Finance   1   F    2    $32,000
12   Ed         Levine       Pres        Sales     4   M    1    $75,000
13   Bill       Mees         Mngmt       Finance   1   M    1    $90,000
14   Cindy      Revel        VP          Finance   3   F    2    $30,000
15   Elaine     Rubenstein   Trainer     Personnel 2   F    3    $27,000
16   Lisa       Salvetti     VP          Mrktg     2   F    2    $30,000
17   Janice     Schooler     Train Spec  Finance   1   F    2    $38,000
18   Glenn      Tucker       Musician    Pub Rel   1   M    2    $25,000
19
20
```

Figure 9.8: Record highlighed with Query Find

To use this command, first specify a condition in the criteria section. Then enter

    / D Q F

The program will highlight the first record in the database that meets the condition. To move to any of the fields in that record, press →; to move to the next selected record, press ↓. To free up the cursor and stop viewing found records, press ←⏎.

A similar procedure is used to delete selected records from the database. It is discussed in the following section.

Deleting Database Records with Query Delete

You will often want to delete certain records from the database. Just as in any query, you first specify a condition in the criteria section. For example, if you wish to delete a resigned employee's record, the condition you enter in the criteria section is the employee's last name.

Save your file before using the Data Query Delete command! If there is an error in the condition, 1-2-3 might delete records you didn't want to delete. You might even delete your entire database. If you save the file before using this command, you can retrieve any deleted data.

Once the file is saved, use the Data Query Delete command to delete the records matching the criteria specified. Once a record is deleted, you cannot recall it.

The next section discusses the most sophisticated query option, called Unique.

Displaying Unique Database Records

Suppose you want a list of all unique positions in the company database. You could sort by position, but in a large company there could be hundreds of records for many of the positions.

The Data Query Unique command reviews each record as it passes through the database, selecting only those records in which the field it is evaluating has a new, unique value.

You specify the field to be evaluated for unique values by modifying the output section so that it contains only that field's name. It is easier to accomplish this by constricting the range name than by erasing the other field names in the output section, because you may want to use those field names for other queries. To constrict the range name OUTPUT, use the Range Name Create command. You could also create a new range name called UNIQUE in another area of the spreadsheet and redefine the output range as UNIQUE.

If you plan to use the command only once, you can call up the Data Query Output range and type in one of the cells that has the same name as the field. Remember to type the field name exactly as it appears in the database.

For this example, the Output section for the Query Unique command looks like:

POSITION

Lotus 1-2-3 will copy all of the unique POSITION fields in the database to the area below the label POSITION. Be wary of using this command in an area that might contain information below the field name; such data will be overwritten when the Query Unique command is carried out.

Before using the command, erase the conditions in the criteria section using the Range Erase command. To use the command, type

/ D Q U Q

The following section introduces a shortcut to using the Data Query command menu.

REPEATING A QUERY WITH THE F7 (QUERY) KEY

Every query, whether Find, Delete, Extract, or Unique, requires a condition (or, in the case of Unique, the removal of any conditions that might be located in the criteria section). When you want to repeat the same queries using different conditions, you can simply change the condition in the criteria section and press the F7 (Query) key. When F7 is pressed, 1-2-3 automatically performs whichever query operation was last used on the new conditions specified.

In the sample problem that follows, you will perform four different Query Extract operations and use the F7 (Query) key to repeat the Query Extract.

SAMPLE PROBLEM: CREATING A REPORT USING QUERY

Problem: The personnel manager has requested four reports for an Equal Opportunity status report: a list of all female employees, a list of all minority employees, a list of all female or minority employees who earn less than $30,000, and a list of all female or minority employees who were hired after January 1, 1984. Use the Data Query Extract commmand to select the records and print the four reports. Ethnic codes of 2, 3, and 4 are used to distinguish minority employees.

Solution: Create the criteria and output section for the database. First, copy the field names to cells A21..J21 for the criteria section and to cells A25..J25 for the output section, using Figure 9.9 as a guide.

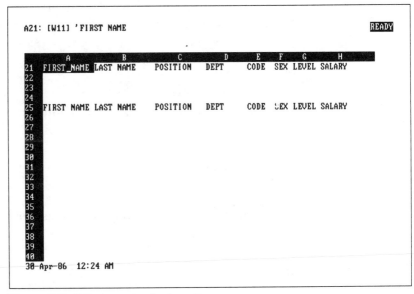

A21: [W11] 'FIRST NAME   READY

	A	B	C	D	E	F	G	H
21	FIRST_NAME LAST NAME		POSITION	DEPT	CODE	SEX	LEVEL	SALARY
22								
23								
24								
25	FIRST NAME LAST NAME		POSITION	DEPT	CODE	SEX	LEVEL	SALARY
26								

30-Apr-86 12:24 AM

Figure 9.9: Criteria and output sections

Now use the Range Name Create command to create three range names: DATABASE, CRITERIA and OUTPUT. Enter

/ R N C DATABASE ◄┘ A2.J18 ◄┘

Repeat this step for CRITERIA, substituting cells A21 to J22 as the range, and for OUTPUT, substituting cells A25 to J25 as the range.

Now name the fields for which conditions will be specified using the Range Labels Down command. Enter

/ R N L D A2.J2 ◄┘

Define the Query ranges database, criteria, and output by using the Data Query command. Enter

/ D Q I

Press F3 twice to call up the list of range names. Select DATA-BASE by highlighting its name; then press ⏎. Enter

C

and press F3 twice.

Select CRITERIA by highlighting its name; then press ⏎. Enter

O

and press F3 twice.

Select OUTPUT by highlighting its name; then press ⏎. Then enter

Q

to quit the Query command.

Start the first report by entering its first condition under the criteria field name SEX as **F** in cell F22.

Now extract the records for all female employees by using the Data Query Extract command. Enter

/ D Q E Q

Your first report should look like Figure 9.10. Because each of the four reports you will create will be displayed successively in the same output section, each report will overwrite the report that preceded it. To preserve a copy of the report, print it out using the Print commands below (assuming, of course, that you have a printer hooked up and on-line). Enter

/ P P R A25.J45 ⏎ A G Q

```
A26: [W11] 'Leon                                                    READY

        A           B           C          D       E    F    G     H
25  FIRST NAME LAST NAME    POSITION   DEPT     CODE SEX LEVEL SALARY
26  Leon  _     Callinan    Counselor  Health      4 F      3 $29,000
27  Judy        Gabriel     Telec Spec Tech        1 F      2 $35,000
28  Alice       Hennetig    Counselor  Personnel   1 F      2 $32,000
29  Cathy       Larson      Auditor    Finance     1 F      2 $32,000
30  Cindy       Revel       VP         Finance     3 F      2 $30,000
31  Elaine      Rubenstein  Trainer    Personnel   2 F      3 $27,000
32  Lisa        Salvetti    VP         Mrktg       2 F      2 $30,000
33  Janice      Schooler    Train Spec Finance     1 F      2 $38,000
34
35
36
37
38
39
40
41
42
43
44
```

Figure 9.10: First report for female employees

To prepare the second report requested, enter the condition in cell E22 for minorities as

$$+ CODE = 2\#OR\#CODE = 3\#OR\#CODE = 4$$

Notice the range name CODE is used instead of a cell location, which makes the formula much easier to read.

Because this report requires no evaluation of gender, erase the condition for SEX in cell F22 by using the Range Erase command.

Press the F7 key, and the Query Extract is repeated, this time using the new condition. The second report should look like Figure 9.11. Notice that the second report overwrites the first. If you had wanted to preserve both reports in the spreadsheet instead of on paper, you would have had to define a second output area for the second query.

For report 3, edit cell E22 to include at the end the condition **#OR#SEX = "F"**, to select female employees. Then, in cell H3

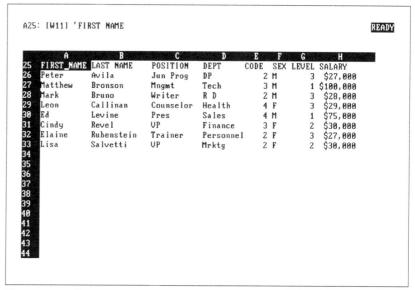

Figure 9.11: Second report for minority employees

under SALARY, enter the formula that will select employees who earn less than $30,000:

   +SALARY<30000

The criteria section should look like Figure 9.12.

Press the F7 key, and the Query Extract is repeated again, using the new condition. The third report should look like Figure 9.13.

The final report uses date arithmetic to select all female or minority employees who were hired after January 1, 1984, regardless of salary.

First, use the Range Erase command to erase the condition in cell H22 for SALARY. Then input the date formula in cell J22 as

   +DATE>@DATE(84,1,1)

Now press F7, and your report should look like Figure 9.14.

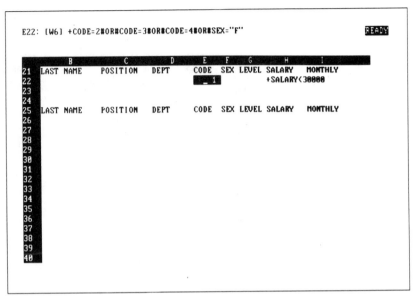

Figure 9.12: Criteria section for female or minority employees who earn less than $30,000

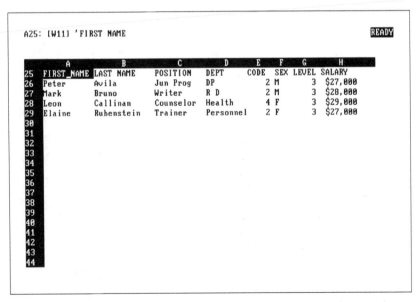

Figure 9.13: Third report for female and minority employees who earn less than $30,000

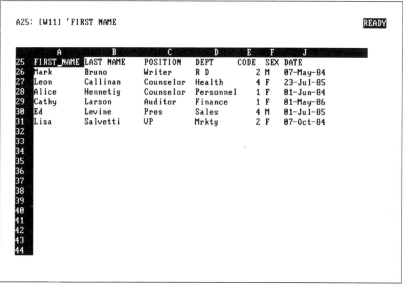

Figure 9.14: Fourth report for female or minority employees hired after January 1, 1984

In this section, you have learned to:

- Automate Query with Data Query command
- Use the Data Query command
- Establish query conditions
- Copy selected database records with Query Extract
- Edit database records with Query Find
- Delete database records with Query Delete
- Display unique database records
- Repeat a query with the F7 (Query) key
- Create a report using Query

Classifying Data Fields into Categories

There is a simple way to categorize values in a field and to determine the frequency of values in a list, called the frequency distribution of data values. Some popular uses for this command include counting and grouping results such as survey responses or student scores into measurement classes. Survey responses, for example, could be classified into "bins" that look like this:

Response	Frequency
1	28
2	18
3	26
4	46

This distribution indicates that 28 people responded with a 1, 18 responded with a 2, and so on.

Student scores could also be classified into bins:

Score	Frequency
60	2
70	10
80	7
90	5
100	3

This distribution indicates that 3 students scored between 90 and 100, 5 between 80 and 90, and so on.

Such distributions in databases could be manually tallied, which would be a tedious prospect at best. Fortunately, the Data Distribution command automates the process, as demonstrated in the following section and the sample problem that follows it.

AUTOMATING CLASSIFICATION: THE DATA DISTRIBUTION COMMAND

The Data Distribution command requires the location of the range to be classified and the location where the results should display, called the *bin range*. As with the Data Sort command, the range to be classified need not be part of a database, although it most often is a field from a database.

The bin range must be numeric and must be a column that has values arranged in ascending order from lowest to highest. In other words, you set up a column and enter each of the values you want to tally, from smallest value in the top row to lowest value in the bottom row. (For large distributions that are of even intervals, you might want to use the Data Fill command to generate the column. The command asks for the starting value, the interval, and the ending value; it then generates all the numbers in between.)

The results of the tally will be displayed to the right of the bin range column. Before executing the command, make sure there are no values in the column to the right of the bin range; they will be overwritten by the results of the command.

SAMPLE PROBLEM:
GROUPING SALARIES INTO CATEGORIES

Problem: You need to determine how many employees earn:

$$0 - \$25,000$$
$$\$25,001 - \$30,000$$
$$\$30,000 - \$35,000$$
$$\text{over } \$35,000$$

Use the Data Distribution command to determine this information.

Solution: First construct the salary bin range. In cells L3 through L6, enter the salary classes shown below:

```
0
25000
30000
35000
```

To compute the frequency distribution, enter

/ D D H3.H18 ↵

to designate cells H3 to H18 as the values range. Then enter

L3.L6 ↵

to designate cells L3 to L6 as the values range and complete the command.

Once the frequency has been calculated, your spreadsheet should look like Figure 9.15.

```
L1: [W13] 'SALARY DISTRIBUTION                                      READY

       F    G      H         I       J       K       L          M
1                ANNUAL            HIRE            SALARY_DISTRIBUTION
2      SEX LEVEL SALARY   MONTHLY  DATE
3      M     3   $27,000   2,250 28-Apr-79                  $0       0
4      M     1  $100,000   8,333 12-Nov-82               $25,000     1
5      M     3   $28,000   2,333 07-May-84               $30,000     6
6      F     3   $29,000   2,417 23-Jul-85               $35,000     4
7      F     2   $35,000   2,917 11-Dec-81     OVER                  5
8      F     2   $32,000   2,667 01-Jun-84
9      M     2   $35,000   2,917 15-Jun-83
10     M     1   $80,000   6,667 23-Dec-85
11     F     2   $32,000   2,667 01-May-86
12     M     1   $75,000   6,250 01-Jul-85
13     M     1   $90,000   7,500 23-Mar-85
14     F     2   $30,000   2,500 15-Mar-83
15     F     3   $27,000   2,250 15-Aug-82
16     F     2   $30,000   2,500 07-Oct-84
17     F     2   $38,000   3,167 01-Feb-82
18     M     2   $25,000   2,083 15-Jul-82
19
20
```

Figure 9.15: Completed salary frequency range

In this section, you have learned to:

- Automate classification with the Data Distribution command
- Group salaries into categories in the sample problem

Using Statistical Analysis with Databases

Databases often contain numeric values for which you might want averages, standard deviations, or any of the other statistical functions that 1-2-3 offers. Like the standard statistical functions, the database functions compute with a single instruction what might otherwise take several formulas to define.

Using these statistical functions you could, for example, determine how many employees are in a database, the average salary for employees, or the standard deviation of the salary for a particular department or the company as a whole.

The database statistical functions are particularly valuable in preparing more sophisticated statistical analyses, such as the analysis of variance discussed in Chapter 4 as well as other various regression and correlation tests. Several of the standard frequency tests can be performed with a combination of the frequency distribution commands introduced in the last section and the statistical functions presented here. Because the functions allow you to specify conditional groups of data (including evaluations based on formulas and logical operations), you can analyze subgroups without having to set up separate ranges for the different groups. This simplifies data entry because the initial order of the data does not matter; it also increases the number of tests you can perform.

AUTOMATING STATISTICAL ANALYSIS: DATABASE FUNCTIONS

You are probably already be familiar with the @SUM, @AVG, @MIN, @MAX, @VAR, @COUNT, and @STD functions from the spreadsheet examples in Chapter 4. These same statistics can be computed for a database using modified versions of these functions:

@DCOUNT	Gives the number of items in a list.
@DSUM	Sums the values of all the items in a list.
@DAVG	Computes the average or mean for a list.
@DMIN	Finds the minimum value in a list.
@DMAX	Finds the maximum value in a list.
@DSTD	Computes the standard deviation of a list.
@DVAR	Computes the variance of a list.

The detailed definition of these statistical functions is not presented in this section; each is the same as its parallel function discussed in Chapter 4.

The general form of these functions is:

@FUNC(*input range,offset,criteria range*)

The input range and criteria range are the same as those used in the Data Query command. The input range is the range where the database is located. The offset indicates which field to use in the computation of the function. It must be a value from 0 to 255, where 0 is the column of the first field, 1 is the value of the second field, and so on. The criteria range is where the conditions by which to evaluate records for inclusion in the function are located. If no conditions are specified, the function selects all the records.

Unlike the query commands, no output section need be specified for database statistical commands. The output is the cell where the function has been placed.

USING DATABASE FUNCTIONS

In specifying the three parameters of a statistical function (the database location, the offset, and the criteria location), it is again a good idea to use range names rather than cell locations. Just as with range names used to specify the database, using range names to specify the database and criteria locations in database functions allows the function to adjust automatically to include new records as the database grows. Also, it is simply easier to remember the word DATABASE than the beginning and ending cell locations.

The offset specified in the function will have to be manually edited when new fields are inserted in the database to the left of the offset field.

To perform a statistical function on a selected group of records, specify the condition in the same area of the criteria section as for a query command, using the same rules.

Suppose, to continue the personnel example used earlier in this chapter, you want to compute the average salary for all the records in the database. First, you would make sure that there are no conditions in the criteria range, so the entire database will be included. Then, in an empty cell, you would enter the function @AVG, the database range name, the offset for salary (in this case, 7) and the criteria range name:

@DAVG(DATABASE,7,CRITERIA)

Now suppose you want an average of the salary for female employees only. You have two choices. First, you can simply add the condition F to the original criteria range. The function will automatically recompute and report salaries for female employees only, overwriting the all-employee calculation and precluding comparison between the two results.

Your second choice is to create a second criteria range (by copying the first criteria range to another location). Give the second range a name, say CRITERIA2. Enter the condition **F** under SEX in the second criteria range. Then, in another empty cell, enter the function:

@DAVG(DATABASE,7,CRITERIA2)

Now you have the average salaries for the company as a whole in one cell and the average salaries for female employees only in another.

A more detailed example is examined in the following sample problem.

SAMPLE PROBLEM: COMPUTING SALARY STATISTICS

Problem: Suppose you want to compute salary statistics such as the total, mean (average), variance, maximum, minimum, and standard deviation for three groups: all employees, all male employees, and all female employees. Use the database functions to compute the statistics.

Solution: You should already have created a range name called DATABASE that refers to cells A3..J18 and another called CRITERIA that refers to cells A21..J22. If not, do so now.

Because SALARY is located in the seventh position to the right of the first field in the database, the offset is 7. Enter the equations for the statistics shown below in your database spreadsheet beginning in cell L11, and the labels beginning in cell M11.

@DSUM(DATABASE,7,CRITERIA)   TOTAL

@DAVG(DATABASE,7,CRITERIA)   MEAN

@DVAR(DATABASE,7,CRITERIA)   VARIANCE

@DMAX(DATABASE,7,CRITERIA)   MAXIMUM

@DMIN(DATABASE,7,CRITERIA)   MINIMUM

@DSTD(DATABASE,7,CRITERIA)   STD DEVIATION

Make sure the criteria section is blank, because this first calculation is for all employees. Format the cells in column L using Currency type and set the column width of column L to 13. Your results should look like Figure 9.16.

```
L9: [W13] 'SALARY STATISTICS - ALL EMPLOYEES                              READY

          H        I        J         K         L          M        N
 1  ANNUAL            HIRE                 SALARY DISTRIBUTION
 2  SALARY   MONTHLY  DATE
 3   $27,000  2,250 28-Apr-79                       $0        0
 4  $100,000  8,333 12-Nov-82                   $25,000       1
 5   $28,000  2,333 07-May-84                   $30,000       6
 6   $29,000  2,417 23-Jul-85                   $35,000       4
 7   $35,000  2,917 11-Dec-81      OVER                       5
 8   $32,000  2,667 01-Jun-84
 9   $35,000  2,917 15-Jun-83              SALARY_STATISTICS - ALL EMPLOYEES
10   $80,000  6,667 23-Dec-85
11   $32,000  2,667 01-May-86                  $713,000 TOTAL
12   $75,000  6,250 01-Jul-85                   $44,563 MEAN
13   $90,000  7,500 23-Mar-85              $612,621,094 VARIANCE
14   $30,000  2,500 15-Mar-83                  $100,000 MAXIMUM
15   $27,000  2,250 15-Aug-82                   $25,000 MINIMUM
16   $30,000  2,500 07-Oct-84                   $24,751 STD DEVIATION
17   $38,000  3,167 01-Feb-82
18   $25,000  2,083 15-Jul-82
19
20
                                                                          CAPS
```

Figure 9.16: Statistics for all employees

To compute the statistics for females, type an **F** in the criteria section under SEX and 1-2-3 will recalculate the results as shown in Figure 9.17. For males, type an **M** in the criteria section under the field name SEX. Results for males are shown in Figure 9.18.

Just as in the previous example, you could also have set up alternate criteria ranges for the male and female studies, and set up separate functions for each of the three evaluations. This choice is more

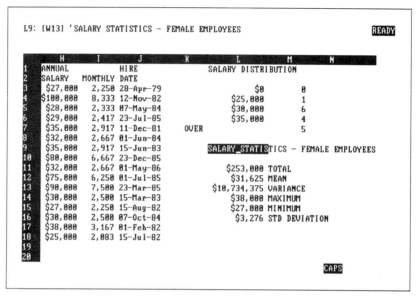

Figure 9.17: Statistics for all female employees

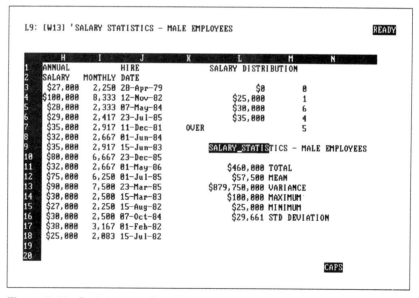

Figure 9.18: Statistics for all male employees

time consuming but does allow the results to be compared and permanently recorded. Another way to preserve the results of each test would be to print out the spreadsheet between each evaluation.

In this section, you have learned to:

- Automate statistical analysis with the database functions
- Use database @ functions
- Compute salary statistics in the sample problem

Using What-If Analysis with Databases

Using 1-2-3's table-building function (of the Data Table command) shown in Chapter 5 is one method of automating "what-if." With a spreadsheet, you use this function to build tables of conditions or values that are input into a formula one at a time.

In a database those conditions can be the already-entered values or labels in database fields. You can build a table of these conditions and substitute them one at a time into the criteria section. Then you can use statistical functions to compute totals or other statistics by categories for the database, expanding the number of conditions that can be evaluated in one report.

For example, you might want to build a table of salaries by department for your database. This table would look like:

Dept	*Total Salaries*
Finance	$150,000
Acctg	$210,000
Admin	$250,000

This function is useful when combined with a regular spreadsheet, referencing totals to compute other results for reports such as a budget, income statement, or payroll.

Accountants also find this feature powerful in summarizing debits or credits for a particular account. An accountant's table might look like:

	Accts Rec	*Accts Pay*
Debit	$20,000	$30,000
Credit	$30,000	$45,000

The database for this example would need an activity field, where you would enter a debit or credit; a type of account field, where you enter the code Accts Rec for Accounts Receivable and Accts Pay for Accounts Payable; and an amount field. The program could then search the database for all records in the each of the four categories and sum the amounts together. The result would then be displayed in the table above.

In summary, the Data Table command can be used with database fields to generate totals or other statistics by categories.

The next section shows how to construct a data table for a database.

AUTOMATING WHAT-IF ANALYSIS: DATABASE FUNCTIONS AND DATA TABLES

You can use the Data Table command to automate the "what-if" process through iteration and then use the database statistical functions to tell 1-2-3 to perform a statistical operation on a database field. The program takes the conditions in the table and substitutes them into the function one by one. To carry out this procedure, 1-2-3 requires the list of conditions to substitute, the function to use, and the area where the results are to be displayed.

This may seem confusing at first, because of the similarity of terms—data table, data command, data function, and so forth. If, as you read, you become confused, don't worry. The table command is simple to execute and obvious after a little practice. The sample problem at the end of this section will help clarify any remaining uncertainty.

All you do to create a data table with a database is to create a standard database criteria section, specify a database statistical function, and set up a table of conditions you want 1-2-3 to test for.

A one-input data table uses one list of conditions; a two-input table uses two lists of conditions. If there is only one list of conditions, the list must be a column and the @ function must be entered in the adjacent right column, one row above the first condition in the list. Again, an example will help clarify. Figure 9.19 shows a data table built for computing totals by department for the employee database.

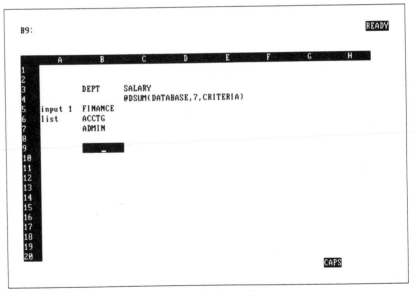

Figure 9.19: Database one-input table for totals

A two-input table lists one set of conditions by column and the other by row. The @ function is entered in the cell that is the intersection of the two lists. (See Figure 9.20.)

Hint: You could use the Data Query Unique command to extract the unique conditions that are substituted in the table.

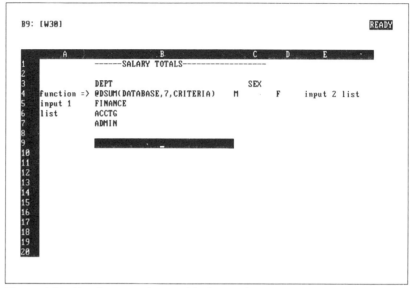

Figure 9.20: Database two-input table for totals

The Data Table command asks for the table area and the input 1 or input 2 cell. The table area consists of the rectangular or square area that is bounded by:

1. The list of inputs
2. The @ function
3. The area where the results should be stored

Input 1 refers to the field name used to derive the input 1 list. To identify this field name, you type the location of the blank cell beneath the field name in the criteria section. For example, if the list is of department names and the field name is DEPT, 1-2-3 requires that the input 1 cell address be the cell below DEPT in the criteria section. The input 2 cell address is identified in the same way—it is the blank cell below the field name in the criteria section that identifies input 2.

USING DATABASE @FUNCTIONS WITH DATA TABLES

The database functions are used in data tables to compute tables for databases. When 1-2-3 sees the @ function, it applies the requested function to the table, just as it applies functions in spreadsheets to ranges.

The values and rules 1-2-3 uses to compute these functions are the same as when they are used without a data table. You supply the database location, the offset position of the field the function is to be performed on, and the criteria section location (where any conditions needed to select records have been entered). The program then searches the database and computes values for the statistic for each input in the table.

SAMPLE PROBLEM: TOTALING SALARIES BY DEPARTMENT

Problem: Construct a table that summarizes salaries by department using the database functions and the Data Table command.

Solution: Enter the list of departments, using Figure 9.21 as a guide. Then enter the @DSUM function in cell M23, which the data table uses to compute the totals, as

@DSUM(DATABASE,7,CRITERIA)

Format cells M24 to M32 in Currency format.

Create a range name TABLE for cells L23 to M32 and INPUT1 for cell D22 by using the Range Name Create command. To create the one-input table, enter

/ D T 1

Press F3 twice to call up the range names. Move the cursor to TABLE to select it as the table location; then press ←. Press F3 twice and move the cursor to INPUT1 to select it as the input 1 cell. Press ← to complete the command.

Once the table has been calculated, your spreadsheet should look like Figure 9.22.

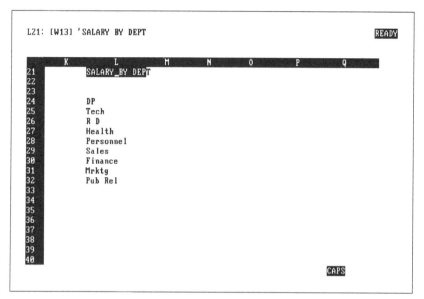

Figure 9.21: Salary data table list of departments

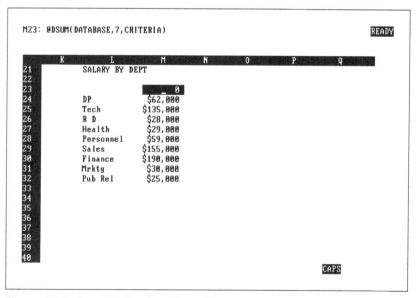

Figure 9.22: Completed salary data table

To verify the results of a data table, enter an @SUM function below the table that sums the salaries in cell M34. The sum of the departments should equal the @DSUM value 713,000.

Hint: You may want to clean up the database for printing by hiding the @DSUM function with the Hide format.

In this section, you have learned to:

- Automate what-if analysis with database @ functions and data tables
- Use database @ functions with data tables
- Compute total salaries by department in the sample problem

Summary

In this chapter, you have learned to sort a database by one or two keys. You have also learned to query a database to find, extract, edit, and delete records based on the criteria you specified. In addition, you have learned to produce analyses of the database as a whole.

The next chapter builds on the basic database skills developed here and introduces the advanced database functions for sharing data.

Chapter *10*

Data Sharing Techniques

In this chapter, you will learn to:

- Link 2 or more 1-2-3 databases
- Parse or break up data in 1-2-3
- Translate 1-2-3 files to and from dBASE II/III

Chapters 8 and 9 introduced techniques for building and accessing a database. Chapter 7 introduced methods for combining spreadsheets. This chapter discusses the methods for combining information in different spreadsheet databases. These are 1-2-3's most sophisticated integration facilities, allowing you to build and use a sophisticated data management system among all your databases.

Throughout this book, the importance of careful and good spreadsheet and database design has been emphasized. In combining databases, this kind of design foresight becomes essential. If you plan each database from a central design, and if your associates use the same design rules, the job of sharing and disseminating information will be much easier. Some of these rules might include establishing spreadsheet naming conventions, so that no two files will have the same name, even if they are created by different users on different computers, and naming spreadsheet files so that the purpose of each file will be obvious to all users from its name.

Similar naming conventions can be invented for column and row headings, range names, and field names in databases. Furthermore, if you and your associates agree to follow set standards for the ordering of fields in databases, for the format and column widths to use, and for the location of databases within a spreadsheet, you will enable yourselves to later create new joint applications from the work you have already done. Without these conventions, creating new databases and spreadsheets from old can become confusing and complicated.

The techniques discussed in this chapter are for data sharing among different databases, even databases created from programs other than 1-2-3. They include linking multiple 1-2-3 databases using @VLOOKUP, importing data from external files using the Data Parse command, and translating files to and from dBASE.

Linking 1-2-3 Databases

Looking up and transferring information from one 1-2-3 database to another is relatively simple. You use a key value in one database to look up the corresponding information in the other database. Once the key value is located in the second database, you can transfer all or part of the information associated with it to the original database.

Suppose the purpose of one database is to manage invoicing customer sales orders, and the purpose of a second is to keep track of customer credit information (such as name, address, phone number, credit history, and the like). You could set up the two databases to work independently by separately entering the information they need to use. In this case, the two databases have in common the need for names and addresses. Rather than enter the addresses twice, you can have the first database look up the address information stored in the second database, based on the customer name, using the @VLOOKUP function described in the following section.

In Chapter 4, @VLOOKUP was used to look up a key value from a list stored in a column, specifying the table location and the column position in the table where the information to be retrieved is located, called the offset. When you use this function with databases, the table becomes the location of the database. The list of key values is the first column in the database, and the offset is the distance the field that contains the information to transfer is located from the first field.

@VLOOKUP is entered in the cell to which the information is to be transferred. The *key value* is the value in this database that should be matched in the second database, the *offset* is the number of columns to the right of the found value in the second database where the desired information is located, and the *range* is the location of the second database. For example, see database 1 in Figure 10.1. There isn't room enough in the figure to display all of the @VLOOKUPs that are actually entered in the database. Instead, an example of a lookup for each field is displayed. In reality, the function is entered in every field where a lookup will take place and is then copied to each record. Lotus 1-2-3 looks up the address, city, state, and zip for each customer using NAME as an index in database 2 (cells L2 through P5, shown in Figure 10.2) based on CUSTOMER last names in column A of database 1. If you enter the @VLOOKUP function for each column once and then copy it to the remaining cells in that column, the results are shown in Figure 10.3.

This powerful combination of 1-2-3's database and spreadsheet functions is possible because of the new way the program treats text cells (see Chapter 12, "Using @ String Functions"). The number of databases that can be linked within a file is limited only by the amount of RAM memory installed in your computer.

In this section, you have learned to:

• Use @VLOOKUPs to link two databases

Translating External Files to Lotus 1-2-3

Often you will want to use data files that contain text and numbers created by other programs or by word processing programs with

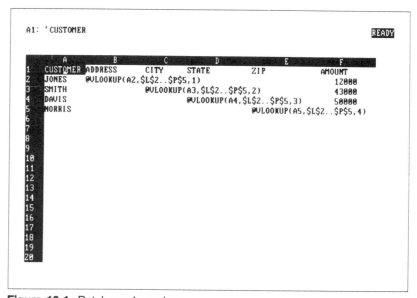

Figure 10.1: Database 1—orders

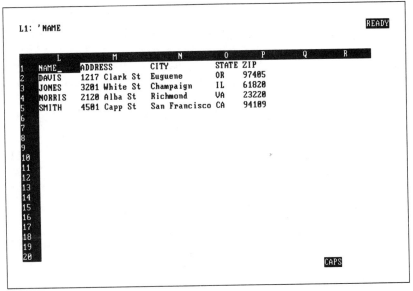

Figure 10.2: Database 2—addresses

L1: 'NAME   READY

	L	M	N	O	P
1	NAME_	ADDRESS	CITY	STATE	ZIP
2	DAVIS	1217 Clark St	Euguene	OR	97405
3	JONES	3201 White St	Champaign	IL	61820
4	NORRIS	2120 Alba St	Richmond	VA	23220
5	SMITH	4501 Capp St	San Francisco	CA	94109

CAPS

Figure 10.3: Resulting database

B2: [W15] @VLOOKUP(A2,$L$2..$P$5,1)   READY

	A	B	C	D	E	F
1	CUSTOMER	ADDRESS	CITY	STATE	ZIP	AMOUNT
2	JONES	3201 White St	Champaign	IL	61820	12,000
3	SMITH	4501 Capp St	San Francisco	CA	94109	43,000
4	DAVIS	1217 Clark St	Euguene	OR	97405	50,000
5	NORRIS	2120 Alba St	Richmond	VA	23220	72,000

1-2-3's database. If the other program stores the data in DIF format, use the Access Translate menu to translate this type of database file. If the file contains only numbers, you can use the File Import Numbers command to break the data into columns. If the file stores the text and numbers in ASCII format, you will want to translate the file to Lotus 1-2-3 by using the File Import Text command.

The File Import Text command enters the imported labels in the column where the cursor is located. They become cell entries only in that single column, even though the data appears to be separate columns of text and numbers. In order to use the imported data as a 1-2-3 database, it has to be broken into columns by using the Data Parse command.

USING THE DATA PARSE COMMAND

There are four steps to setting up the Data Parse command.

1. Create a format line that is used as a guide to divide the column of data.

2. Edit the format line for the type of data and length of data blocks.

3. Specify the column where the data is to be parsed on the spreadsheet.

4. Specify a range to store the parsed data on the spreadsheet.

To create a format line, position the cursor in the first row in the column that contains the imported data. Each cell's contents will be preceded with an apostrophe ('), visible in the control panel when the cursor is located in the cell. For example, an imported file will appear as long labels in column A of Figure 10.4.

You create a format line with the Data Parse Format-Line Create command. The format line controls the way this one long label will be divided into separate columns. Make sure the cursor is in the first row of data and in the imported column. The format line created automatically by 1-2-3 uses the blank spaces between the first row's numbers and text to guess where breaks in the data ought to

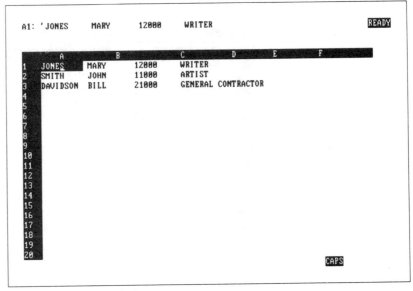

Figure 10.4: Imported data

go. Each separate block of data is identified as a label, value, date, or time with the symbol L, V, D, or T, respectively.

The format line is also a label; it is preceded by a split vertical bar. Additional symbols are used to specify information in a format line. S skips the character and > represents a continuation of the character. An * represents a blank space between the blocks. A format line created during parsing is shown in Figure 10.5.

Notice that this format line is based on the data below it. The first label entered in the first column will be last names, the second first names, the third numbers, and the last job descriptions. However, because 1-2-3 guesses the most likely format by looking at the first row only, it guessed the wrong width for the last column, which needs to be longer to allow for the last entry, GENERAL CONTRACTOR.

You can edit the format line to correct the type of data and column width by using the Format-Line Edit option. Move the cursor to the incorrect data type symbol and type the correct symbol

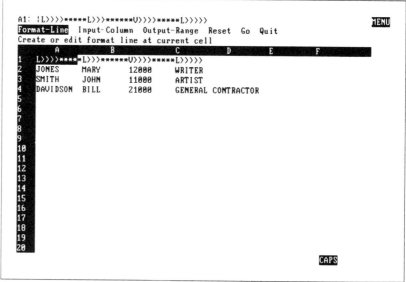

Figure 10.5: Format line

over it. To make the columns that will be created wider, insert spaces in the format line by pressing the Ins key and then typing the symbol for a space (>) as necessary. An edited version of the example format line is shown in Figure 10.6.

For more on using the Format-Line Edit option, refer to the 1-2-3 *Reference Manual,* page 163. You might need to insert an additional format line for a block of data that does not match the original data type.

The next step is to use the Data Parse Input-Column command to specify the format line and the entire column range that contains data to parse.

The final step is to use the Data Parse Output-Range command and specify the area of the spreadsheet to copy the parsed data to. Then select Go from the menu to tell 1-2-3 to process the data and parse it into columns. Make sure there is enough space in the area you specify as the output range for the data that will go there. Once the parsing is complete, delete the format lines with the Worksheet Delete Row command.

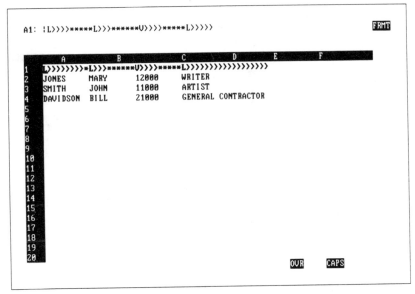

Figure 10.6: Edited format line

To adjust a column containing parsed data, use the Worksheet Column Set-Width command, as you would for any other column. The final result of our example is shown in Figure 10.7.

In this section, you have learned to:

- Use the Data Parse Command

Transferring Data to and from Other Database Products

Database programs like dBASE II and dBASE III use several files of related information and consequently are called *relational databases.* While 1-2-3 does have some facilities for sharing data between files, they are awkward for complex relational applications. To get around the problem, you can use other relational database programs like dBASE II and dBASE III to work with your 1-2-3 databases. You might also want to translate to dBASE II or dBASE III to increase the number of fields beyond 1-2-3's limit of 256. Because dBASE II is

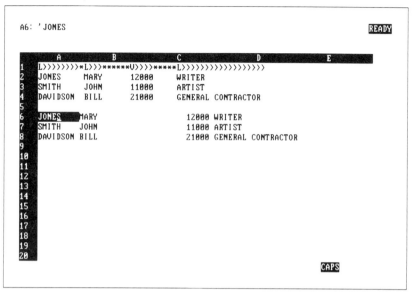

Figure 10.7: Completed parsed data

restricted to 64 fields, you would probably use dBASE III, which doesn't have the 64-field limit.

If you have a great many 1-2-3 database and dBASE files, you will want to systematize transferring them back and forth. You may want to keep a log of the files you create, including the creation date, last date revised, location (on floppies or on the hard disk) and what is done with the file each time it is used. If the contents of one file depend on another, you may also want to devise a checklist system so that you can manage the steps that must occur with one file before you use another.

The Translate utility is located on the 1-2-3 Access menu. It transfers files from 1-2-3 databases to dBASE II or dBASE III files and vice versa. The Translate option is discussed in detail at the end of Chapter 7. What is discussed here are the special concerns of translating files when databases are involved.

Most database program files have a special extension called .DBF and can be translated using the Access Translate to or from dBASE II/dBASE III option. There are a few twists and cautions to look out for when translating between 1-2-3 and dBASE II or III. After understanding and allowing for them, you will be ready to use the Translate option of the Access menu. The Access program is discussed in Chapter 7 in greater detail.

TRANSLATING 1-2-3 FILES TO dBASE

When two 1-2-3 files are to be linked with a database program like dBASE, it is essential that a key field is used in each 1-2-3 file to link the information they have in common. For example, if you have a 1-2-3 file that contains customer sales records and another 1-2-3 file that contains customer addresses, the key field each file must contain is customer name, and the customer names must match exactly for the link to work.

If your 1-2-3 database is a part of a spreadsheet that contains other information (like a spreadsheet or macros), or if your 1-2-3 database begins anywhere other than cell A1, you'll want to translate only the portion of the spreadsheet that actually contains the database. You extract to another file the portion of the spreadsheet you want to translate by using the File Extract command. This portion must include the field names at the top of the 1-2-3 database. The field names in the 1-2-3 database must match the field names in the dBASE II/III database. Follow the appropriate dBASE documentation to create proper field names in your dBASE database. The Lotus-to-dBASE II/III option first matches the field names and translates data until it reaches a blank row.

Before translating the file, make sure that your dBASE II/III field lengths are the same as the number of characters in the matching spreadsheet fields. For example, if the field CUSTOMER NAME in column A is 25 characters wide, the field CUSTOMER NAME in the dBASE file must be 25 characters wide as well.

The number of decimals in each numeric field in the dBASE file is determined by the format of the first cell in that field in the 1-2-3 file. For example, if the first cell under the column header SALE AMOUNT contained the number 100.25 and this cell uses General format, then the field SALE AMOUNT in dBASE would have two decimal places. If this cell contained the same number, 100.25, but was formatted to Fixed with zero decimal places and appeared in the cell as 100, the field SALE AMOUNT in the dBASE file would have zero decimal places. The value displayed in the 1-2-3 cell is the value used in dBASE.

Lotus 1-2-3 databases can contain dates stored as the number of days, which are used for calculations. The dBASE II/III programs do not store dates in this way, and 1-2-3 dates have to be converted from the Lotus form to the dBASE II/III form. The best way is to print the range of Lotus dates to a file so that the label is stored rather than the value. For example, if the date 1/1/86 is stored using @DATE(86,1,1), printing it to a special .PRN file using the Print File command will convert the value to the label

'1/1/86

Then you can copy the .PRN file with the column of date labels back to the column in the original 1-2-3 database by using the File Import command. (This command is explained in detail in Chapter 7.) Once translated to dBASE II/III, the date label can then be converted back into an arithmetic date by using dBASE II/III date-handling routines.

TRANSLATING dBASE FILES TO LOTUS

There are several restrictions on translating dBASE files into 1-2-3 files. Because dBASE II and III allow many more records than 1-2-3, be careful not to try to bring a dBASE file that is too large into 1-2-3. Instead, first split up the dBASE file into smaller files. Even then, you may find that the problems of managing the 1-2-3 database across several spreadsheets may be more trouble than it is worth. Although dBASE is a powerful database program, it is not as fast as 1-2-3 when it comes to sorting and finding individual records. The dBASE programs also lack 1-2-3's graphics and financial and mathematical functions. When you want these features, transferring dBASE files to 1-2-3 may be worthwhile.

One last caution: because the width of each field in a 1-2-3 database is determined by the width of the same field in the dBASE file, you may have to expand the column width of narrower fields before the full field name and contents will display in 1-2-3.

In this section, you have learned to:

- Translate Lotus 1-2-3 files to dBASE
- Translate dBASE to Lotus 1-2-3

Summary

In this chapter, you have examined the possibilities of using several personal computer packages to manipulate and manage files, moving back and forth among the programs as each offers the best solution to particular problems you encounter. Sharing a database between dBASE II/III and Lotus 1-2-3 was the example used here, but you are by no means limited to this example. If you want to work with a file using other database, spreadsheet, or word processing packages, you can probably do so using the general rules outlined in this chapter and the documentation of the other package you want to use. In general, if the package expects to receive a flat ASCII file and produces a flat ASCII file, you should have no problem sharing with Lotus 1-2-3. If the package will not work with and does not produce flat ASCII files, check its documentation for translation utilities.

The next chapter introduces how you can automate data entry and routine spreadsheet chores by setting up and using Lotus 1-2-3 macros.

Part IV

Macros and Advanced Commands

Chapter *11*

Macros

In this chapter, you will learn to:

- Create simple macros
- Plan the location of macros
- Debug macros
- Build a reusable macro library
- Build a menu step by step
- Make a macro automatic
- Automatically retrieve a file
- Distinguish between /X commands and Advanced Command Language equivalents
- Build simple ACL macros
- Combine ACL macros

Macros are probably 1-2-3's biggest work-saving feature. A macro is a special cell (or group of cells) containing text that represents a series of 1-2-3 commands. Using a macro, you can perform repetitive tasks that require dozens of keystrokes by pressing a single key in combination with the Alt key.

Although macros save time in the end, they do take time to learn, time to construct, and time to debug. The examples used in this chapter are proven time-savers. Even if you never construct a macro on your own, you can copy these macros into your spreadsheets and put them to work. Building on these macros and adapting them to your own work is the easiest bridge to inventing new ones of your own.

Many 1-2-3 users believe that you have to be a programmer to write sophisticated macros. This is not true. If you can perform a task using 1-2-3 commands, you can create a macro to do that task for you. But, at least in the beginning, your macros may not always do what you expect, so keep the backup copies of your spreadsheet current, and save often while testing your first macros.

Experienced 1-2-3 users will find the new 1-2-3 Command Language more flexible in performing complex tasks and programs. Advanced macros can transform a spreadsheet into a customized applications program complete with print options, update options that transfer information from other spreadsheet files, and data entry screens. Security features can be built into macros to protect novice users from accidents and prevent them from carrying out unauthorized procedures.

The best way to approach macros is to break down the overall job into the discrete steps the job requires. A collection of simple macros that work together is easier to design and test as well as more efficient than one long complex macro. Often the elementary macros can be used again and again in different applications.

1-2-3's new Advanced Command Language (ACL) uses special key words instead of abbreviated keystrokes to perform tasks. The 1-2-3 Reference Manual gives detailed examples for each ACL command. Rather than repeat that information here, the section "New ACL Commands" introduces the commands within sample macros in the combinations in which they are actually used.

One of the most useful macros is one that creates a menu for jobs that you do often in 1-2-3. This chapter, in the section "Building a Custom Menu," illustrates how to link simple macros using just such a custom menu.

Simple 1-2-3 Macros

A macro cell contains a label consisting of various text symbols that act as a shorthand notation for 1-2-3 commands normally typed at the keyboard. The macro cell is assigned a name using a character between A and Z. When you ask for the macro to be executed (by entering the macro's letter name and pressing the Alt key), the commands represented in the macro cell are automatically "typed" by the 1-2-3 program.

Use these six basic steps to design and build macros:

1. Decide what task you want 1-2-3 to do.

2. Map out the keystrokes that are required to perform the task manually.

3. Allocate an area (a cell or range) of the spreadsheet to store the keystrokes.

4. Enter the keystrokes in the cell (or range) exactly as you would type them manually.

5. Using the Range Name Labels Right command, assign a name to the macro cell or range that consists of a slash (\) and a character from A–Z.

6. Test the macro by holding down the Alt key and the assigned character; make any corrections that are neeeded.

For example, suppose you want to create a very simple macro that will save the current file. The macro would look like this:

'/FS ˜

First, you enter this macro in a cell exactly the way you would enter any other text label: by typing a label prefix followed by the characters in the label. The apostrophe keeps the / from calling up the menu as you enter the macro. You can also use a double quote (") or a caret (^) to begin a label, but you must use one of the three whenever the macro begins with a non-text character. This safeguards against the program's interpreting the characters as numbers or commands to be executed at once and allows them to be stored for later use.

The next four characters represent the command used to save a file. /FS is the abbreviation of / File Save and ˜ is used to signal <enter>, to represent the ⏎ you press after you select a file to save.

Using the six steps above, build this macro.

1. Determine the task: Save a file.

2. Specify the keystrokes:

'/FS ˜ ⏎

3. Select where to store the keystrokes: Cell B1.

4. In cell B1, enter the exact keystrokes specified in step 2:

'/FS ˜ ⏎

In cell A1, enter:

'\F ⏎

Note the apostrophe that must precede the menu keystroke.

5. Assign the macro task a name:

   / R N L R A1 ⏎

6. Test the macro: hold down the Alt key and press the F key.

Special symbols can be used to indicate keystrokes for nonalphabetic keys. For example, the above macro can be altered to include pressing the Home key:

   '{HOME}/FS ˜

This tells 1-2-3 to move the cursor to the Home position before saving the file. Table 11.1 shows the macro text symbols for the PC keyboard's nonalphabetic keys. In using these text symbols in macro-named cells, either upper- or lowercase letters are acceptable. Observe the use of the nonalphabetic symbols carefully, because many of the problems with macros that fail to work the first time can be traced back to errors with them (such as failing to distinguish between brackets and parentheses, or between the left and right apostrophes). Remember to include the Enter symbol (˜) in macro command sequences when it is required, and observe the unorthodox spelling of such symbols as PGUP and PGDN. The best way to write complex macros is to type out the keystrokes needed for the operation, making notes that can be later transcribed into the special symbols of macro text.

Non-Alphabetical Key	Macro Symbol
Alt-F1	{COMPOSE}
Alt-F2	{EDIT}
Alt-F3	{NAME}
Alt-F4	{ABS}
Alt-F5	{GOTO}
Alt-F6	{WINDOW}
Alt-F7	{QUERY}

Table 11.1: Macro Text Symbols for Special Keys

Non-alphabetical key	Macro Symbol
Alt-F8	{TABLE}
Alt-F9	{CALC}
Alt-F10	{GRAPH}
BACKSPACE	{BS}
ENTER	~
ESCAPE	{ESC}
HOME	{HOME}
END	{END}
PAGE UP	{PGUP}
PAGE DOWN	{PGDN}
DELETE	{DEL}
TAB	{BIGRIGHT}
SHIFT-TAB	{BIGLEFT}
↑	{UP}
↓	{DOWN}
→	{RIGHT}
←	{LEFT}
MENU (Command/Slash key)	'/

Table 11.1: Macro Text Symbols for Special Keys (continued)

PLANNING THE LOCATION OF MACROS

When Lotus 1-2-3 executes a macro, it interprets the symbolic text commands in the macro cell and proceeds to read down the column, cell by cell, looking for additional instructions until it reaches a blank cell, which stops the macro's execution.

Because macros are nothing more than text cells named with the backslash character and a letter from A to Z, they can be located anywhere on the spreadsheet. It is best to put them in a remote section of the spreadsheet, where they won't be accidentally overwritten.

Also take special care when deleting or adding rows and columns. A safe place to locate regularly used macros is in column A, either above or below the area in which most spreadsheet work is being performed.

You can further protect macro areas by using the Range Protect commands or by using Release 2's new Worksheet Column Hide command, which will "hide" columns from view, reducing the chances that someone will unintentionally overwrite macro cells while entering information.

If you locate a macro cell directly below another macro, both macros execute with a single keystroke. For example, say you add another macro that moves the cursor to cell A5 in cell B2 (remember, the File Save macro is in cell B1). This macro looks like:

{GOTO}A5 ˜

When you type Alt-F, 1-2-3 saves the file first and then executes the "GOTO" macro, moving the cursor to cell A5.

When you do not want macros to execute together, make sure you leave a blank row between the end of one macro and the beginning of another.

DEBUGGING MACROS

Mistakes are almost inevitable when creating macros. Fortunately, 1-2-3 has a convenient debugging tool that allows you to test macros in slow motion: the Step function key. Instead of executing instructions at full speed, the macro can be told to wait for you to press a key before it executes each step. By observing what is happening on the screen as your macro goes through its operation one step at a time, it is comparatively easy to isolate any problems that may be affecting performance.

To use the Step function key, hold the Alt key down and press the F2 function key. (Release 1A users may remember that the F1 key was the Step command.) A "STEP" indicator appears in the bottom part of the screen. To start a macro, press the Alt key and the macro's letter key. To advance to the next step, press the space bar. While you step through a macro, the "STEP" indicator is replaced by a flashing "SST" indicator. To cancel the Step function, press the Alt key and the F2 key again.

THE DATE-STAMP MACRO

Another simple macro can be used to date-stamp a spreadsheet file, making it easier to see when the spreadsheet was last updated with new information. Place this date stamp in cell C1, where it can readily be seen. Because the File Save macro is in cell B1, place this macro in cell B3, two cells below, so that the two macros won't execute together.

1. In cell B3, enter

'{home}{RIGHT 2}@NOW{edit}{calc} ˜ /RFD4 ˜

The symbols and commands in this macro do the following:

- Send the cursor to the "home" position (cell A1).
- Send the cursor two columns to the right (cell C1).
- Type the formula @NOW into that cell.
- Convert the formula @NOW into a number, by using the EDIT (F2) and CALC (F3) function keys.
- Enter the resulting value into cell C1.
- Format the date to MM/DD/YY Date format.

2. Assign the macro task a name. Enter

\D ⏎

into cell A3 and type

/ R N L R A3 ⏎

3. Test the macro by holding down the Alt key and pressing the D key.

The cursor now highlights cell C1, where the Date-Stamp macro has entered today's date.

AUTOMATING PRINTING WITH MACROS

Macros can be particularly effective for automating printing of multiple-page reports. For example, suppose you have a spreadsheet file consisting of three distinct spreadsheets, each of which must be printed on a separate page in the final report. Rather than manually define and print each spreadsheet separately, you can create range names for each page and enter a simple macro that will print all three pages with one Alt-P keystroke combination.

First, create the range names for each page. Move the cursor to the upper-left cell of the first page to be printed. Using the Range Name Create command, attach the name "PAGE 1" to the range of cells that include this spreadsheet. Assume that the spreadsheet PAGE 1 is the range A1 to F15, PAGE 2 is the range A16 to F30, and PAGE 3 is the range A31 to F45. Name the second spreadsheet "PAGE 2" and the third spreadsheet "PAGE 3".

Now enter the following text into cell B5:

'/pp

to select the Print command menu. Enter

ca

to clear any previous print settings. Enter

rPAGE 1 ~

to select PAGE 1 as the current print range. Enter

agp

to align the printer, print PAGE 1, and advance the paper to the top of the next page for printing. Enter

rPAGE 2 ~

to select PAGE 2 as the current print range. Enter

agp

to print PAGE 2 and advance the paper. Enter

rPAGE 3 ~

to select PAGE 3. Enter

agpq

to print PAGE 3, advance the paper, and quit printing.

Then assign the macro task a name. Enter

'\P ⏎

into cell A5 and type

/ R N L R A5 ⏎

To test the macro, hold down the Alt key and press P.

To use this macro, first prepare the printer so that it is online and the printer paper is lined up with the top of the form; then execute the macro. The macro now prints the three pages. You can modify the macro to print one page by deleting **rPAGE2˜** and **rPAGE3˜** from the macro. To add pages, just insert an additional **rPAGE** and **agp** into the macro. Make sure to create a range name for each page before testing the macro.

Because you will sometimes want to print one page only, and sometimes want to print all three pages, create a macro in cell B7 that as part of its execution asks you which page to print. Enter

'/pp ca r{Name} {Name} {?} ˜agpq

This selects the Print command menu, clears any previous print settings, lists range names on the screen, and then pauses for the user to select a range name. It then completes the selection, aligns the printer, prints the selected range, advances the paper to the top of the next page for printing, and quits the menu.

Then assign the macro task a name. Enter

'\L ⏎

into cell A7, and type

/ R N L R A7 ⏎

To test the macro, hold down the Alt key and the character L.

Note that this macro uses the {?} symbol to force a pause in execution until the range name has been selected. The macro resumes execution after ⏎ has been pressed.

CREATING HEADERS

Many spreadsheets are built to hold information for 12 months, which means that you often find yourself entering January through December as a header for each new spreadsheet. A macro can be created to do this for you. Because this macro will be used over and over again in new spreadsheets, you might want to store it in a spreadsheet of its own and call it into each new spreadsheet where it is needed. This section will show you how to create the macro; the next section will show how to store macros in a library such as that shown in Figure 11.1.

Enter the header macro shown in cells B9 to B12 of Figure 11.1 and assign it the name \H. The macro begins entering the label where you position the cursor, moves one column to the right, and enters the next label. When finished, the cursor returns to the first label.

BUILDING A REUSABLE MACRO LIBRARY

Once you have created several macros, you will find that some are going to be useful again and again, and you will want to build a macro library for them. A macro library is a 1-2-3 file that contains several macros, including the name associated with each macro. Figure 11.1 shows the file of macros you have created so far. These macros should be entered in column B, with their labels in column A, and saved in a separate file called something like LIBRARY.

To copy all of the macros to another spreadsheet, retrieve the spreadsheet you want the macros to be in and place the cursor where you want the library to appear. Then use the File Combine Copy Entire-File command to copy the macros to the spreadsheet from the file LIBRARY.

Once you have copied the library file into your new spreadsheet, the macros have to be renamed in the new spreadsheet, using the

```
C1: (D4) 31517.014919                                        READY

          A       B          C         D        E        F        G        H
1   \F         /FS~      04/15/86
2
3   \D         {home}{right 2}@NOW{edit}{calc}~/RFD4~
4
5   \P         /ppcarPAGE 1~agprPAGE 2~agprPAGE 3~agpq
6
7   \L         /ppcar{Name}{Name}{?}~appq
8
9   \H         JAN{RIGHT}"FEB{RIGHT}"MAR{RIGHT}"APR{RIGHT}
10             MAY{RIGHT}"JUN{RIGHT}"JUL{RIGHT}"AUG{RIGHT}
11             SEP{RIGHT}"OCT{RIGHT}"NOV{RIGHT}"DEC{RIGHT}
12             {END}{LEFT}
13
14
15
16
17
18
19
20
17-Apr-86   08:17 AM
```

Figure 11.1: Macro library

Range Name Labels Right command. For example, move the cursor to cell J1 in a blank spreadsheet. Enter

/ F C C E LIBRARY ↵

This designates LIBRARY as the file to copy from. Then enter

/ R N L R J1.J9 ↵

This designates the cells to receive range names and designates the cells that contain range name labels.

To repeat this command sequence in another file, you need only substitute **J1.J9** with the first cell where the macros begin and the 9th row below. For example, if your macros will begin in column AA, substitute **AA1.AA9** for this step.

You can retrieve individual macros from the LIBRARY file if you have assigned each macro a range name in the LIBRARY file. Then you can use the File Combine Copy Named/Specified-Range command to copy only the macro you want into a spreadsheet.

For example, the sequence below will copy only \P to the current worksheet in cell J1. Watch the prompts on screen as you enter this relatively complex sequence that copies the print macro to the current spreadsheet.

/ F C C N \P ↩ LIBRARY ↩ ← ′\P ↩ / R N L R ↩

the print macro to the current spreadsheet.

When ranges are combined into a worksheet, their cells are copied but not their range names. The second \P in the above sequence relabels this macro for the current spreadsheet.

In this section, you have learned to:

- Create simple macros
- Plan the location of macros
- Debug macros
- Date-stamp a file with a macro
- Automate printing with a macro
- Create headings with a macro
- Build a reusable macro library

Building a Custom Menu

Macros can also be used to create customized user menus, with which you can create sophisticated menu-driven applications for the 1-2-3 spreadsheet. The familiar 1-2-3 menu system (selected by pressing the command/slash key) can be reproduced through the use of the the macro symbol /XM.

Figure 11.2 shows a spreadsheet that incorporates macros similar to the ones previously created. However, rather than designate each macro with a separate name such as \F, \P, etc., these macros have been organized into a user menu system.

The user-defined menu feature of 1-2-3 macros is obviously a powerful tool. Used in conjunction with the 1-2-3 macro Command Language (more on that later) the 1-2-3 program becomes as versatile as a high-level programming language in generating applications.

A thriving market has developed for macro-driven templates of 1-2-3 spreadsheets for applications that include complex sequences of instructions. This market will continue to develop as a result of the flexibility and usefulness of 1-2-3's macro and menu capabilities.

The process of creating and using such a user-defined menu system can be broken into six steps:

1. Start the menu.

2. Create the menu options.

3. Add keystroke instructions.

4. Tell each option how to return to the menu.

5. End the menu.

6. Execute the menu.

The following sections illustrate these steps in building a custom menu.

STARTING THE MENU USING THE /XM COMMAND

In a cell, /XM or "execute menu" is the text symbol used for generating user-defined menus.

The /XM command has the form of /XM(menu range), where "menu range" is the upper-left cell of a range designed by the user as a selection of menu choices.

Using the Range Name Labels Right command and a character from A–Z, create a range name that will later be used to call up and start the macro. The cell location of the range name must be the cell with the /XM command.

For example, suppose you wanted to construct a menu beginning in cell B4 (Figure 11.3). You could enter the menu starter /XM in cell B1. The menu starter range could refer to a range name such as "MAINMENU" attached to it in this spreadsheet (Figure 11.4). This is a more efficient way to reference the beginning of the menu, because it allows the menu to be moved without editing the beginning cell location of the menu in the /XM command. The Range Name Labels Right command is used to name cell A4 MAINMENU and cell A1 \M.

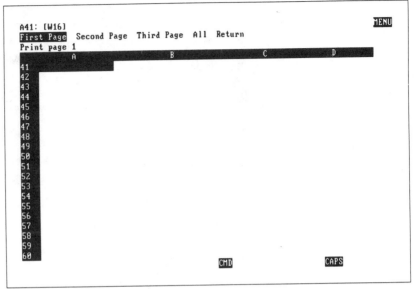

Figure 11.2: Macro Print menu

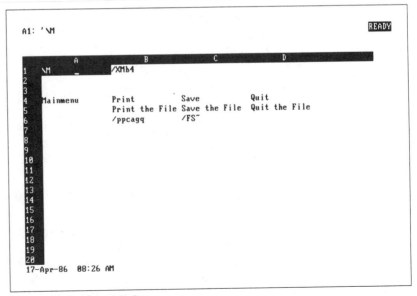

Figure 11.3: Menu starter

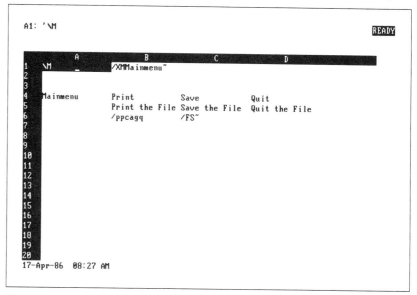

Figure 11.4: Range name menu starter

CREATING THE MENU OPTIONS

Menu options are simply cells that contain single words which describe commands (e.g., Save) followed by English messages (e.g., Save spreadsheet) and the symbolic macro text to match these instructions (e.g., /FS). The single-word options are arranged vertically in a row, one per column, and the brief message follows below, as in Figure 11.4.

Some planning is necessary to organize the horizontal menu choices. Make sure no two choices begin with the same letter, and limit the number of choices to eight for each menu.

To display the choices, press the Alt key and the M key simultaneously. Pressing Ctrl-Scroll Lock or Ctrl-Break will cancel the menu.

ADDING KEYSTROKE INSTRUCTIONS

Instructions can either follow below the message or be stored elsewhere on the spreadsheet as a subroutine. A *subroutine* is a complete set of instructions that the menu goes to, executes, and then returns from. The command to instruct a menu to go to a subroutine is /XC, the subroutine call command. The /XC command requires that you enter the location of the keystroke instructions that make up the subroutine.

For example, you can construct the previous menu using a subroutine call as shown in Figure 11.5. PRINT and SAVE are the range names for the subroutines in which the keystroke instructions are stored for printing and saving, respectively. They might, for example, be located in cells B8 and B10.

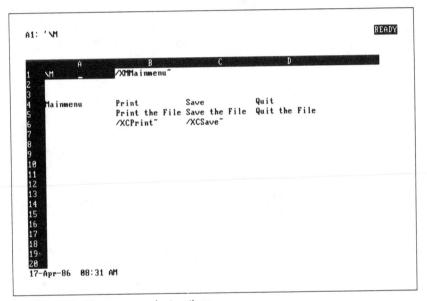

Figure 11.5: Macro menu instructions

To return to the menu from a subroutine, enter the /XR command after the keystroke instructions, as shown in Figure 11.6.

When keystroke instructions are long and use up a lot of space, it is better to use a subroutine. Also, the same subroutines are often repeated in a menu, and it is more efficient to enter only one set of instructions as a subroutine, rather than enter the same instructions over and over again.

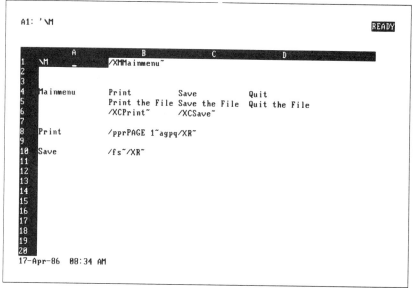

Figure 11.6: Print and Save subroutines

RETURNING FROM AN OPTION
TO THE MENU

Once a menu option has been chosen and performed, the user may choose another option from the menu. Lotus 1-2-3 must be told to offer the menu options again after it performs a task selected from the menu. The command for returning to the menu is /XG, the "go to" command. The /XG command must be told where the menu starter /XM entry is located. For example:

'/XGB1 ˜

This tells the "go to" command /XM that the menu starter is in cell B1. Because this menu starter also has a range name associated with it, you could enter:

'/XG\M ˜

The \M is the range name that has been assigned to call up the menu. The "go to" command must be entered at the end of each possible menu choice, so that the user will always be returned to the menu starter (see Figure 11.7). Use the Copy command to copy the command to each choice.

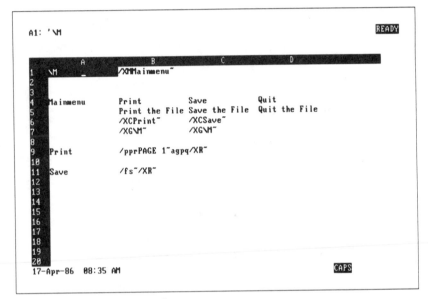

Figure 11.7: /XM command

You can create submenus by calling up another menu inside the first with the '/XM command, specifying the location of the first menu choice in the submenu.

ENDING THE MENU USING THE /XQ COMMAND

The final step in building the menu is ending it with the /XQ command, which is entered below the last menu option. Note in Figure 11.8 that the symbol ˜ for <enter> is used to complete this command.

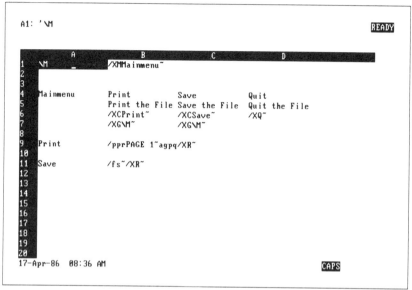

Figure 11.8: /XQ command

EXECUTING THE MENU

After you have built a macro menu, execute it by holding down the Alt key and pressing the key you have assigned to start the menu.

Observe the command line at the top of the screen. The single-word entries you entered in row 4 have become an active 1-2-3 menu! Move the cursor to the right and observe that the brief messages change along with the highlighted menu choices. Your user menu works in exactly the same way as the built-in command menus in the 1-2-3 program. When you make a selection by pressing ←┘ (or typing the first letter of a menu choice), the macro instructions entered in row 6 will execute, carrying out your command and returning you to the menu you have created.

SAMPLE PROBLEM: CREATING A MENU

Problem: Create a menu that will print three different sections of a spreadsheet.

Solution: Enter the spreadsheet in Figure 11.9 into a blank spreadsheet, using the rows and columns as a guide to entering text. For clarity, you may wish to set the column widths as follows:

Column	Suggested Width
A	10
B	16
C	25
D	16
E	16

Be sure to attach the names \M, MAINMENU, and PRINT-MENU to the cells A1, A8, and A15, respectively, by using the Range Name Labels Right command.

User menus can be linked, as was done with the "Print" selection in cell D8. Notice that this choice uses cell D10 below to call another menu (PRINTMENU) using the /XM command. This use of secondary menus is also analogous to the way 1-2-3's built-in command menus work. By carefully linking customized user menus, you can simplify the use of spreadsheets and make them accessible to others not familiar with the program's standard commands.

In this section, you have learned to:

- Start a custom menu
- Create menu options
- Call up routines from menu options
- End a custom menu
- Execute a menu
- Build a menu step by step

Making a Macro Automatic

Most macro cells are named with the alphabetic keys A–Z, but the numeral zero (0) can be used as a macro name as well. There

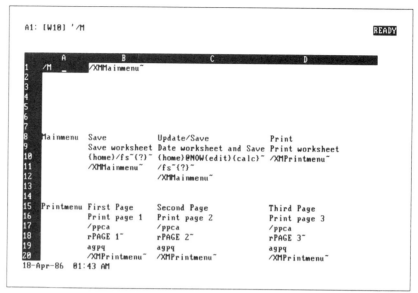

Figure 11.9: Macro worksheet

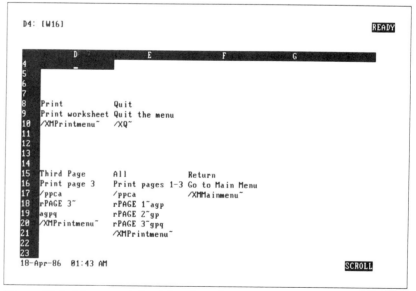

Figure 11.9: Macro worksheet (continued)

is one important distinction: a macro \0 is an automatic macro. That is, whenever you retrieve a spreadsheet file with a macro cell named \0, the commands in that macro will automatically begin to execute as the spreadsheet is loaded into memory.

You cannot manually invoke an automatic \0 macro by pressing the Alt and 0 (zero) keys together as you can with macros named with the alphabetic characters A–Z. For this reason, it is often convenient to attach an additional macro (using an alphabetic character) pointing to the automatic macro cell, so that you have the option of invoking the macro by its alternate name with the Alt key.

Automatic \0 macros are useful for date-stamping a file being retrieved for revision or for initiating user-defined menus in spreadsheets customized for special applications.

Automatically Retrieving a File

Any spreadsheet file with the name AUTO123 will automatically be retrieved into memory when 1-2-3 is loaded. This file must be located in the startup, or default, directory. A useful way to start a 1-2-3 work session automatically is to create a spreadsheet named AUTO123 that contains a \0 (automatic) macro that initiates some common startup task, such as processing a user menu. In this way, loading the 1-2-3 program causes AUTO123 to be retrieved; then the \0 macro goes to work, displaying a menu—all automatically.

For example, an AUTO123 spreadsheet can be constructed to prompt you automatically to choose a directory for retrieving files when 1-2-3 is loaded. Such a spreadsheet is shown in Figure 11.10. Name cell A1 \0 and cell A4 MENU by using the Range Name Labels Right command.

In the last sections, you have learned to:

- Make an automatic macro
- Automatically retrieve a file

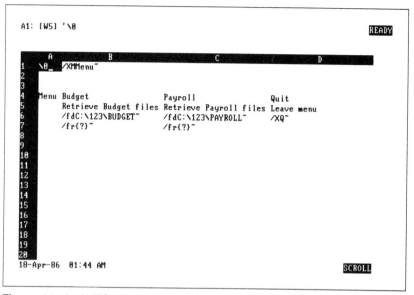

Figure 11.10: AUTO123 spreadsheet with AUTO \0 macro

Advanced Command Language Commands with /X Equivalents

The real power of macros in 1-2-3 goes beyond the high-speed "replay" of keystrokes discussed thus far. Lotus 1-2-3 includes a full-featured programming language, part of which has already been discussed in the creation of user menus. The /XM, /XC, /XR, /XG and /XQ commands used to create user menus are part of the Advanced Command Language (ACL) of 1-2-3, Release 2.

Table 11.2 lists the various macro programming commands available, for both Release 1A and Release 2. The * indicates /X commands that were previously discussed in building a menu.

Many of the Advanced Command Language commands in Release 2 have functional equivalents in the /X commands in both Release 1A and Release 2. This next section will focus on the new ACL commands that resemble /X commands. The new commands follow in the last section, "New ACL Commands."

Advanced Macro Command—Release 2	Release 1A,2 /X Equivalent	Description
*{MENUBRANCH location} {MENUBRANCH location}	/XMlocation ~	Process user menu
*{BRANCH location}	/XGlocation ~	Go to location; continue
*{actual routine name}	/XClocation ~	Call to subroutine
*{RETURN}	/XR	Return from subroutine
*{?}	{?}	Pause for number/text input
*{QUIT}	/XQ	Stop macro processing
{IF condition}	/XIcondition ~	Conditional IF-THEN
{GETNUMBER message, location}	/XNmessage ~ location ~	Prompt for numeric input
{GETLABEL message, location}	/XLmessage ~ location ~	Prompt for text input

Table 11.2: Macro Programming Commands

GETLABEL, GETNUMBER, AND IF

The GETLABEL and GETNUMBER commands are equivalent to the /XL text input and /XN number input commands of 1-2-3 Release 1A and Release 2. The GETLABEL and GETNUMBER commands execute faster than the /XL and /XN commands. You should note that the command syntax (i.e., the placement of punctuation symbols and arguments) is different for both GETLABEL and /XL and GETNUMBER and /XN versions of this command.

The GETLABEL Command

{GETLABEL *"prompt-message",location*} ~

Pause for text input, and store at 'location' cell.

/XL*"prompt-message",location* ~

The purpose of the GETLABEL command is to prompt the user to type in text at the 1-2-3 Control panel at the top of the screen.

Macro execution pauses as the "prompt-string" message appears in the Control panel. This message is most often a request for information, such as "Enter name of customer: ". When you type in a response and press ⬅, that response is stored as a label entry in the 'location' cell.

The GETNUMBER Command

{GETNUMBER *"prompt-message",location*} ˜

Pause for numeric input, and store at 'location' cell.

/XN *"prompt-message", location* ˜

The purpose of the GETNUMBER command is to prompt the user to type in a number at the 1-2-3 Control panel at the top of the screen, in response to the "prompt message". The main difference between the GETNUMBER and the GETLABEL commands is that input from a {GETNUMBER "prompt-string",location} macro statement will always be stored as a numeric entry at the 'location' cell, and the input from the GETLABEL command is stored as a label in the 'location' cell.

COMBINING GETNUMBER AND GETLABEL

The data entry macro shown in Figure 11.11 shows how the GETLABEL and GETNUMBER commands might be combined to create input prompts, store data in cells D1 to D5, copy the column to a row in a database that begins in row 10 by using the Range Transpose command, and then insert a new row between row 10 and row 9. Note that the symbols enclosing the getlabel and getnumber commands are surrounded by brackets { }, not by parentheses ( ).

Cell B1 is assigned the range name \N. To invoke the macro, type **Alt-N.** Lotus 1-2-3 will ask you to type a name in response to the prompt message. For example, you could type:

Smith, J.

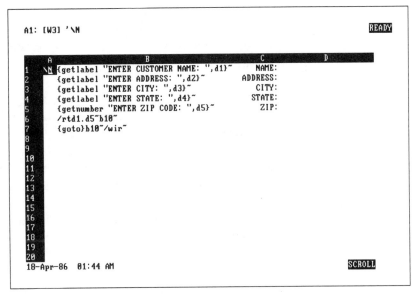

Figure 11.11: Data entry macro

This will be copied to cell D1, and a new prompt message will appear: "ENTER ADDRESS: ". By continuing to enter an address, a state, and a zip code in response to the prompt messages, you will automatically fill cells D1 to D4 with labels and D5 with a value.

When the data has been entered, it is copied and a new row is inserted. The macro will stop after inserting the row.

The IF Command

    {IF *condition*}

An "if/then" statement that tests for a TRUE or FALSE condition in the spreadsheet and then transfers control to another macro command, based on the result of the test.

    /XI *condition* ˜

An IF statement is used within a set of macro commands to direct program flow depending on whether the 'condition' argument is evaluated as TRUE (1) or FALSE (0). The condition argument can be expressed as a number, a string value, or the result of a calculation.

The data security spreadsheet in Figure 11.12 contains an automatic macro \0, which uses the BREAKOFF macro command to keep users from cancelling the macro and uses an IF statement to determine whether to allow a spreadsheet to be edited. The condition of the IF uses a calculation to determine whether the last file date in cell B1, named Last Update is within 15 days of the current date. If so, the macro does not allow the user to make changes and erases the spreadsheet using Worksheet Erase Yes. Cell B1 uses the function @date(86,2,3) to store the date as a number.

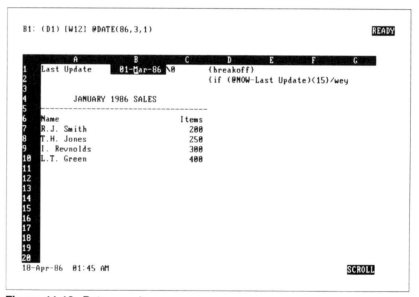

Figure 11.12: Data security macro

Each time that this spreadsheet is updated and saved, the current date needs to be entered in cell B1. Normally, once the sales figures for January are entered and the file is saved, no adjustment in the sales figures should be made. By using this macro, a manager in charge can confirm that no unauthorized adjustments had been made in the last 15 days, for example.

In this section, you have learned to:

- Distinguish between /X commands and Advanced Command Language equivalents
- Use GETLABEL, GETNUMBER, and IF
- Build simple ACL macros

New ACL Commands

Many new macro commands in Release 2 of 1-2-3 allow for keyboard interaction, controlling program flow, manipulating data, working with files, and controlling the screen.

Because macro commands are so interdependent, discussing them out of the context of their use is not very useful. The sections that follow divide the Advanced Command Language commands into five groups and briefly define them. Instead of giving an example of each command separately, the commands will be demonstrated and explained together in the problem at the end of the chapter. For detailed examples of each command, see the 1-2-3 Reference Manual.

ALLOWING KEYBOARD INTERACTION

New keyboard interaction macros allow you to make a macro pause during execution to enter data and perform other manual procedures. This list includes safeguards that keep users from interfering with a macro that is executing. GETLABEL, GETNUMBER, MENUBRANCH, MENUCALL, BREAKOFF, and {?} have been covered in the previous section "Advanced Command Language Commands with /X Equivalents."

{BREAKOFF}   Disables the Ctrl-Break key sequence to stop macro.

{BREAKON}	Enables the Ctrl-Break key sequence to stop macro.
{GET *location*}	Halts macro execution temporarily to store a single character in a location. It does not prompt the user to enter the information; instead, it retrieves information from a location. GET can be thought of as a "copy" command: it copies the contents of a cell to a location.
{LOOK *location*}	During a macro, checks to see if a certain character has been typed in a specified location.
{WAIT *time-serial number*}	Suspends macro execution for a specified time. You must use @TIME and @NOW to reference the internal clock with this command.

CONTROLLING THE SCREEN WITH COMMAND LANGUAGE

The following commands are used to change the appearance of the screen display and to sound the bell (beep tone). Many users become confused when they see the screen flashing or commands flying by on the status line during macro execution. This problem can be solved by using the commands below to hide the screen images.

{BEEP}	Sounds the computer's beep or tone.
{INDICATE *new indicator*}	Changes the indicator in the upper-right corner of the screen.
{PANELOFF}	Keeps the control panel (menus and messages) from being displayed.
{PANELON}	Restores the control panel.

{WINDOWSOFF}   Keeps the display from being redrawn with new information.

{WINDOWSON}   Restores standard screen redrawing.

CONTROLLING PROGRAM FLOW WITH COMMAND LANGUAGE

Several new commands are useful for controlling the flow of macro command language. Branching and looping are two common techniques used in programming languages that can be performed by these commands. (ROUTINE-NAME and RETURN are excluded from this list; they are covered in the previous section under /XC and /XR.)

{BRANCH *location*}   Continues executing macro instructions located in a different cell.

{DEFINE *location 1:type 1, location 2:type 2 . . . .*}   Specifies cells that store arguments in a subroutine call.

{DISPATCH *location*}   Branches indirectly to a specified destination.

{FOR   *counter-location, start-number,stop-number,- step-number,starting location of routine to repeat*}   Repeats a macro subroutine for a fixed number of iterations. Counter-location uses a range name referring to a single cell. Stop-number may be a range name that represents a fixed number input by the user with the GETNUMBER command.

{FORBREAK}   Cancels execution of {FOR} loop.

{ONERROR   *branch- location, <message- location>*}   Stops execution of current macro and continues execution at specified branch location if a 1-2-3 error occurs. The normal 1-2-3 error message may be copied to an area of the spreadsheet called message-location. This is an optional parameter.

{RESTART}

Continues to process the current subroutine steps that follow the command.

MANIPULATING DATA

The following commands are used to copy and store data in particular formats (as labels or numbers), to erase data, and to force recalculation of specified rows and columns during macro execution.

{BLANK *location to blank*}

Erases the contents of a specified cell or range.

{CONTENTS *destination-location, source-location, <width-number>, <format-number>*}

Places the contents of one cell in another cell as a label. The current column width and format of the source-location cell can be overidden with width- and format-number options.

{LET *location,number or string*}

Stores a label or number in a specified cell.

{PUT *location, col-number,row-number,number, or string*}

Copies a label or number located in one cell to a specified range where the first column is numbered 0 in that range.

{RECALC *location, <condition>,<iteration number>*}

Recalculates the formulas in a specified range, row by row. The condition and iteration number are optional. The condition tells 1-2-3 to recalculate until the value of that condition is FALSE. Iteration-number specifies the number of times to recalculate.

| {RECALCCOL *location,* <*condition*>, <*iteration-number*>} | Recalculates the formulas and functions in a specified range, column by column. Condition and iteration are used in the same manner as RECALC. |

WORKING WITH ASCII FILES

The following file-handling commands allow you to open and close files and to read and write data into those files. Note that the files should be ASCII-type files.

{OPEN *filename, R or W*}	Opens a specified file for reading, writing, or both.
{FILESIZE *location*}	Determines the number of bytes in the currently open file specified and displays the size in the specified location.
{SETPOS *file-position*}	Sets a new position for the file pointer in the currently open file at a character number. The first character is 0 in the file.
{READLN *location*}	Copies a line of characters from the currently open file into a specified cell location in the spreadsheet.
{READ *bytecount,- location*}	Reads a fixed number of characters (bytecount) from a file into the specified cell location.
{GETPOS *location*}	Determines the current position of the file pointer in an open file and puts the value in the specified cell location.
{WRITELN *string*}	Adds a carriage-return line-feed sequence to a string of characters and writes the string to the ASCII file.

{WRITE *string*}

Copies characters into an open file without a carriage return. This is used to write multiple strings to a line in the ASCII file.

{CLOSE}

Closes a file that was opened with the {OPEN} command. You need not specify the file name.

COMBINING GET AND IF

{GET *location*}

Pause for single-character input, and store at designated cell 'location'.

This command can be used in place of a user-defined macro menu when a conditional response to a prompt for user input involves only two or three choices. When a {GET} command is executing, a "CMD" indicator is displayed at the bottom of the screen. Pressing any key thereafter will cause the character value of that keystroke (such as A–Z, 0–9, etc.) to be placed into the location cell.

The single-character input for a {GET} command can be any alphabetic or numeric key. The {GET} command is not case dependent for text input, so m and M are treated as the same.

You can simplify the choice of saving and/or exiting a spreadsheet. Instead of using the standard File Save <filename> sequence, use the following exit macro \E that combines GET and IF:

Macro Commands	*Explanation*
{goto}A100 ˜	Move cursor to location A100
Save this Worksheet? (Y)es or (N)o	Present Y or N choice to user
{get ANSWER}	Put Y or N response in cell ANSWER
{if ANSWER = "y"} {branch SAVE}	Execute SAVE routine if ANSWER = Y
{if ANSWER = "n"} {branch QUIT}	Execute QUIT routine if ANSWER = N

{beep}{branch \E}	If ANSWER isn't Y or N, try again
ANSWER	(The {get} command puts a Y or N here)
SAVE /fsEXAMPLE ~	SAVE routine saves EXAMPLE.WKS
QUIT /wey	QUIT routine exits without saving

SAMPLE PROBLEM: CREATING A COMMAND LANGUAGE FILE TRANSFER MACRO

The following problem is used to demonstrate 1-2-3's ACL commands in a custom menu. The menu gives the user options to transfer monthly distributions for investors from another file, add new investors to the spreadsheet report, print the report, and save the new file. To understand this macro routine, you should be familiar with the concepts of combining files, inserting rows, printing, and saving. The example makes use of some functions for manipulating strings of text. Some of these string functions are available only in Release 2 of 1-2-3. For a detailed discussion of the structure and application of string functions, see Chapter 12. The completed menu and report are shown in Figure 11.13.

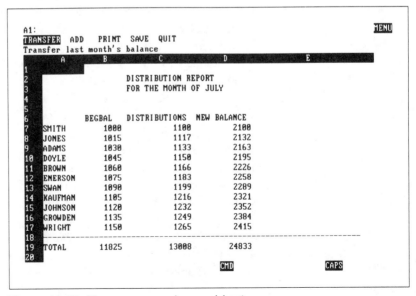

Figure 11.13: Macro menu and spreadsheet

Problem: Construct a menu that transfers the ending balance from a previous month's spreadsheet to the current month's beginning balance in a spreadsheet. The user will be asked to input the name of the previous month, which will be used to combine the proper file. If the file is not on disk, an error message is displayed informing the user to check that the correct disk is in the drive.

A second menu option allows the user to add new investors to the report. A new row is inserted into the spreadsheet, and the user inputs each new name. The macro then copies the ending balance formula automatically. The add option uses a looping macro to continue adding rows.

A third option prints the report, asking the user to input the current month name, which is automatically copied to a special heading on the report. This heading uses string arithmetic to display a heading that changes each time a new month is entered.

The fourth option saves the file either in a new file or by replacing the existing file. The user tells the macro if this is the first or second time the file has been saved. Depending on the result of this IF test, the option calls up one of two saving routines. If it is a first-time save, the user enters the current month again. If it is a second-time save, the current file is replaced automatically.

The final option quits the menu and restores the panel, screen display, and upper-right corner indicator to the normal 1-2-3 display.

Solution: Construct the main menu as shown in Figure 11.14. Then use the Range Name Labels Right command to specify range names for cells G1 to G6. The macro menu should appear on your screen when you press Alt-M.

The next section breaks down the four subroutines used to perform the transfer, add, print, and save functions. The first routine is called TRANS.

Enter TRANS in the spreadsheet using columns G and H (Figure 11.15). You need not enter the explanation for the macro to work, but documenting the macro will make it easier for you and other users to understand and debug.

The section shown in Figure 11.16 is used to store the error messages for the ONERROR command. The text displayed is copied from the OOPS routine to this area of the screen so the user can see the message clearly.

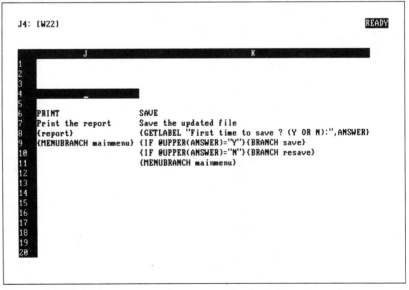

```
G4: [W9]                                                          READY

         G              H                          I
 1  \M          {MENUBRANCH mainmenu}
 2
 3
 4          _
 5
 6  MAINMENU TRANSFER                         ADD
 7           Transfer last month's balance  Add investor(s)
 8           {trans}                         {add}
 9           {MENUBRANCH mainmenu}           {MENUBRANCH mainmenu}
10
11
12
13
14
15
16
17
18
19
20
```

Figure 11.14: Main macro custom menu

```
J4: [W22]                                                        READY

          J                          K
 1
 2
 3
 4          _
 5
 6  PRINT                 SAVE
 7  Print the report      Save the updated file
 8  {report}              {GETLABEL "First time to save ? (Y OR N):",ANSWER}
 9  {MENUBRANCH mainmenu} {IF @UPPER(ANSWER)="Y"}{BRANCH save}
10                        {IF @UPPER(ANSWER)="N"}{BRANCH resave}
11                        {MENUBRANCH mainmenu}
12
13
14
15
16
17
18
19
20
```

Figure 11.14: Main macro custom menu (continued)

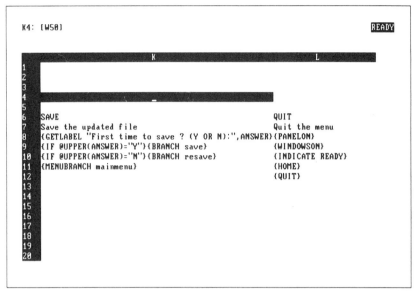

Figure 11.14: Main macro custom menu (continued)

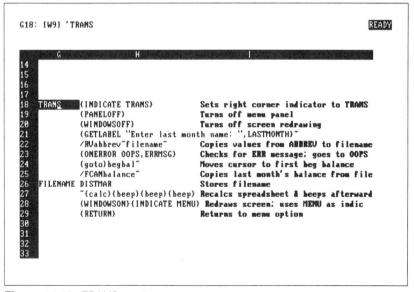

Figure 11.15: TRANS routine

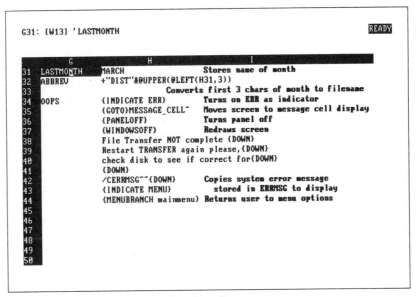

Figure 11.15: TRANS routine (continued)

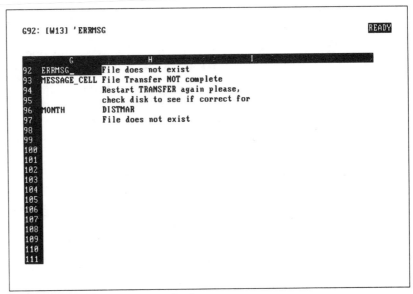

Figure 11.16: Error message display area

The next routine is ADD, which inserts rows for new investors into the spreadsheet (Figure 11.17). Note the position of the routine, cells N1 to O16. When you use the Worksheet Insert command in a FOR loop, you must position the routine in rows *above* the insert range. Otherwise, a minor glitch in 1-2-3 causes the loop to continue infinitely. The stop value NEWNUM must also be adjusted by subtracting 1 from the desired number of new investors or the routine inserts an extra row, perhaps because this is a subroutine call.

After the FOR loop stops, there is no need for {RETURN} because 1-2-3 will automatically go back to the main menu. If you insert a {RETURN} in the FOR loop, 1-2-3 will incorrectly return to the menu after each row is inserted.

You must use the Range Name Labels Right command to name the ranges ADD, INSERT, NEWNUM, COUNTER, and NEWNAME in cells N1 to N16 for the ADD routine.

The REPORT macro (Figure 11.18) subroutine asks the user to label the report with the current month before printing the report REPORT1. It also uses INDICATE and WINDOWSON for the same purpose as the above macros.

The two routines SAVE and RESAVE (Figure 11.19) are used to save the file. SAVE requires the user to enter the name of the current month and uses the string function @LEFT to create the file name. RESAVE uses a simple /FS ˜ R macro.

Use the Range Name Labels Right command to identify the range names in cells G18 to G96. Construct the spreadsheet using Figure 11.20 as a guide.

The formula for NEW BALANCE is +B7+C7. This must be copied to the rows below in column D. @SUM(B7.B18) is used to total BEGBAL, and is copied to DISTRIBUTIONS and NEW BALANCE. The heading cell in C3 uses the string formula:

+"FOR THE MONTH OF"&CURRENT MONTH

The final step is to create the range names BEGBAL, BOTTOM, FORMULA1, and BALANCE as shown in the figure

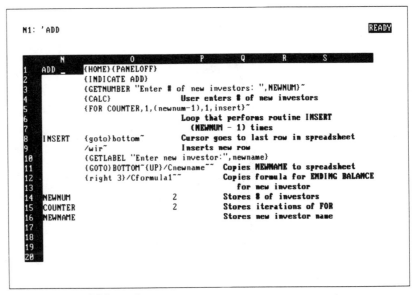

Figure 11.17: ADD routine

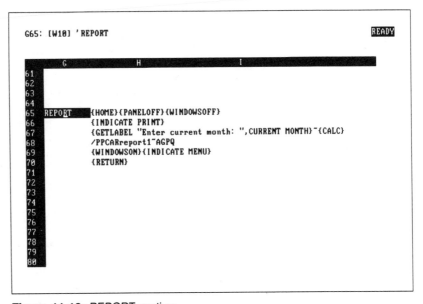

Figure 11.18: REPORT routine

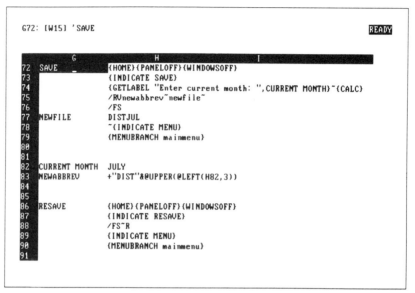

Figure 11.19: SAVE and RESAVE routines

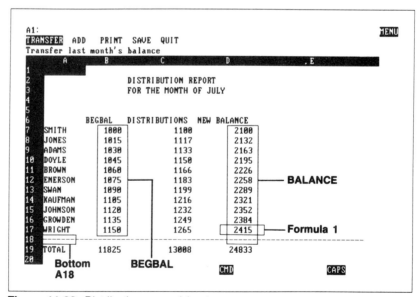

Figure 11.20: Distribution spreadsheet

by using the Range Name Create command. As a final check before testing the macro, create a Range Name Table in cell Y1. The table should appear as in Figure 11.21. Save the file using the name DISTJAN.

In this section, you have learned to:

- Control the screen
- Allow for keyboard interaction
- Control program flow
- Manipulate data
- Work with files
- Use GET with IF
- Combine Advanced Command Language macros

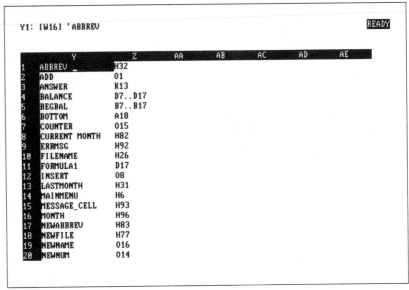

Figure 11.21: Range name table

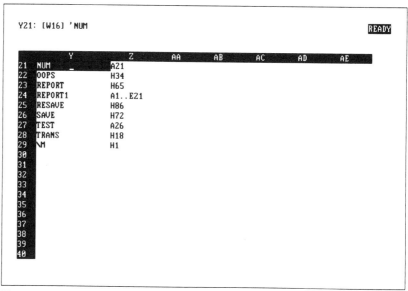

Figure 11.21: Range name table (continued)

Summary

In this chapter, you have seen how macros can be constructed that automate common 1-2-3 tasks. Taking the time to build up a good macro library pays off in the end, freeing you to manage your work instead of attending to troublesome and repetitive typing.

The next chapter introduces the new (with Release 2) string functions that manipulate alphanumeric text labels. These functions are especially useful for maintaining database records and converting data from one form to another.

Chapter 12

Using @ String Functions

In this chapter, you will learn to:

- Convert text to UPPER, lower, or Proper case
- Break down text with substring functions
- Change values to labels and vice versa
- Create special characters

Lotus 1-2-3 @ string functions perform many of the same operations on text that the program performs on numbers. Some of the string functions allow you to manipulate words and phrases in unique and interesting ways. Lotus 1-2-3's string functions are:

@UPPER	@EXACT
@LOWER	@REPEAT
@PROPER	@STRING
@LENGTH	@VALUE
@TRIM	@N
@CLEAN	@S
@LEFT	@ISSTRING
@RIGHT	@ISNUMBER
@MID	@CODE
@FIND	@CHAR
@REPLACE	

Among the operations you can perform on strings of text are:

- Changing case from upper to lower and back for consistency of records in a database: @UPPER, @LOWER, @PROPER
- Returning the length of a string for logical or formatting purposes: @LENGTH
- Stripping special characters and leading zeros from imported text: @TRIM and @CLEAN
- Returning parts of strings: @LEFT, @RIGHT, @MID, @FIND
- Replacing strings of text recurring in a database with other strings: @REPLACE

- Filling specified parts of a cell with repeating values: @REPEAT
- Converting values to labels and vice versa automatically, @STRING, @VALUE, @N, and @S
- Returning logical values (true, false, equals) for the existence of labels or values in particular cells: @EXACT, @ISSTRING, and @ISNUMBER
- Converting ASCII codes to Lotus LICS characters and vice versa: @CHAR and @CODE.

The chapter ends with a discussion of how to use the function keys and ASCII codes to produce characters not available on the keyboard, including the British pound sign (£), and French and Spanish accents.

Changing the Case of Text

Three functions—@UPPER, @LOWER, and @PROPER—can be used to change the case of all or part of the letters in a label. These functions are particularly useful when you want to transform a label into a standard form for comparison with items in a database.

The functions have no effect on numeric labels. If you enter

@UPPER("123")

the value of the function is the *label* 123. If you attempt to apply the same function to a number (not enclosed in quotes) the function returns ERR. For example, if cell A1 contains the number 10, the function @LOWER(A1) returns the ERR message.

@UPPER

@UPPER(*label or cell address*)

Example: @UPPER(A2)

@UPPER transforms all of the letters in a label into uppercase. The argument of a label function can be either a label enclosed in double quotes or a reference to a label cell. For example:

@UPPER("david norris")

The value of this function is the label DAVID NORRIS.

@LOWER

@LOWER(*label or cell address*)

Example: @LOWER(A2)

@LOWER is the opposite of the @UPPER function. @LOWER transforms all of the characters in a string into lowercase. For example:

@LOWER("DAVID NORRIS")

The value of this function is the label david norris.

@PROPER

@PROPER(*label or cell address*)

Example: @PROPER(A2)

@PROPER changes only the first letter in every word in a label into uppercase. For example:

@PROPER("david norris")

The value of this function is the label David Norris.

The @PROPER function works on most names, but there are exceptions that it can't handle: de la Cerna, McDougal, MacIntosh, and the like. These names would have to be edited by hand.

In this section, you have learned to use:

- @UPPER to convert lowercase text to UPPER case

- @LOWER to convert UPPERCASE text to lower case
- @PROPER to convert any case text to Proper case

Breaking Down Text with @ Substring Functions

Lotus 1-2-3 includes several functions that can be used to break a string down into smaller parts. You might, for example, want to set up a database for your records in a spreadsheet that stores first and last names in one column, while in the database you want the first and last names in separate fields. You might also want the data stripped of leading spaces, and if the file is imported from a word processing program, you may need to clean out special print control characters embedded in the text.

Lotus 1-2-3 now includes several new functions that allow you to operate on strings or portions of strings (called substrings) in these ways. These functions are:

@LENGTH	@MID
@TRIM	@FIND
@CLEAN	@REPLACE
@LEFT	@EXACT
@RIGHT	@REPEAT

@LENGTH

@LENGTH(*label or cell address*)

Example: @LENGTH(A2)

The simplest string function is @LENGTH. This function returns the length of the string named in the argument. As with the other string functions, the argument can be either a label enclosed in double quotes or a reference to a label cell. For example:

@LENGTH("War and Peace")

This function returns the value 13, the number of characters in the string. Just as with other string functions, if a cell containing a value is used as an argument of @LENGTH, an ERR message is returned.

@LENGTH can be very useful in testing labels to make sure they will fit in columns or fields they may be copied into. For example, suppose you want to write a macro that gets a set of labels from the keyboard and stores them in a database. The first field of the database is 15 characters wide, and you want to be sure that no label wider than 15 characters is entered in this field. Your macro could contain:

```
{GETLABEL Enter a Label:,INPUT}
{IF @LENGTH(INPUT)>15}{BRANCH AA1}~
```

The first line requests the user to enter a label and then stores that label in the cell that has been named INPUT. The second line tests the length of the string in INPUT; if the string is longer than 15 characters, the macro continues to process at cell AA1, which contains a message that requests the user to reenter the label.

@TRIM AND @CLEAN

```
@TRIM(string)
@CLEAN(string)
```

@TRIM and @CLEAN are two new 1-2-3 functions that let you remove unwanted characters from labels. @TRIM is designed to remove preceding and trailing spaces from a label. For example:

```
@TRIM(" first name ")
```

The result of this function is "first name". The leading and trailing spaces have been removed, but the space between the first and last name has not.

@TRIM can be used in a macro to compress imported text from a word processed file that produced leading left spaces. It can also be used to convert a label that has been accidentally entered with leading spaces, especially in databases whose sort order depends on the labels being left-aligned. For example, suppose cell A1 contains:

'First Name

The function @TRIM(A1) would return the left-justified label:

'First Name

@CLEAN is used to strip control codes from labels. (Control codes are ASCII codes below 32.) Word processing files imported into 1-2-3 with the File Import command often contain embedded control codes that enable and disable special printing features, like boldface and underline. Control codes are also sometimes included in text received from data communications packages.

@LEFT, @RIGHT, @MID

@RIGHT(*string,X*)
@LEFT(*string,X*)
@MID(*string,X,Y*)

Lotus 1-2-3 includes three functions that will extract a substring from a string. @LEFT allows the user to create a substring that consists of the leftmost characters in the string. @RIGHT returns a substring containing the rightmost characters in the string. @MID returns a substring from any part of the string, starting at a specified offset from the beginning of the string.

The argument X of the @LEFT and @RIGHT functions tells the function how many characters should be included in the substring. This argument must be greater than or equal to 0. If the X argument is equal to or greater than the total number of characters in the string, the entire string will be returned. For example:

Function:	*Result:*
@LEFT("Mr. David Norris",3)	"Mr."
@LEFT("Mr. David Norris",9)	"Mr. David"

Function:	*Result:*
@LEFT("Mr. David Norris",20)	"Mr. David Norris"
@RIGHT("Mr. David Norris",6)	"Norris"
@RIGHT("Mr. David Norris",12)	"David Norris"

@MID is slightly more complicated than @LEFT and @RIGHT. The X argument is the position of the first character to be included in the substring, and Y is the length of the string. The X and Y arguments in the @MID function should both be greater than or equal to 0.

An X argument of 0 instructs 1-2-3 to start in the leftmost column and makes the @MID function the functional equivalent of @LEFT.

If the X argument is greater than the length of the string (for example, if the instruction is to start in column 15 and the string only contains 12 characters), the function will return a blank.

A Y term of 0 causes the function to return 0 characters, also a blank. If the Y argument is greater than the total length of the string, the entire remainder will be returned. For example:

Function:	*Result:*
@MID("Mr. David Norris",4,5)	"David"
@MID("Mr. David Norris",0,3)	"Mr."
@MID("Mr. David Norris",4,0)	" " (blank)
@MID("Mr. David Norris",4,30)	"David Norris"

@RIGHT can be combined with @FIND and @LENGTH to do some surprisingly complex housekeeping, as described in the example at the end of the chapter.

@FIND

@FIND(*string 1,string 2,offset*)

@FIND is a new 1-2-3 function that is used to return the locations of a particular string in a longer string. The function finds

string 1 within string 2, beginning with the offset specified
for string 2. For example:

Function: *Result:*

@FIND("b","abcabcabc",0)   1

The function returns the value of 1, the first found location of "b"
in "abcabcabc". The count always begins at 0, so the "a" is
located in position 0 and "b" is in position 1.

The offset term is included to make it possible to find multiple
occurrences of a string within a longer string. For example:

Function: *Result:*

A1:@FIND("b","abcabcabc",0)   1 (location of 1st b)
A2:@FIND("b","abcabcabc",A1 + 1)   4 (location of 2nd b)
A3:@FIND("b","abcabcabc",A2 + 1)   7 (location of 2nd b)

Because the value of cell A1 is 1, the offset in A2 is A1 + 1 = 1
+ 1 = 2, and 1-2-3 starts the search for "b" at the second offset
position, which is the first occurrence of "c". The first "b" after
this is in the fourth offset from the start of the string, so the value
4 is returned.

Because the value of cell A2 is 4, the offset of cell A3 is A2 + 1
= 4 + 1 = 5, and the search for "b" starts at the second occurrence of "c", the fifth offset from the beginning of the string. The
first "b" after this is in the seventh offset position, so the value 7 is
returned.

When the string being searched for does not occur in the larger
string at all, the ERR message is returned.

This function is seldom used outside of sophisticated macro programming, where branches of the macro steps sometimes depend
on complicated evaluation conditions.

@REPLACE

@REPLACE(*string 1,offset,*X,*string 2*)

This function is the most complicated of the string functions. It allows you to substitute one string for a portion of another string. The function deletes X characters beginning at the offset in string 1 and substitutes string 2 into string 1 at the offset position. Note that the value is not returned in the original string 1 but is returned to the cell where the function is located. For example:

Function: *Result:*

@REPLACE("Lotus Symphony",6,8,"1-2-3")   "Lotus 1-2-3"

The function deleted 8 characters beginning with offset position 6 (the letter S) and replaced them with the string "1-2-3".

Suppose that column A were composed of text strings, and that some but not all of the strings were "Lotus Symphony". To replace "Lotus Symphony" with "Lotus 1-2-3" in the original column A cells, you would first place the @REPLACE function just used in the first cell of column B (assuming column B is empty.) Next, you would copy that function to the remaining cells in column B. If you then wanted to replace the string "Lotus 1-2-3" into the original cells in column A, you would set up a macro that evaluates each cell in column B and copies it to column A only if it is not equal to 0. Of course, the procedure is hardly worthwhile unless there are hundreds, perhaps thousands, of cells to be evaluated.

In the @REPLACE function, you cannot specify more characters for deletion than the number that exist between the offset starting point and the end of the string. If the number of characters to be deleted (the X argument) is 0, the function will insert the replacement string at the location specified by the offset. If the replacement string is blank (" "), the original string is merely deleted from the total string.

One of the most common uses of this function is to replace hyphens in dates with slashes, so that text dates can be converted to arithmetic dates with the functions @DATEVALUE and @TIMEVALUE, discussed in Chapter 4.

@*EXACT*

The @EXACT function compares two strings to determine if they match. If the two strings match exactly, the function returns the value TRUE; otherwise, the function returns the value FALSE. If one of the cells referred to by the @EXACT function contains a value instead of text, the function returns the ERR message.

@EXACT is usually used as a conditional test in a logical function. For example:

@EXACT("first name","first name")

Because this is true, an example @IF statement might be:

@IF(@EXACT("first name","first name"),"correct","incorrect")

If the strings match, print the message "correct"; otherwise, print the message "incorrect". @EXACT is similar to the the logical operator =. The difference is that @EXACT insists on an exact match between the two strings, while = can tolerate differences in case. For example:

Function:	*Result:*
@EXACT("First name","first name")	FALSE
"First name" = "first name"	TRUE

@REPEAT

@REPEAT(*string,X*)

@REPEAT duplicates a string within a single cell, where the argument X is the number of times you want the string to be repeated. For example:

Function:	*Result:*
@REPEAT(" ˜ * ˜ ",3)	" ˜ * ˜ ˜ * ˜ ˜ * ˜ "

This is similar to the repeating label prefix \. The difference between the two is that \ always repeats the label enough times to fill the column width exactly. @REPEAT repeats the label only as many times as you specify with the X argument.

COMBINING SUBSTRING FUNCTIONS

Lotus 1-2-3's string functions have a great deal of power. But you may not be sure about how to put that power to work for you. Following is a an example of the string functions @FIND and @RIGHT.

Problem: Suppose your database contains both client first and last names located together in one cell, like David Jenkins. You need to break out only the last name for each client so that the database can be sorted into last-name order. Assume client names begin in cell A2. Break the last name out in cell B2.

A2:'David Jenkins

Solution: Enter the function below that will extract the right-most characters from the string in cell A2, beginnning one character to the right of the space in the label in A2. The length of the string is found by the @LENGTH function. The location of the space is determined by the @FIND function. To find the number of characters from the right needed by the @RIGHT function, @FIND is subracted from @LENGTH. You also subtract 1 from @LENGTH because the @FIND function starts its count with 0, not 1. Enter the function below in cell B2.

@RIGHT(A2,@LENGTH(A2) – @FIND(" ",A2,0) – 1)

Remember the syntax of these functions:

@RIGHT(*string,X*)
@FIND(*string 1,string 2,offset*)
@LENGTH (*label or cell address*)

First, the @LENGTH function finds the length of the string A2:

@LENGTH(A2)

For the string "David Jenkins", the length is the value 13. The @FIND function looks in the string A2, starting in the first position, and counts forward until it finds the space:

@FIND(" ",A2,0)

For the string "David Jenkins", the result of the find is the value 5.

Then the @RIGHT function takes the 13, subtracts 5 and 1 from it, and counts to the seventh offset position from the right, the J. It returns everything in the string starting at the J to the end of the string:

@RIGHT(A2,13 – 5 – 1) =
@RIGHT(A2,7)

and "Jenkins" is the text returned by the function.

You could now copy this function to each cell in column B, extracting the last name for the remaining database records, and then sort the database on the last-name column you have just created.

Hint: One very useful application of the @ string functions FIND, LENGTH, and MID is to transform comma-delimited databases into 1-2-3 databases. First, use @LENGTH and @FIND to return the position of each comma; then use that position as the offset for @MID and use the position of the previous comma as the delimiter for the @MID function.

In this section, you have learned to:

- Return the @LENGTH of a string
- @TRIM leading and trailing spaces
- @CLEAN special characters from word processed files
- Return the @LEFT portion of a string
- Return the @RIGHT portion of a string
- Return the @MID portion of a string
- @FIND one string in another string
- @REPLACE one string with another in the function cell location

- Compare two strings and see if they match with @EXACT
- @REPEAT a string a given number of times in a cell
- Combine the substring functions @RIGHT, @FIND, and @LENGTH

Special Transforming @ Functions

@STRING(*value,number of decimal places*)
@VALUE(*numeric label*)
@N(*first cell.last cell of range*)
@S(*first cell.last cell of range*)

Lotus 1-2-3 includes four more functions—@STRING, @VALUE, @S, and @N—that perform special transforming operations on cells containing text or values.

@STRING

@STRING(*value,number of decimal places*)

Example: @STRING("123.45",1)

@STRING transforms a value into a numeric string. The argument for a string can be any value: a number, a function, or a formula. The second part of the argument specifies the number of decimal places to be included in the string. For example:

Function:	*Result:*
@STRING(500,0)	'500

Results of @STRING are not numbers and cannot be used in formulas. This function transforms the right-justified default for numbers to the left-justified default for labels.

This new function saves a great deal of time. In previous releases of 1-2-3, the label prefix in front of text numbers had to be manually edited out, one cell at a time, to transform values into labels.

When @STRING is used with functions, 1-2-3 returns the value of the function as a label, not a value or a function. For example, if the sum of cells A1 to A5 is 500:

Function: *Result:*
@STRING(@SUM(A1.A5),0)   '500

Note that the result is '500, not '@SUM(A1.A5) or the value 500.

@VALUE

@VALUE(*cell or "label"*)

@VALUE changes a numeric string into a value. In effect, @VALUE is the opposite of @STRING. This function is useful in transforming fraction labels ('12 5/8) such as stock prices into values for calculations. For example:

Function: *Result:*
@VALUE('4 1/2)   4.5

@N AND @S

@N(*range*)
@S(*range*)

The @N and @S functions return the value of the cell in the upper-left corner of a range. @S is used if the range contains labels; @N is used to return numeric values. They can both operate on a single cell, but the argument must always be in the form of a range.

One use of this function is to protect against the ERR messages that arise when you accidentally add two cells together, one containing a label and the other a value. For example:

+A1+A2

If A2 contains a label, an ERR message appears in this cell. To correct this, use the function:

+A1 + @N(A2)

@ISSTRING AND @ISNUMBER: TESTING FOR A LABEL OR VALUE

@ISSTRING(*cell*)
@ISNUMBER(*cell*)

The @ISSTRING and @ISNUMBER functions can be used to determine whether a cell contains a label or a value. Like @ISERR and @ISNA, these conditional functions are true if the cell being tested contains the sought entry type and false if the cell contains a different type of entry or is blank. For example:

@IF(@ISSTRING(A1),"label","value")

This function displays "label" if cell A1 contains a string or label; it displays "value" if cell A1 contains a value or blank.

@ISNUMBER is used to determine whether a cell contains a value. If a cell contains a value, the conditional function @ISNUMBER is true. If a cell contains a label or blank, then @ISNUMBER is false.

Just as with other logical evaluations, true is equal to 1 and false is equal to 0, which can be used to initialize macros and counters, and to count occasions of values in a statistical analysis where @COUNT proves inappropriate because it counts any non-blank cell.

Notice that although @ISSTRING and @ISNUMBER are nearly opposite, they both test false if the cell being tested is blank. Therefore, a false result from either does not mean that a cell contains a label or value.

These functions are most frequently used as conditional tests in conjuction with the 1-2-3 Command Language command {IF} and macros. For more on macros, see Chapter 11, "Macros."

In this section, you have learned to:

• Transform a value into a string with @STRING

- Transform a string into a value with @VALUE
- Return the value of the upper-left cell in the range with @N and @S
- Test for values and strings with @ISSTRING and @ISNUMBER

Creating Character Sets

Computers use a code to represent the numbers and letters you see on the screen. The most commonly used code in the world of personal computers is called ASCII, or American Standard for Character Information Interchange. ASCII assigns a code to every letter, numeral, and punctuation mark. For example, the letter a is represented by the ASCII code 97. The numeral 1 is represented by the code 49. The ASCII codes from 0 to 32 are used to represent special characters that do not appear on the screen, like Control-G (bell) and Escape. The standard ASCII character set uses the numbers between 0 and 127.

Although all computers use the ASCII codes from 0 to 127 in the same way, the codes between 127 and 256 (called the "upper 128" codes) are not standardized. Many computers use these codes to represent special graphics characters. In 1-2-3, these upper 128 codes are used to represent characters used in foreign alphabets and other special symbols, like the British pound sign. Lotus 1-2-3 calls these codes the LICS, or Lotus International Character Set. For a complete listing of LICS codes and characters, see pages 306 through 309 in the Lotus Reference Manual.

Lotus 1-2-3 includes two functions that can convert a character into its ASCII equivalent or an ASCII code into a character. The @CODE and @CHAR functions are most useful to users of the most advanced aspects of the 1-2-3 Command Language.

@CODE: CONVERTING CHARACTERS TO ASCII

@CODE(*string*)

This function returns the ASCII value of the first character in a string. For example:

Function:	*Result:*
@CODE("Mr.")	77
@CODE("The")	84
@CODE("Zebra")	90
@CODE("Apple")	65

@CHAR: DISPLAYING CHARACTERS

@CHAR(*value*)

@CHAR is used to convert a three-digit ASCII value into the Lotus character it represents. The value can be any number between 0 and 256. For example:

Function:	*Result:*
@CHAR(115)	s
@CHAR(74)	J
@CHAR(163)	British pound sign
@CHAR(162)	cent sign

COMPOSING KEYS TO REPRESENT INTERNATIONAL CHARACTERS

The F1 (Compose) key can be combined with a series of keystrokes to enter characters not available on the keyboard, like the British pound sign (£), the French accents grave (`) and acute (´), and the Spanish cedilla (ç).

Select the special character you want to enter and the sequence that represents it from the LICS appendix on pages 306–309 of the Lotus Reference Manual.

For example, the sequence for the British pound sign is L = or the ASCII code 163. You can enter the sequence in one of two ways:

- Press Alt and F1 (Compose) at the same time, and type **L =**
- Type **@CHAR(163)**

Either sequence will place the pound sign on your screen. The most cumbersome part of this sequence is that when you press Alt-F1, nothing appears to prompt you to enter the L = . It would be helpful if an indicator would light up at the bottom of the screen.

When special characters will be used frequently, you can use macros to call them up with Alt and a letter key. Suppose you use the Compose key to place a British pound sign in cell A1. Using the Range Name Labels Right command, name this cell \L. Then, wherever you want a pound sign to appear, press **Alt** and **L** simultaneously. Because there are 26 letters available to use as macros, the maximum number of special characters you can create in one spreadsheet is 26, assuming you enter no other macros in the file.

Hint: You can also use @CHAR to store a special character in a cell instead of using the Compose key. Then use a macro to name a key to call up the character.

Chapter 11, "Macros," explains more on how to create macros. For more on composing characters, refer to page 304 of the Lotus Reference Manual.

In this section, you have learned to:

- Convert characters to ASCII with @CODE
- Display characters with @CODE
- Compose keys to represent international characters

Summary

In this chapter, you have explored the use of Lotus 1-2-3 string functions. Most of the time, you will find that these functions are not particularly useful, especially standing alone, but in combination with other functions, they can sometimes be invaluable.

Release 2 of Lotus 1-2-3 can be used with a wide selection of printers, monitors, and computer models, including many that could not be used with Release 1A. Before you can use 1-2-3, you will have to run the Install program, where you will tell the program what kind of equipment you have. After you have installed 1-2-3, you will also need to change the default directory to drive B (for a floppy system) or drive C (for a hard disk system). This appendix contains instructions for these procedures; for more details, see your 1-2-3 *Getting Started* manual.

Install Checklist

When you use the Install program, you will need the following information about your equipment:

Computer Model: IBM, COMPAQ, AT&T, IBM 3270-PC
or certified compatible:_____
A minimum of 256K RAM memory: Yes   No
One or more floppy disk drives: Yes   No
Monitor type: Color, Monochrome, Single-Color
Graphics card type:_____
Text printer model(s):_____
Graphics printer model(s):_____

Once you have completed this checklist, use the lists of monitors and printers in the following sections to verify that your equipment will work or is supported by the Lotus 1-2-3 program. If you find that your equipment is not on the list, contact your dealer, who may be able to help you identify a monitor or printer that is on the list or that is sufficiently like yours to be interchangeable.

Determining How Much RAM You Need

If you have been using Version 1A of Lotus 1-2-3, you may only have 196K of RAM. You will need to buy at least another 60K to run Release 2.

To determine how much memory is installed in your computer, use the DOS command CHKDSK. At the A> prompt, enter **CHKDSK.** You will receive a message similar to that which appears in Figure A.1.

```
A>chkdsk

    362496 bytes total disk space
     22528 bytes in 2 hidden files
    144384 bytes in 30 user files
    195584 bytes available on disk

    524288 bytes total memory
    495136 bytes free


A>_
```

Figure A.1: DOS CHKDSK message

If you have 256,000 bytes of total memory, you have enough to run Lotus 1-2-3, Release 2. If not, you will need extra RAM.

While 256K is sufficient to run the 1-2-3 program, it is advisable to have more than the minimum RAM available. Extra RAM increases the size of the spreadsheets you can construct.

The maximum amount of RAM you can use with Lotus 1-2-3, Release 2 is 4 million bytes (4 MB), when you also have installed the Lotus/Intel expanded memory board. However, for most uses of 1-2-3, between 512K and 640K of RAM is adequate.

Monitor Checklist

There are several types of monitors available that will work with 1-2-3. Among those types there are several dozen models to choose from. You need to know both the type of monitor you have (color or monochrome) and whether your monitor has graphic capabilities before using the Lotus 1-2-3 Install program. Unfortunately, the only place in the 1-2-3 manuals and programs where you can get a list of the monitors that will work with 1-2-3 is in the Install program. In order to run the Install program, you must already have purchased both 1-2-3 and the monitor. The middle of the installation procedure is hardly the place to find out the monitor you just bought won't work.

The following section lists the types and models that will work with Lotus 1-2-3. If your monitor is not on this list, consult with Lotus technical support or an authorized Lotus dealer.

Lotus 1-2-3 does not require that you use either a monitor or printer with graphics capabilities. If your system doesn't support graphics, select equipment for text only.

COLOR MONITOR COMBINATIONS

Color monitors can display red, blue, green, and white characters, and can display graphics (circles, bar graphs, and the like). Some color monitors can display more colors than others, depending on the sophistication of the monitor and the adapter card installed in your computer. Below is a list of color monitor and adapter combinations that can be used with Lotus 1-2-3, Release 2:

Lotus supported color text/color card combinations (IBM PC unless otherwise stated)

Color monitor, IBM color graphics adapter card
Color monitor, Plantronics graphics card
Color monitor, Tecmar graphics adapter
IBM enhanced monitor, IBM enhanced graphics adapter
    card
COMPAQ, color monitor, IBM graphics adapter
AT&T 6330, color monitor, IBM graphics adapter
IBM 3270-PC, color monitor, IBM graphics adapter

Monochrome Monitor Combinations

Monochrome monitors are divided into two categories: those without graphics capabilities (called high-resolution text monitors) and those with graphics capabilities. Most monochrome monitors can handle graphics capabilities if you install a graphics adapter card in your computer.

Below is a list of monochrome monitor and adapter combinations that can be used with Lotus 1-2-3, Release 2 to produce monochrome text and single-color graphics.

Monochrome text/single-color graph combinations (IBM PC unless otherwise stated)

High-resolution monochrome monitor, Hercules card
Single-color monitor, graphics card
Single-color monitor, Tecmar GM adapter card
COMPAQ, single-color monitor, IBM graphics adapter
AT&T 6330, single-color monitor, IBM graphics adapter
IBM 3270-PC, single-color monitor, IBM graphics adapter
IBM Portable Computer

Printer Checklist

Lotus 1-2-3 distinguishes between two basic types of printers: text and graphics. When you install Lotus 1-2-3 you will indicate the printer model(s) you will be using. With Release 2, you can choose more than one printer model for text printers. This means that you can use one printer for draft copies (usually a parallel printer), and another for letter quality (usually a serial printer).

Release 2 allows you to move back and forth between the two printers using the Worksheet Global Default Printer Name command. See Chapter 7 for specific instructions about this command.

If your printer isn't on the following list, consult Lotus Technical Support or an authorized Lotus dealer, preferably the dealer from whom you bought 1-2-3. An experienced computer user or technician can custom install many printers that are not on the list.

(See the section on "Setting 1-2-3 Defaults" later in this appendix for more details on custom installations.)

TEXT PRINTER MODELS

Check the model(s) that you wish to install:

Anadex DP-9620A SilentScribe
C. Itoh Prowriter 8510A
Canon A-1210/ PJ 1080A Color Ink Jet Printer
DEC LA100
Diablo 630
Epson FX, RX series, JX series, LQ-1500, MX series
GE/Genicom 3000 B&W or color
HP 2225 ThinkJet series or 2930 series/ 2686A LaserJet
IBM Graphics Printer, Jet Printer, PC Color Printer,
    QuietWriter
IDS Prism 80, 132
Inforunner Riteman 280
Infoscribe 1200
MPI PrintMate 150
NEC 8023
Okidata Microline 82A, 83A, 84, 92, 93, Pacemark 2410
Printek 920
Printronix MVP 150B
Quadram Quadjet Color Printer
Qume Sprint 11/40
Star Micronics Gemini 10x/15x
TI 850,855
Toshiba P1350 Series
Transtar 315 Color Printer

There is also an Unlisted option, used to install a printer not listed above.

1. Complete capability
2. Forced Auto-LF
3. No BS
4. No BS, Forced Auto-LF

You can choose more than one graphics printer model and designate the model you are currently using with the PrintGraph Select Hardware command (see Chapter 7).

GRAPHICS PRINTER/PLOTTER MODELS

Check the model(s) that you wish to install:

Amdek II Plotter
Anadex DP-9620A SilentScribe
C. Itoh Prowriter 8510A
CalComp Model 84 Plotter
Canon A-1210/ PJ 1080A Color Ink Jet Printer
DEC LA100
Diablo C150
Epson FX, RX series, JX series, LQ-1500, MX series
GE/Genicom 3000 B&W or color
HP 2225 ThinkJet series or 2930 series/ 2686A LaserJet,
    7470A, 7475A, 7550A Plotters
IBM Graphics Printer, Jet Printer, PC Color Printer
IDS Prism 80, 132
Inforunner Riteman 280
Infoscribe 1200
MPI PrintMate 150
NEC 8023
Okidata Microline 82A, 83A, 84, 92, 93, Pacemark 2410
Printek 920
Printronix MVP 150B
Quadram Quadjet Color Printer
Star Micronics Gemini 10x/15x
TI 850,855
Toshiba P1350 Series
Transtar 315 Color Printer

Installing 1-2-3

You have now arrived at the point where you are ready to tell 1-2-3 what type of equipment you will be using. This is done in the

Install procedure, which must be carried out before you can run Lotus 1-2-3's spreadsheet, database, or graphics programs successfully.

Unless you buy new equipment, you will not need to use the Install program again.

The Install program simply asks you to type in the information on the checklist you just filled out. You should review the Lotus manual titled *Getting Started* before you install Lotus 1-2-3 on your computer.

INSTALLING 1-2-3 ON A FLOPPY SYSTEM

To prepare a floppy disk system:

1. Make backups of all Lotus 1-2-3 disks.
2. Format a data diskette to store 1-2-3 data files.
3. Copy the command.com file onto the 1-2-3 disks.

Because you are using a floppy system, it is possible for your disks to be damaged or lost. Make sure you have backup copies of all Lotus 1-2-3 disks—the 1-2-3 System disk, the Utility disk, the View of 1-2-3 disk, the Library disk, and the PrintGraph disk.

For step-by-step instructions on preparing a one-drive floppy system, read pages 4-8 of the 1-2-3 *Getting Started* manual. For a two-drive system, read pages 8-12.

To install the program, you will use the Utility disk. Have your Lotus disks ready, and remove any write-protect tabs for this Install procedure.

INSTALLING 1-2-3 ON A HARD DISK SYSTEM

To prepare a hard disk system:

1. Make the subdirectory where the Lotus 1-2-3 programs will be stored.
2. Make a subdirectory where the 1-2-3 data files will be stored.
3. Copy the Lotus 1-2-3 program files to the Lotus program directory.

If you are using a hard disk, you will need to make two sub-directories on it. One is used to store the data files and the other to store the Lotus 1-2-3 program. To make a subdirectory called data, where your actual spreadsheets will be stored, start your computer and at the DOS C> prompt enter

    md\data ◄┘

Using the same command, make a directory called 123. Then change the current directory to 123. Finally, copy all of the Lotus 1-2-3 disks into the subdirectory. You should keep the original floppies as backups in case your hard disk files are damaged.

For step-by-step instructions in preparing a hard disk system, read pages 12–13 in the 1-2-3 *Getting Started* manual.

Experienced 1-2-3 users will be relieved to learn that with Release 2, the Lotus floppy doesn't have to be in drive A to load the 1-2-3 program any more. The new COPYON utility program allows you to copy the key from the Lotus 1-2-3 System disk to your hard disk. Instructions for using the COPYON utility are presented later in this appendix.

To install 1-2-3 on a hard disk system, make sure you are looking at the directory you called 123. (To move to that directory, enter **cd \123**.)

STARTING THE INSTALL PROGRAM

With either system, to start the install program, just type

    INSTALL

You will be instructed by the program to select the monitor, text printer, and graphics printer you will use. Figure A.2 shows the Install menu.

For more details on using the Install program, read pages 15-27 in the 1-2-3 *Getting Started* manual. When you finish the procedure, the Install program saves this information either on your original Lotus disks or on the hard disk.

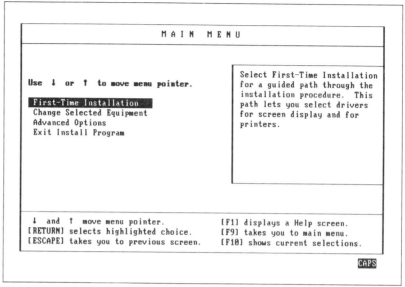

Figure A.2: The Install menu

INSTALLING 1-2-3 ON A SECOND COMPUTER SYSTEM

You can use Lotus 1-2-3 on more than one computer system— for example, if you have a COMPAQ portable as well as an IBM PC. To use Lotus 1-2-3 on both systems, you simply install an extra *driver set* (set of monitor and printer models) by repeating the Install procedure for the other computer system's monitor and printer types.

The Install program allows you to create a name for the second computer's driver set (such as COMPAQ for a COMPAQ computer, COLOR for a color system, or whatever is easiest for you to remember). The name must be eight characters or fewer and can't begin with a number. Your first installed driver set is called LOTUS by default. The install program saves this second driver set in a file on each of the Lotus disks with the name you specify.

To use Lotus 1-2-3 with this second driver set, type the name of the program and driver set you created. For example, if you called

the second driver set COMPAQ, you would type at the A>
prompt:

123 compaq

Lotus will look for the driver set called COMPAQ and use the
hardware you specified to display and print Lotus 1-2-3 spreadsheets, databases, and graphs. For more on saving driver sets, see
page 19 and page 25 in the 1-2-3 *Getting Started* manual.

USING THE COPYON PROGRAM FOR A HARD DISK SYSTEM

After installing Lotus 1-2-3 on your hard disk, you will want to
use the new COPYON program so that you won't need to put the
original System disk in the floppy drive every time you use the program. In your 1-2-3 documentation, there is a pamphlet called
"How to Start 1-2-3 Directly from a Hard Disk." It outlines the
COPYON, COPYOFF, COPYHARD, and COPYHARD/U
routines with which you copy the protected information from your
1-2-3 System disk to the hard disk of the IBM XT or IBM AT.
(Previously, 1-2-3 Release 1A users had to keep the original 1-2-3
system disk in drive A to load 1-2-3.)

However, do *not* use COPYON with the IBM AT. Use the
COPYHARD utility for the AT double-sided 360K drive, and
COPYHARD /U for the AT high-density drive.

WARNING: Some of the early shipments of Release 2 contain a
bug that makes it impossible to load other software programs after
exiting from 1-2-3 to the DOS prompt, once you have used one of
the COPYON utilities. The bug occurs only when you have not
saved the current worksheet and then select the System command
and attempt to load certain other software.

If you encounter this problem, reboot the computer after you
exit 1-2-3. Then try to load the software you want to run. If it still
will not load, turn the computer off, wait 15 seconds, and then turn
it back on.

Check the size of the 123.cmp file on your 1-2-3 system disk
with the DOS DIR command. If the size shown is not 133848

bytes, you should request replacement disks from Lotus. Write to Lotus at the following address with your request. Include your name, address, daytime phone number, and the letters and numbers on the bar code sticker located on the bottom of the 1-2-3 Release 2 package. Also include the serial number that appears on your screen when you load 1-2-3. The address is:

Customer Service, Department 2
Lotus Development Corporation
55 Cambridge Parkway
Cambridge, MA 02142

Starting Lotus 1-2-3

To start 1-2-3 after you have installed it, first load DOS into your computer system. Unfortunately, there is not enough space on the 1-2-3 System disk to store the file that will boot your computer. Every time you start your computer, you must load DOS from a second bootable floppy (which contains command.com and on which the SYS command has been performed). Store the second floppy near your 1-2-3 System disk, so that both are always handy.

After you boot the computer using the DOS disk, remove it and put in the 1-2-3 System disk. With the cursor at the A> prompt, type

    123

to enter the 1-2-3 program.

On a hard disk system, you need only change the subdirectory to 123, since your 1-2-3 System disk has already been copied to the hard disk. Start 1-2-3 by typing

    123

at the system prompt.

If you are using a hard disk system, you will probably want to set up an autoexec file that will bring you directly into 1-2-3 when you turn on the computer. Using either the DOS Edlin utility or your word processing software, create a file on the root directory (the \ directory). Call it autoexec.bat. If you already have an autoexec file, add the lines below to the end of it. (Several of the commands may already be in the file. Don't enter them again if they're already there.) Enter the following lines:

```
Date
Time
Prompt $P $G $C
Path c:\;c:\123;c:\DOS
cd\123
123
```

If you have a clock installed, you will want to enter the clock prompt (like "setclock") instead of the date and time prompts.

The Prompt $P $G $C command causes your computer to display the name of the directory you are currently working in at the system prompt. It is convenient, but not strictly necessary.

You will have to tailor the Path c:\;c:\123;c:\DOS command to fit your own system. Where DOS appears, put the name of the directory where your DOS files are stored. Also add the directory names where other software programs you use often are stored, so that you can access them from the 123 directory. After the word DOS (or the directory name), add a semicolon and the name of the directories.

The last lines, cd\123 and 123, cause your computer to go straight into the 1-2-3 program every time you boot the system. If you use other software often, you may want to omit this line.

For more help in starting your system, read pages 30-35 in the 1-2-3 *Getting Started* manual.

ENTERING THE 1-2-3 SPREADSHEET DIRECTLY

There are two ways to enter Lotus 1-2-3. You may directly enter the spreadsheet program by typing

123

at the A> or C> prompt. This saves an extra keystroke or two. The second way is to first enter the Lotus Access menu.

ENTERING THE LOTUS ACCESS MENU

At either the A> or C> prompt, type

lotus

This command brings up the Access menu. It contains the option that allows you to enter the spreadsheet as well as several other 1-2-3 programs. The Lotus Access menu appears as shown in Figure A.3.

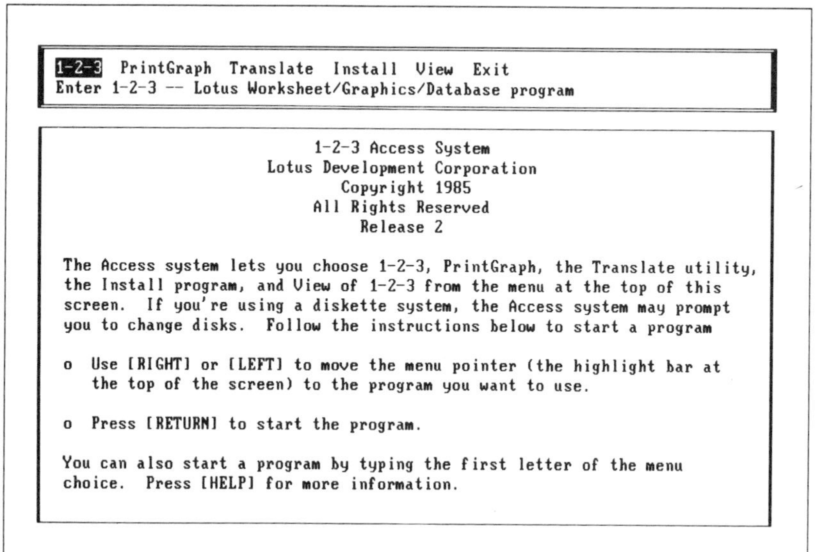

```
 1-2-3  PrintGraph  Translate  Install  View  Exit
 Enter 1-2-3 -- Lotus Worksheet/Graphics/Database program


                        1-2-3 Access System
                    Lotus Development Corporation
                          Copyright 1985
                         All Rights Reserved
                            Release 2

 The Access system lets you choose 1-2-3, PrintGraph, the Translate utility,
 the Install program, and View of 1-2-3 from the menu at the top of this
 screen.  If you're using a diskette system, the Access system may prompt
 you to change disks.  Follow the instructions below to start a program

 o  Use [RIGHT] or [LEFT] to move the menu pointer (the highlight bar at
    the top of the screen) to the program you want to use.

 o  Press [RETURN] to start the program.

 You can also start a program by typing the first letter of the menu
 choice.  Press [HELP] for more information.
```

Figure A.3: The Lotus Access menu

The options available on this menu are:

- 1-2-3—the spreadsheet, database, and graphics programs.
- PrintGraph—the special program used to print graphs.
- Translate—the program that transfers data to and from other software programs.

- Install—the program used to select and alter hardware used.
- A View of 1-2-3—a tutorial to help you learn about 1-2-3.
- Exit—the command that takes you out of the 1-2-3 program and into the operating system.

Setting 1-2-3 Defaults

The ways in which 1-2-3 handles files, printers, dates, and formats routinely are called the 1-2-3 *defaults*. This section will discuss the defaults that you can change, but you will only be concerned here with actually making one default change required to use 1-2-3: changing the default directory where your data will be stored. As you use 1-2-3, however, you may want to make other changes from time to time.

THE DEFAULT STATUS SCREEN

Figure A.4 illustrates the default status screen, which you can see by typing

W G D S

for **W**orksheet **G**lobal **D**efault **S**tatus.

Listed below are the defaults you can change. For more information on printer settings, see Chapter 7.

- Printer Interface: Change the printer default to access a second printer installed on a second port of the computer.
- Auto-Linefeed: Change when the second printer's auto-linefeed requirement is the opposite of the first printer's requirement.
- Margins: Change for different sizes of spreadsheets or paper.
- Page Length: Change for different paper lengths.
- Wait: Change to Yes when you are printing on single sheets rather than continuous forms. 1-2-3 will then pause during printing while you insert each page.

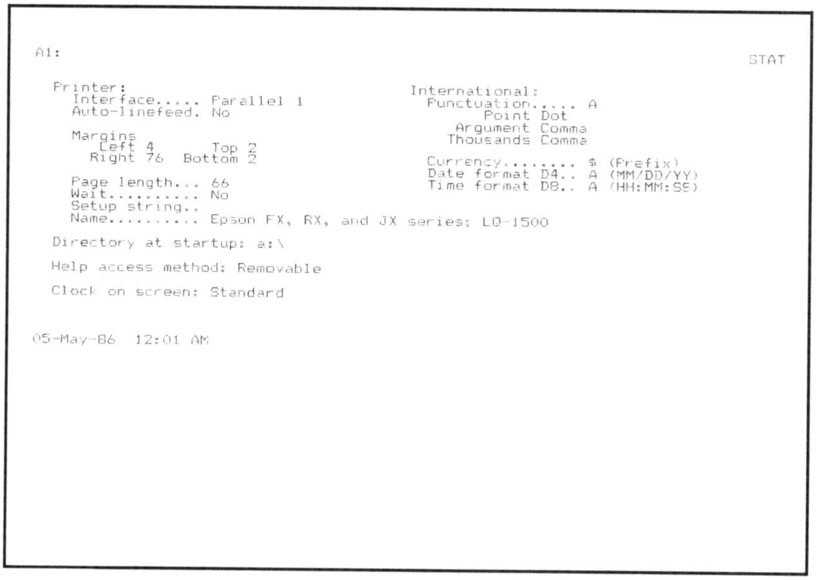

```
A1:                                                                STAT

  Printer:                                International:
    Interface..... Parallel 1               Punctuation..... A
    Auto-linefeed. No                          Point Dot
                                            Argument Comma
    Margins                                 Thousands Comma
       Left 4        Top 2
       Right 76   Bottom 2                  Currency........ $ (Prefix)
                                            Date format D4.. A (MM/DD/YY)
    Page length... 66                       Time format D8.. A (HH:MM:SS)
    Wait.......... No
    Setup string..
    Name.......... Epson FX, RX, and JX series: LQ-1500

  Directory at startup: a:\

  Help access method: Removable

  Clock on screen: Standard


  05-May-86  12:01 AM
```

Figure A.4: The default status screen

- Setup String: Change for different default font and type styles, using codes from your printer manual. Also change to custom install a printer not on the Install menu, entering the initial sequence of codes 1-2-3 should send to your printer. Check your printer manual for the sequence to enter.

- Name: Names the printer. To install a different printer, use the Install program.

- Directory at startup: Change when you want 1-2-3 to find and save files to a different disk drive, or to a different directory on the hard disk. You must do this if you have a two-disk-drive or hard disk system, before you can use 1-2-3. (Instructions are in the following section.)

- Help Access Method: Change to Instant to have Instant Help. (The Help disk must stay in the floppy drive when you select this option for a floppy drive system. If you have a hard disk, you will almost always choose Instant Help.) Change to Removable to have 1-2-3 prompt you to insert the Help disk whenever you ask for help.

- Clock on screen: Select Standard or International.
- International: Change the Puncuation, Currency, Date and Time formats from standard American to one of the several International formats offered for each.

Whenever you make a change to a default, you then select Update to permanently record the change in your Lotus program.

CHANGING THE DEFAULT DATA DRIVE

Release 2 of 1-2-3 now not only allows the use of a one-drive system but also defaults to one-drive. For some unfortunate reason, Lotus Development assumed that most people use systems with only one drive and will therefore store their data in the A drive. In reality, one-drive systems are the minority. Most users have two disk drives and store data in drive B.

If your system has either two drives or a hard disk, you will have to change the default directory where the 1-2-3 program will store your data to drive B and drive C, respectively. You will also specify the name of the data directory you have set up for a hard disk system.

The command to specify the destination of your data is / **Work**sheet **G**lobal **D**efault **D**irectory.

If you have a two-disk-drive system, remove the write-protect tab from your system disk so that 1-2-3 can permanently write the data destination information on the System disk. You should have the 1-2-3 spreadsheet on your screen.

To change the default drive from drive A to drive B, type

    / W G D D

Then press Esc to cancel drive A as the startup directory. To complete the process, enter

    B:\ ↵ U Q

If you have a hard disk, you may want to use the DOS Make Directory command (MKDIR or MD) to make a data subdirectory on your hard disk if you have not done so already. Type, at the C>:

MD C:\DATA

and enter

C:\DATA

as the startup directory using the procedure outlined above.

Appendix *B*

Add-ons to 1-2-3

Every software package has its limitations, and 1-2-3 is no exception. Some things it simply can't do; others it does in a very limited way. This is not necessarily a drawback; packages that attempt to do everything are often so unwieldy that their integration rapidly becomes a burden.

The problem remains: how do you do the things that need to be done that 1-2-3 doesn't do?

The solution has been the opening of a market for separate standalone packages called "add-ons" that work side by side with 1-2-3. Report Writer, Spotlight, and The Cambridge Spreadsheet Analyst are three such add-on packages that can be used to augment the features of 1-2-3.

Report Writer does what its name implies: it generates reports from 1-2-3 spreadsheets and databases. These reports can be summaries, mailing labels, or even form letters.

Spotlight is a desktop manager similar to the popular SideKick. Using Spotlight, you can access desk accessories called an Appointment Book, Calculator, DOS Filer, Index Card File, Note Pad, and Phone Book.

Each of these add-ons is reviewed in the following sections. New packages that are coming on the market almost daily will continue to expand the range of applications for 1-2-3 until eventually you will be able to build around 1-2-3 a complete business management system.

Report Writer

Report Writer is a formatting tool for 1-2-3 databases. It creates customized reports, forms, and mailing labels. For example, from a database of all employees, you can choose only those in a particular department who are within a certain salary range. Report Writer allows you to specify a format for information from a database and then print the selected database information.

Report Writer is a menu-driven program that uses the slash key to call up commands, as 1-2-3 does. Many of the Report Writer commands are similar to 1-2-3 commands. The on-line Help feature, prompts, mode indicators, and line and column indicators are like those in 1-2-3 as well.

HOW REPORT WRITER WORKS

You use Report Writer independently from 1-2-3; all you need are the data files created with 1-2-3, not the 1-2-3 program disks. Report Writer can use 1-2-3 or Symphony data that does not necessarily have to be defined as a database (in terms of having an input, criteria, or output range). It can work with any columns that have field names and any rows that are labeled. Each horizontal row should contain only one record. Report Writer can work with a database or range with up to 100 fields and as many records as are in the database—up to 8,091 records in the current Release 2 of 1-2-3.

Before using Report Writer, you must first install it for the type of monitor and printer you have, using the Install program included with Report Writer.

Once installed, use the original Report Writer disk to start the program. The disk is copy-protected.

CREATING A REPORT

When you start the program, Report Writer asks you for the name of the 1-2-3 database file you will use. It then displays the file's fields in their current order. You won't see the file itself. To display the file, leave Report Writer, start 1-2-3, and retrieve the file.

Once the fields appear on the screen, you can modify their layout. You can reposition or remove fields, or change the format for values or labels. You are also able to recall a field if later you decide to insert it back.

When the report layout is complete, you can print the report. You can review it on the screen before you print it on paper. Report Writer takes information from the database and prints it in the layout specified. Changes in the layout do not affect the original database. You could rename a field in the report without changing it in the database.

Suppose you want to create a report for the employee database from Chapter 8. The report layout would look like Figure B.1. The first line of the report layout shows the field names, and the second line contains placeholders for the data in each field. These are used to indicate the width, format, and type of data for the field. Labels are small boxes, values are # signs, and dates are MM/DD/YY.

```
Field: FIRST NAME                      Line:  4 Col:  6                        READY
Type / for 1-2-3 Report Writer commands.  Press F1 for help.

àààààààaaaaaaaaaaaaaaaaaaaaaaaaaaaaaaaaaaaaaaaaaaaaaaaaaaaaaaaaaaaàaaaaaaaaaa
FIRST NAME  LAST NAME     POSITION      DEPT       CODE SEX  LEVEL
'ˆˆˆˆˆˆˆˆˆ 'ˆˆˆˆˆˆˆˆˆˆˆˆ 'ˆˆˆˆˆˆˆˆˆ 'ˆˆˆˆˆˆˆ ##### 'ˆˆ #####
        SALARY      MONTHLY    DATE
($###,###,###) (#,###,###) DD-MMM-YY
```

Figure B.1: Employee database report layout

REARRANGING FIELDS ON THE PAGE

You can move a field to any position on the screen. You can use the line and column indicators in the upper right of the screen as a guide for positioning fields for special forms. Report Writer prints the fields on the page exactly as you see them on the screen. A special command lets you print or display a test pattern of the report so that you can see the actual number of spaces allowed for each field, because data is often narrower than the maximum field width. In the test pattern, squares represent the maximum width so that you can change the report layout.

Field data can be moved independently of the field name. Suppose you want the employees' first and last names to appear above their jobs in the report. Figure B.2 shows how to position the field names and field data in the report layout to achieve this.

PRODUCING TOTALS

Report Writer can perform many calculations and display the results at the end of a report (grand totals) or between categories

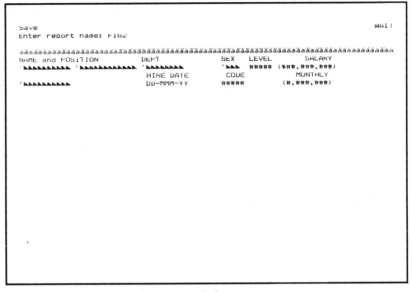

Figure B.2: Modified field names and data

(subtotals). It can keep track of the number of entries in a particular field (the count), calculate sums, averages, and high/low (min/max) values for a field of numbers.

For example, you can calculate total salary by department for the employee database. To calculate a total, you highlight a field and then execute the Current-Field Totals command. An indicator in the control panel shows you which type of total you have chosen for the field, either subtotal or grand total. The totals appear when you generate the report by printing it or displaying it on the screen.

ADDING DESCRIPTIVE HEADERS AND FOOTERS

You can add a header and a footer of up to five lines each by using menu selections. The program moves the report layout up or down, allowing room for the text of the header and footer. Report Writer uses the same special characters as 1-2-3 and Symphony to center (|) or right-align (||) text and to insert dates (@) and page numbers (#).

SELECTING RECORDS WITH QUERY

The Query command lets you define a special set of conditions for the program to look for when selecting records to include in a report. The conditions you construct take the form of simple English sentences.

For example, to produce a report that selects records of all employees who earn less than $35,000, you would construct a condition that reads "Select all records where Salary is less than 35000" where Salary is the name of the field.

You can specify up to 24 conditions and group them in a variety of combinations.

SORTING RECORDS

Report Writer can sort records in ascending or descending alphabetic or numeric order. You can specify up to four sort keys; 1-2-3 permits only two.

PRINTING THE REPORT

When you want to view the data in the report, use the Print command. Report Writer will display a model page that shows the current dimensions of a page within the report. You can change margins, page length, number of copies, spacing between records, and the start and end pages. The number of fields and records printed is also shown. When you change any of these, the model page is redrawn to display the modifications. Figure B.3 shows a model page.

You can use print enhancements such as boldface, underscoring, italics, or a combination of the three, depending on the capabilities of your printer.

PRINTING MAILING LABELS

Report Writer easily produces mailing labels. A special Print Mailing-labels menu lets you specify the size of the labels and indicate how many to print across the page, up to four labels. When

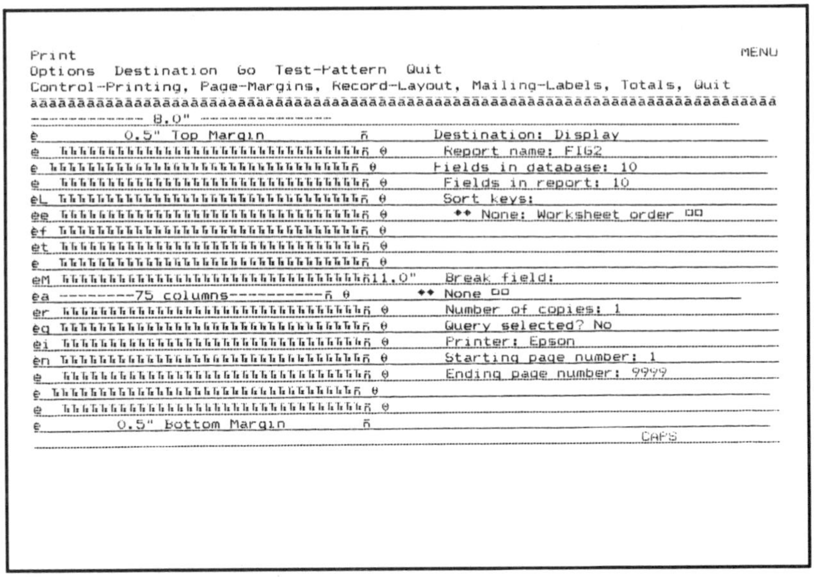

```
Print                                                                MENU
Options  Destination  Go  Test-Pattern  Quit
Control-Printing, Page-Margins, Record-Layout, Mailing-Labels, Totals, Quit
aaaaaaaaaaaaaaaaaaaaaaaaaaaaaaaaaaaaaaaaaaaaaaaaaaaaaaaaaaaaaaaaaaaaaaaaaaaa
----------------- 8.0" -----------------
e        0.5" Top Margin           n      n      Destination: Display
e   bbbbbbbbbbbbbbbbbbbbbbbbbbbbbbbn  o       Report name: FIG2
e  bbbbbbbbbbbbbbbbbbbbbbbbbbbbbbbbn  o        Fields in database: 10
e  bbbbbbbbbbbbbbbbbbbbbbbbbbbbbbbbn  o        Fields in report: 10
eL bbbbbbbbbbbbbbbbbbbbbbbbbbbbbbbbn  o        Sort keys:
ee bbbbbbbbbbbbbbbbbbbbbbbbbbbbbbbbn  o          ** None: Worksheet order  oo
ef bbbbbbbbbbbbbbbbbbbbbbbbbbbbbbbbn  o
et bbbbbbbbbbbbbbbbbbbbbbbbbbbbbbbbn  o
e  bbbbbbbbbbbbbbbbbbbbbbbbbbbbbbbbn  o
eM bbbbbbbbbbbbbbbbbbbbbbbbbbbbbbbbn11.0"      Break field:
ea --------75 columns---------n  o       ** None  oo
er bbbbbbbbbbbbbbbbbbbbbbbbbbbbbbbbn  o        Number of copies: 1
eg bbbbbbbbbbbbbbbbbbbbbbbbbbbbbbbbn  o        Query selected? No
ei bbbbbbbbbbbbbbbbbbbbbbbbbbbbbbbbn  o        Printer: Epson
en bbbbbbbbbbbbbbbbbbbbbbbbbbbbbbbbn  o        Starting page number: 1
e  bbbbbbbbbbbbbbbbbbbbbbbbbbbbbbbbn  o        Ending page number: 9999
e  bbbbbbbbbbbbbbbbbbbbbbbbbbbbbbbbn  o
e  bbbbbbbbbbbbbbbbbbbbbbbbbbbbbbbbn  o
e        0.5" Bottom Margin          n
                                                             CAPS
```

Figure B.3: Model page

the program prints mailing labels, field names and any blank spaces between records are automatically eliminated.

PRINTING ON CUSTOM FORMS

Preprinted custom forms that vary in size such as invoices, bills, or checks can be used with Report Writer for report layouts. Because the layout process is visual, trial and error might be necessary. To avoid wasting expensive custom forms, let paper copies serve as test forms.

A report can have a maximum width and length of 14 inches (either direction), and you may specify either 6 or 8 lines per inch.

REPORT WRITER AT A GLANCE

- Retail price: $150
- Compatibility: 1-2-3 Release 1A, 2; Symphony Release 1.0, 1.1

- RAM memory required: 256K
- Disk drives: Two floppy or one floppy/hard disk combination
- DOS level: 2.0, 2.1, 3.0, or 3.1
- Hardware: IBM PC, XT, AT, Portable PC, and 3270 PC (in standalone PC mode); the Compaq Portable, Plus and DeskPro; or the AT&T PC 6300

Spotlight

Spotlight is a desktop organizer that lets you use your computer the way you use materials at your desk, picking up what you need at the moment and then returning to what you were doing before. Spotlight contains six individual programs called desk accessories that perform unique organizing functions. They include the Appointment Book, the Calculator, the DOS Filer, the Index Card File, the Note Pad, and the Phone Book.

Once Spotlight has been loaded, you can call up any combination of desk accessories at almost any time, even when you are using another program. When the accessory is called up, it appears in a window that takes up about half of the screen. When you have finished using the accessory, you are returned to the program and files you were previously using.

For example, suppose you are entering data in a spreadsheet and discover that you need some numbers from the sales manager, whose phone number you have forgotten. With two keystrokes, you call up the Phone Book. Then you ask for his phone number and call him, arranging to meet with him the following day. You call up your Appointment Book and enter the meeting. Then you escape from Spotlight and you are returned to the very cell you were editing before you asked for Spotlight.

Any of the data stored in Spotlight can be copied or "pasted" into a 1-2-3 spreadsheet or into most other program files you might be working with.

Spotlight is a menu-driven program that uses the Esc key to select accessories, similar to the 1-2-3 slash key. Many commands are similar to 1-2-3 commands, and the program includes a 1-2-3-like on-line Help feature.

HOW SPOTLIGHT WORKS

Spotlight can be called either from DOS or from within any program. It consists of two parts: the core program and the individual accessories. The core program may be copied to the disk you use to boot your computer. It remains in memory until you turn off the computer or reboot DOS.

To call up an accessory, hold down the Shift and Alt keys and type the first letter of the accessory you want. The core program temporarily suspends what you are doing and calls up the accessory. To call up the accessory menu, press the Esc key and type the first letter of the option you want. To quit an accessory, press the Esc key and type **Q.**

Depending on how much RAM the program you are in uses, you can call up several accessories. When Spotlight tells you there is not enough memory to load an accessory, just remove one of the other accessories temporarily from the screen.

If you do not have a hard disk, you must keep the disk that contains the Spotlight files in one of your drives. This makes using Spotlight in conjunction with programs that also require that disks be in the drives somewhat cumbersome.

Spotlight can be used on a color or monochrome monitor. You need not install it with a special program. To use color, type **slcolor,** for monochrome, **sl.** Spotlight will display an array of hues for color monitors. You can change these colors by calling up the Kaleidoscope feature (Shift-Alt-K).

CREATING A NOTE

When you call up the Note Pad, Spotlight will display a note pad as shown in Figure B.4. There are eight pages for writing notes. The PgDn key is used to go to the next page. The notes can be printed to a file or to a printer. To call up the Note Pad, hold down the Shift and Alt keys and press **N.**

When you quit the Note Pad, notes are saved in RAM temporarily. Unless you copy them to a file before you next turn off the computer, they will be lost.

When you want to write, just begin typing. The Del key is used to erase characters. To call up the Note Pad menu, press the Esc key and type the first letter of the option you want.

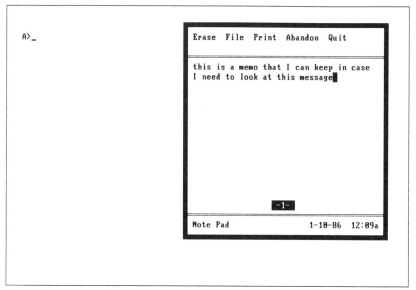

Figure B.4: Note Pad

To copy the note to another program's file, save the contents in a text file and copy the text file into the other file. For example, in 1-2-3 you use the File Import Text command to copy text. This is useful in adding text notes to a spreadsheet.

USING THE CALCULATOR

The Calculator (Figure B.5) allows you to do calculations quickly at your computer. The numeric keypad on your computer is converted into a calculator with 12-digit display, memory and constants. To call up the Calculator, type Shift-Alt and press **C**.

A handy feature of the Calculator is its ability to "paste" or copy the result of a calculation either directly to the file you were previously using or to the Note Pad. You press the Esc key and type **P** for Paste. If the Note Pad is still on the screen, the result is copied to it. Otherwise, it is copied to a text file.

The +, −, *, and / keys are used for addition, subtraction, multiplication, and division, respectively. Special keys on the keypad of your computer are assigned the other functions of the calculator, which are mapped out in detail in the Spotlight documentation.

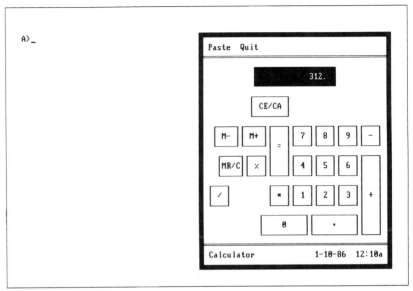

Figure B.5: The Calculator

USING THE APPOINTMENT BOOK

The Appointment Book keeps track of meetings, appointments, and daily activities. You can set up regular meetings with reminders, move meetings from one time to another, and set an audio alarm to remind you of your meetings. This audio alarm, which relies on the DOS clock to tell the time, will sound regardless of which program you are using. To call up the Appointment Book, hold down Shift-Alt and press **A**. To save your appointments permanently, you must save them in a file before the computer next loses power. You can print them out by using the Print command.

This accessory contains several menu options that take up two rows on the screen. At first glance, you may not realize that there are 13 menu options in the Appointment Book. The daily calender first appears on the screen as shown in Figure B.6. To enter a daily appointment, use the arrow keys to move to the time. Type any notes or reminders; press ◄─┘ to complete the appointment. To schedule a meeting for a time that is not listed, use the Insert command. You can then enter the exact starting time.

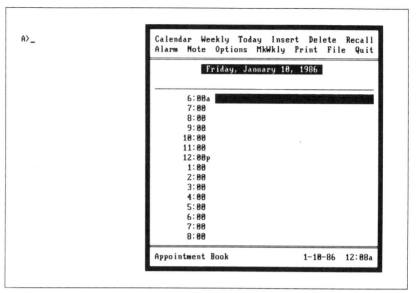

Figure B.6: Daily calendar

You can delete meetings or recall them if you accidentally delete them by using the appropriate menu command (Delete or Recall). In addition, you can create regular weekly meetings by using the MkWkly command. To review regular weekly meetings, call up the Weekly calendar, which looks like Figure B.7. Figure B.8 shows the monthly calendar.

The PgUp and PgDn keys move you backward and forward six weeks at a time. To view appointments for a date on the calendar, move the cursor to the date desired and press ←┘. The Appointment Book will appear on the screen.

CREATING A PHONE BOOK

The Phone Book allows you to keep alphabetical lists of names and phone numbers, along with text notes such as addresses and contacts. You can store as many as 500 names in a list and create 36 separate phone lists. As with the other accessories, you must save the entries in a file. The best way to do this is to save the file every time

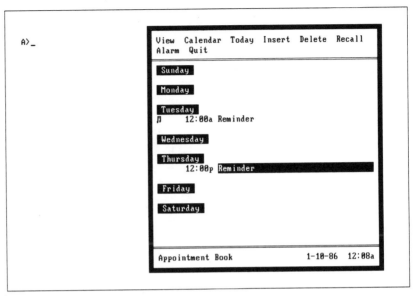

Figure B.7: Weekly calendar

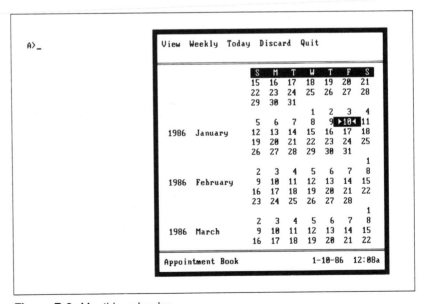

Figure B.8: Monthly calendar

you make an entry. To permanently save the Phone Book file, use the Esc-Q command. You can also print the Phone Book, as you can the other accessories. To call up the Phone Book, hold down Shift-Alt and press **P.**

You can search the list for certain characters by using the Search command or move to an entry beginning with a particular character by using the Goto command.

The Phone Book has two views. The first view that appears on the screen looks like Figure B.9. The second view is used to describe or view information about the phone number in more detail. It is called up by moving the pointer to the number and selecting the command View-Card. A card is shown in Figure B.10.

To return to the phone index, use the View-Index command. Use the Alternate command to create or retrieve separate phone lists, named using a letter (A–Z) or a number (0–9).

CREATING AN INDEX CARD FILE

The Indexer or Index Card File is a general-purpose version of the Phone Book accessory. It is used to create an indexed list of

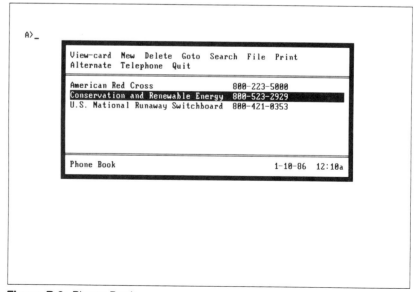

Figure B.9: Phone Book

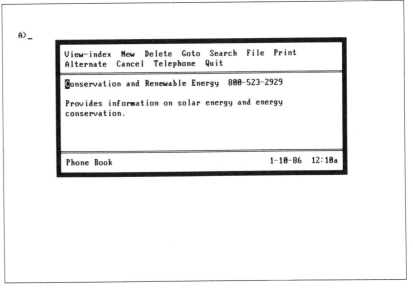

Figure B.10: Phone number card

information that can be used for keeping a list of activities to do, organizing a collection of hints, or documenting cell formulas in your spreadsheet. To call up the Indexer, hold down Shift-Alt and press **I**.

There are two views in the Indexer, similar to the Phone Book: the Index (Figure B.11) and the Index Card (Figure B.12). The commands and the limits are identical to the Phone Book; the limits are 500 cards per list and 36 separate lists. You can search for text by using the Search command and move to a list of cards beginning with a similar character by using the Goto command. Printing and saving are done through the menu.

USING THE DOS FILE HANDLER

The Filer (Figure B.13) lets you view and manage the files and directories on your disks. DOS functions such as copying, renaming, erasing, and looking at files are available. The files are displayed in alphabetical order. To call up the Filer, hold down Shift-Alt and press **F**.

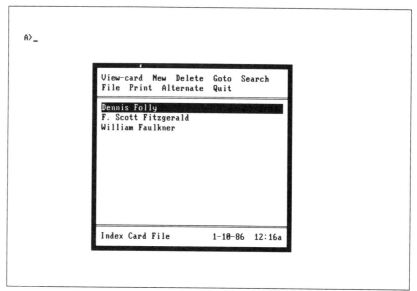

Figure B.11: Indexer list

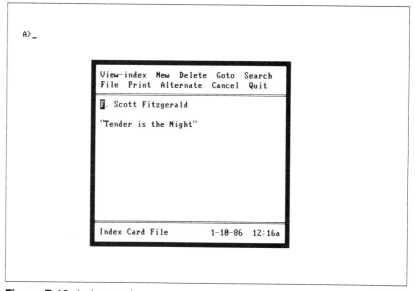

Figure B.12: Index card

```
A>_

    ┌──────────────────────────────────────────────┐
    │ View  Up Home  Sort  Other...  Delete        │
    │ Copy  Rename  Mkdir  Paste  Quit             │
    ├──────────────────────────────────────────────┤
    │               A:\                             │
    │ CHAP6     WK1   12119   12-31-85    4:45a     │
    │ CHAP9     WK1    4344   12-23-85    1:39a     │
    │ COLORBAR  PIC    1084   12-10-85    3:40a     │
    │ DEPREC    WK1    9030   12-15-85   12:43a     │
    │ DT2       WK1   12250   12-31-85    4:55a     │
    │ GRID      PIC    1583   12-10-85    3:40a     │
    │ GRIDSCAL  PIC    1754   12-10-85    3:40a     │
    │ LINE1     PIC    1373   12-10-85    3:39a     │
    │ LINLAB    PIC     773   12-10-85    3:39a     │
    │ LN        WKS    1920   12-13-85   12:02p     │
    │ LOG1      PIC    1152   12-13-85   11:33a     │
    │ LOG2      PIC    1152   12-13-85   11:33a     │
    │ LOG3      PIC    2645   12-13-85   12:01p     │
    │ MACMENU   WKS    2176   12-15-85    1:10a     │
    ├──────────────────────────────────────────────┤
    │ Filer                   1-10-86   12:11a      │
    └──────────────────────────────────────────────┘
```

Figure B.13: DOS Filer

You can look into subdirectories or other disk drives by using the View command. You can also use the Filer to review disk space information, such as the number of files or available bytes, by selecting the Other Info command. Another useful feature of File is the View Wrap command to review the contents of a file. You can sort files for review by file name, extension, size, or time last modified, similar to the 1-2-3 Release 1A ACCESS menu File-Manager.

Formatting, which is included in the Other menu, allows you to format a disk from within an application program such as 1-2-3. Changing directories, another option of the Other menu, can also be done from within an application program.

The Paste command copies a file name to another program file such as a document or spreadsheet. You could, for example, paste a list of spreadsheet names into a spreadsheet and use it as a reference.

SPOTLIGHT AT A GLANCE

- Retail price: $75
- Compatibility: Most popular software for the IBM

- RAM memory reserved: 75K
- Disk drives: One or two floppy or one floppy/hard disk combination
- DOS level: 2.0, 2.1, 3.0, or 3.1
- Hardware: IBM PC, XT, AT, the Compaq computers

The Cambridge Spreadsheet Analyst

The Cambridge Spreadsheet Analyst is a debugging and documentation tool for 1-2-3 spreadsheets. The package is interactive, allowing you to direct the flow of analysis and pause to make changes as you locate errors. The commands are similar to Lotus 1-2-3 commands in appearance and structure, and a 1-2-3 emulator allows the spreadsheet being reviewed to appear as it does within 1-2-3. The package's on-line Help is similar to the 1-2-3 Help.

When you scan through the spreadsheet and locate a suspicious cell, you use the function key XREF to locate all other cells that refer to it. The PROBE key logically traces its flow through the spreadsheet. The SHEET key presents a graphic trace of the cell through the spreadsheet, and the REPORT options allow you to print various aspects of the spreadsheet, such as global settings, cross references, or ranges of cell formulas or values.

AUTOMATIC SCAN

The automatic scan feature allows you to review the entire spreadsheet. It looks for and reports any unusual situations that may indicate that errors exist, such as circular references and actual ERR messages. The scan pauses at each possible error site, so that you can make corrections on the spot.

CIRCULAR REFERENCE LOCATOR

The Circular Reference Locator identifies all formulas caught in endless loops created by circular cell references. It displays all the formulas that are dependent on the circular reference.

CROSS REFERENCE

The Cross Reference feature shows where and how a specified cell, range, named range, or function is used in formulas throughout the worksheet. This is enormously valuable for locating indirect circular references, correcting mistakes in absolute and relative cell references after copies, and finding all iterations of a number, formula, or function that contains an error.

INTERACTIVE PROBE

The Interactive Probe explores the logic of a spreadsheet, tracing the formulas and intermediate values that flow into a specified cell.

REPORTS

The Report feature allows flexible printouts not available in 1-2-3, so that you can print global settings, range analysis, cross references, integrated maps, and two-dimensional cell contents (that is, printing the formulas and functions in cells and their results at the same time).

THE CAMBRIDGE SPREADSHEET ANALYST AT A GLANCE

- Retail price: $149
- Compatibility: Most popular software for the IBM
- RAM memory reserved: 192K
- Disk drives: One or two floppy or one floppy/hard disk combination
- DOS level: 2.0, 2.1, 3.0, or 3.1
- Hardware: IBM PC, XT, AT, the Compaq computers
- Toll-free order and information numbers:
  (800) 446-1238
  Within Massachusetts call:
  (617) 576-5744

- Produced by Cambridge Software Collaborative
  University Place Suite 200
  Cambridge, MA 02138

INDEX

Selections from The SYBEX Library

Integrated Software

SIMPSON'S 1-2-3 MACRO LIBRARY
by Alan Simpson

300 pp., illustr., Ref. 314-7

This book provides many programming techniques, macro examples, and entire menu-driven systems that demonstrate the full potential of macros. The full power of 1-2-3 version 2 is laid out in powerful, time-saving business solutions developed by bestselling author Alan Simpson.

ADVANCED BUSINESS MODELS WITH 1-2-3
by Stanley R. Trost

250 pp., illustr., Ref. 159-4

If you are a business professional using the 1-2-3 software package, you will find the spreadsheet and graphics models provided in this book easy to use "as is" in everyday business situations.

THE ABC'S OF 1-2-3 (New Ed)
by Chris Gilbert and Laurie Williams

225 pp., illustr., Ref. 168-3

For those new to the LOTUS 1-2-3 program, this book offers step-by-step instructions in mastering its spreadsheet, data base, and graphing capabilities. Features Version 2.

MASTERING SYMPHONY
by Douglas Cobb (2nd Ed)

763 pp., illustr., Ref. 224-8

This bestselling book has been heralded as the Symphony bible, and provides all the information you will need to put Symphony to work for you right away. Packed with practical models for the business user. Includes Version 1.1.

SYMPHONY TIPS & TRICKS
by Dick Andersen

325 pp., illustr. Ref. 247-7

Organized as a reference tool, this book gives shortcuts for using Symphony commands and functions, with troubleshooting advice.

BETTER SYMPHONY SPREADSHEETS
by Carl Townsend

287 pp., illustr., Ref. 339-2

For Symphony users who want to gain real expertise in the use of the spreadsheet features, this has hundreds of tips and techniques. There are also instructions on how to implement some of the special features of Excel on Symphony.

MASTERING FRAMEWORK
by Doug Hergert

450 pp., illustr. Ref. 248-5

This tutorial guides the beginning user through all the functions and features of this integrated software package, geared to the business environment.

ADVANCED TECHNIQUES IN FRAMEWORK
by Alan Simpson

250 pp., illustr. Ref. 257-4

In order to begin customizing your own models with Framework, you'll need a thorough knowledge of Fred programming language, and this book provides this information in a complete, well-organized form.

MASTERING THE IBM ASSISTANT SERIES
by Jeff Lea and Ted Leonsis

249 pp., illustr., Ref. 284-1

Each section of this book takes the reader

through the features, screens, and capabilities of each module of the series. Special emphasis is placed on how the programs work together.

DATA SHARING WITH 1-2-3 AND SYMPHONY: INCLUDING MAINFRAME LINKS
by Dick Andersen
262 pp., illustr., Ref. 283-3

This book focuses on an area of increasing importance to business users: exchanging data between Lotus software and other micro and mainframe software. Special emphasis is given to dBASE II and III.

MASTERING PARADOX
by Alan Simpson
350 pp., illustr., Ref. 334-1

Everyone's introduction to this unique, menu-driven dbms, from essential operations to complex uses including PAL programming techniques. There are valuable real-world illustrations including a complete mailing lists system, and an inventory, sales, and purchasing system with automatic multiple-table updating.

MASTERING EXCEL
by Carl Townsend
454 pp., illustr., Ref. 306-6

This hands-on tutorial covers all basic operations of Excel plus in-depth coverage of special features, including extensive coverage of macros.

APPLEWORKS: TIPS & TECHNIQUES
by Robert Ericson
373 pp., illustr., Ref. 303-1

Designed to improve AppleWorks skills, this is a great book that gives utility information illustrated with every-day management examples.

JAZZ ON THE MACINTOSH
by Joseph Caggiano and Michael McCarthy
431 pp., illustr., Ref. 265-5

Each chapter features as an example a business report which is built on throughout the book in the first section of each chapter. Chapters then go on to detail each application and special effects in depth.

MASTERING APPLEWORKS
by Elna Tymes
201 pp., illustr., Ref. 240-X

This bestseller presents business solutions which are used to introduce Apple-Works and then develop mastery of the program. Includes examples of balance sheet, income statement, inventory control system, cash-flow projection, and accounts receivable summary.

PRACTICAL APPLEWORKS USES
by David K. Simerly
313 pp., illustr., Ref. 274-4

This book covers a breadth of home and business uses, including combined-function applications, complicated tasks, and even a large section on interfacing AppleWorks with the outside world.

Computer Specific

IBM PC AND COMPATIBLES

OPERATING THE IBM PC NETWORKS
Token Ring and Broadband
by Paul Berry
363 pp., illustr., Ref. 307-4

This tells you how to plan, install, and use either the Token Ring Network or the PC Network. Focusing on the hardware-independent PCN software, this book gives readers who need to plan, set-up, operate, and administrate such networks the head start they need to see their way clearly right from the beginning.

THE ABC'S OF THE IBM PC
by Joan Lasselle and Carol Ramsay
143 pp., illustr., Ref. 102-0

This book will take you through the first crucial steps in learning to use the IBM PC.

THE IBM PC-DOS HANDBOOK
by Richard Allen King
296 pp., Ref. 103-9
Explains the PC disk operating system. Get the most out of your PC by adapting its capabilities to your specific needs.

BUSINESS GRAPHICS FOR THE IBM PC
by Nelson Ford
259 pp., illustr. Ref. 124-1
Ready-to-run programs for creating line graphs, multiple bar graphs, pie charts and more. An ideal way to use your PC's business capabilities!

THE IBM PC CONNECTION
by James Coffron
264 pp., illustr., Ref. 127-6
Teaches elementary interfacing and BASIC programming of the IBM PC for connection to external devices and household appliances.

DATA FILE PROGRAMMING ON YOUR IBM PC
by Alan Simpson
219 pp., illustr., Ref. 146-2
This book provides instructions and examples for managing data files in BASIC Programming. Design and development are extensively discussed.

THE MS-DOS HANDBOOK
by Richard Allen King (2nd Ed)
320 pp., illustr., Ref. 185-3
The differences between the various versions and manufacturer's implementations of MS-DOS are covered in a clear straightforward manner. Tables, maps, and numerous examples make this the most complete book on MS-DOS available.

ESSENTIAL PC-DOS
by Myril and Susan Shaw
300 pp., illustr., Ref. 176-4
Whether you work with the IBM PC, XT, PC jr. or the portable PC, this book will be invaluable both for learning PC DOS and for later reference.

Software Specific

SPREADSHEETS

MASTERING SUPERCALC 3
by Greg Harvey
300 pp., illustr., Ref. 312-0
Featuring Version 2.1, this title offers full coverage of all the sophisticated features of this third generation spreadsheet, including spreadsheet, graphics, database and advanced techniques.

DOING BUSINESS WITH MULTIPLAN
by Richard Allen King and Stanley R. Trost
250 pp., illustr., Ref. 148-9
This book will show you how using Multiplan can be nearly as easy as learning to use a pocket calculator. It presents a collection of templates for business applications.

MULTIPLAN ON THE COMMODORE 64
by Richard Allen King
250 pp., illustr. Ref. 231-0
This clear, straightforward guide will give you a firm grasp on Multiplan's function, as well as provide a collection of useful template programs.

WORD PROCESSING

PRACTICAL WORDSTAR USES
by Julie Anne Arca
303 pp., illustr. Ref. 107-1
Pick your most time-consuming office tasks and this book will show you how to streamline them with WordStar.

THE COMPLETE GUIDE TO MULTIMATE
by Carol Holcomb Dreger
250 pp., illustr. Ref. 229-9
A concise introduction to the many practical applications of this powerful word processing program.

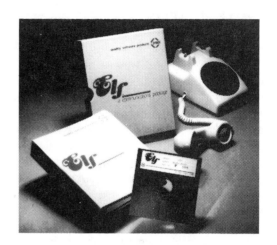

SYBEX COMPUTER BOOKS

are different.

Here is why . . .

At SYBEX, each book is designed with you in mind. Every manuscript is carefully selected and supervised by our editors, who are themselves computer experts. We publish the best authors, whose technical expertise is matched by an ability to write clearly and to communicate effectively. Programs are thoroughly tested for accuracy by our technical staff. Our computerized production department goes to great lengths to make sure that each book is well-designed.

In the pursuit of timeliness, SYBEX has achieved many publishing firsts. SYBEX was among the first to integrate personal computers used by authors and staff into the publishing process. SYBEX was the first to publish books on the CP/M operating system, microprocessor interfacing techniques, word processing, and many more topics.

Expertise in computers and dedication to the highest quality product have made SYBEX a world leader in computer book publishing. Translated into fourteen languages, SYBEX books have helped millions of people around the world to get the most from their computers. We hope we have helped you, too.

For a complete catalog of our publications:

SYBEX, Inc. 2344 Sixth Street, Berkeley, California 94710
Tel: (415) 848-8233   Telex: 336311